When Hens Begin to Crow

When Hens Begin to Crow

Gender and Parliamentary Politics in Uganda

Sylvia Tamale

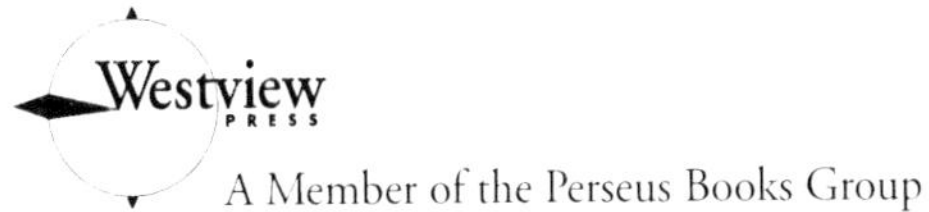

Copyright © 1999 by Westview Press, A Member of the Perseus Books Group

Published in 1999 in the United States of America by Westview Press, 5500 Central Avenue, Boulder, Colorado 80301-2877, and in the United Kingdom by Westview Press, 12 Hid's Copse Road, Cumnor Hill, Oxford OX2 9JJ

Library of Congress Cataloging-in-Publication Data
Tamale, Sylvia (Sylvia Rosila)
    When hens begin to crow : gender and parliamentary politics in
Uganda / Sylvia Tamale.
        p.   cm.
    Includes bibliographical references and index.
    ISBN 0-8133-3462-4 (hc) —ISBN 0-8133-3896-4 (pb)
    1. Women in politics—Uganda.   2. Women legislators—Uganda.
3. Uganda—Politics and government—1979–   . I. Title.
HQ1236.5.U33T35   1999
320'.082—dc21   98-28629
                                                                                    CIP

The paper used in this publication meets the requirements of the American National Standard for Permanence of Paper for Printed Library Materials Z39.48-1984.

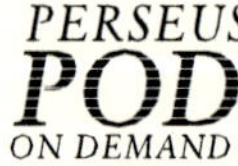

10   9   8   7   6   5   4   3

*To all African women in the struggle for emancipation . . .
past, present, and future*

Contents

Tables and Figures

Acronyms

AA	affirmative action
ACFODE	Action for Development
AR	Army Representative
CA	Constituent Assembly
CAD	constituent assembly delegate
CBO	community-based organization
CP	Conservative Party
CS	county seat
DP	Democratic Party
FIDA	Association of Women Lawyers
FOWODE	Forum for Women in Democracy
FRELIMO	Front for the Liberation of Mozambique
HDI	human development index
IAT	intra-African traders
IPFC	Inter-Party Political Forces Cooperation
KY	Kabaka Yekka (The King Alone)
LC	local council
Legco	legislative council
LRA	Lords Resistance Army
MGCD	Ministry of Gender and Community Development
MP	member of parliament
NAWOU	National Association of Women's Organizations in Uganda
NCC	National Consultative Council
NCW	National Council of Women
NGO	nongovernmental organization
NGP	national gender policy
NRA	National Resistance Army
NRC	National Resistance Council (interim national parliament, 1986–1996)
NRM	National Resistance Movement
NWC	National Women's Council
OAU	Organization of African Unity
PAL	Public Accounts Committee
PPC	Presidential Party Commission
PRA	People's Resistance Army

RC	Resistance Council (Committee)
RDA	resident district administrator
SAP	Structural Adjustment Program
STC	state trading corporation
UAUW	Uganda Association of University Women
UAWL	Uganda African Women's League
UAWO	Uganda Association of Women's Organizations
UCW	Uganda Council of Women
UNLA	Uganda National Liberation Army
UPC	Uganda People's Congress
UPM	Uganda Patriotic Movement
UWESO	Ugandan Women's Effort to Save Orphans
UWFCT	Uganda Women's Finance and Credit Trust
UWONET	Uganda Women's Network
UWOPA	Uganda Women Parliamentarians Association
WC	Women's Council (Committee)
WID	Women in Development
YWCA	Young Women's Christian Association
YWG	Young Wives Group

Preface and Acknowledgments

The topic of women and politics has only recently attracted attention in general political discourse and intellectual analysis. For this reason, relatively little has been written on the subject, and studies that have been conducted on women in Africa have largely neglected the areas of government, statecraft, and politics. Nevertheless, as the numbers of women politicians steadily increase in national legislatures, more and more studies are conducted on the subject. Notably, the bulk of these studies have been conducted in the Western world. This book is only a small contribution to recent attempts at filling this yawning gap.

Perhaps the most enriching and humbling experience for me during this study was my encounter with the older pioneer women of the contemporary Ugandan women's movement. Their oral histories (herstories) constitute a fascinating recounting of women's activism in an era of conservative, colonial oppression. Many women of my generation tend to believe that the *real* struggles for women's emancipation started only recently. We fall into the trap of associating incipient women's groups with an exclusively apolitical, welfare-oriented agenda. Such thinking exposes our ignorance of a historical fact and also impugns the basic feminist notion that "the personal is political." In our struggle for political, economic, social, and cultural emancipation, we—the young shoots sprouting from roots embedded in the first half of the twentieth century—have a great deal to learn from our predecessors.

Employing primarily qualitative methods of research, this book addresses a specific question: How does *gender* (as opposed to sex) affect women in politics, and how does that dynamic contribute to shaping the character of contemporary Ugandan politics? The conceptual framework adopted in the study takes into account the nuances of African gender relations resulting from neocolonialism and the process of imperialism. Inspired by a 1989 affirmative action policy guaranteeing the election of a minimum of thirty-nine women district representatives to the national legislature, this study is the first detailed examination of the gender dynamics of women's participation in the legislative process in an African country. The book situates the experiences of politically active women in the context of sociohistorical processes and structural contradictions that have shaped gender dynamics in Ugandan politics. It also explores the different strategies adopted by female legislators in empowering themselves and in resisting male domination.

The research was conducted between September 1995 and August 1996, and again between June 1997 and March 1998. Field notes from observations in the National Assembly and transcripts from intensive interviews with forty female legislators and fifteen male legislators form the primary data set. To explore links among the female political elite, women's activist networks, and women at the grassroots, additional interviews were conducted with eight leaders from women's organizations and twenty women from the rural sectors of Uganda.

The increased numbers of women legislators in the National Assembly clearly altered the profile of parliamentary politics in Uganda. Tangible benefits have already begun to be registered for Ugandan women in the form of legislation. However, the impact of the women legislators is limited by two important factors: first, the overall patriarchal structure within which parliament exists and operates and, second, the fact that the affirmative action policy was imposed from above and was not the result of a bottom-up grassroots women's movement. This second factor made some women legislators susceptible to co-optation and complacency. At the same time, because the Ugandan parliament is institutionally and compositionally male dominated, female legislators constantly practice conciliatory politics, pragmatically finding ways of negotiating the various barriers that stand in their way.

For African people struggling for the emancipation of women on our continent, the task often appears too daunting; we despair in the face of pervasive patriarchy and debilitating underdevelopment. For me, writing this book was an exercise in revitalized energy, renewed hope, and rekindled commitment. I am thus eternally grateful to the following agencies and people who, in various ways, helped in the process that started as a doctoral dissertation and finally led to this book.

Thanks to the J. William Fulbright Foundation and the John D. and Catherine T. MacArthur Foundation for their generous financial support. The Center for Basic Research (CBR) and the National Documentation Center extended to me the use of their facilities at Kampala. Ronald Aminzade and Susan Geiger gave me more of their time than I had a right to expect. Barbara Laslett, Jennifer Pierce, and Jean Allman took time to read draft chapters and kindly gave me the benefit of their professional expertise. Several friends and colleagues helped me clarify issues and arguments, among them, Amina Mama, Nelson Kasfir, Jehoash Sendege, Janet Spector, Pamela Aronson, Deborah Engelen-Eigles, Sharon Preves, Marit Berntson, Sharilyn Geistfeld, and Erik Larson.

I am indebted to the staff of the National Assembly in Kampala, in particular, Andrew Walube, Gloria Nakebu, and Abby Kagoye, who graciously offered me shortcuts through the bureaucratic maze. I owe much to Serina Nyakoojo for her patience in enduring the arduous job of transcribing the long interviews that formed the core of my study. Heartfelt thanks go to Jennifer Nalweyiso, who acted as my guide when I visited the welcoming homes of peasant women in Nkozi village.

I wish to acknowledge with thanks Laura Parsons, editor of Westview Press, who encouraged me to pursue this project and lent me all the necessary support. The same goes for the anonymous reviewer who worked with Westview Press in providing useful comments and to Justus Mugaju, associate editor of Fountain Publishers.

The feminism, scholarship, and editorial ingenuity of my partner in the struggle and in life, Joe Oloka-Onyango, are all positively reflected in this book. I want to recognize my sons, two-year-old Kwame Sobukwe Ayepa and one-month-old Samora Okech Sanga, who were my number one incentive in expeditiously concluding this project. My parents, Evelyn and Balaba Tamale, have been solid pillars of support throughout my life, always encouraging me to reach out for that which appeared to be unreachable. Finally, to the women and men who participated in this study, I owe my greatest debt.

Sylvia Tamale

1

Introduction

Female chickens normally do not crow. At least popular mythology claims that they cannot. Hence, in many African cultures a crowing hen is considered an omen of bad tidings that must be expiated through the immediate slaughter of the offending bird. During the 1996 general elections to Uganda's national legislature, a male observer at a campaign rally reminded a woman candidate of this old African apothegm: *Wali owulide ensera ekokolima?* "Have you ever heard a hen crow?" The message was clear: Women have no business standing for political office. The rowdy applause from the other men at the gathering signaled their broad sympathy and support for their colleague's observation.[1] It is popularly believed that women are not supposed to speak up or express their opinions in public, a view that is deeply embedded in African patriarchal values, which relegate women to the domestic arena of home and family.[2] Such a view assumes that men are the anointed link between the home and the public world; they are the "natural" players in the game of politics. However, women are increasingly negating the metaphor of the crowing hen. They are defying custom, culture, discrimination, and marginalization to join formal politics in Uganda. That process is the subject of this book.

Field research for this book coincided with a momentous event in the political history of Uganda: the 1996 parliamentary and presidential elections. Two "firsts" were associated with these events. Presidential elections had never been held in the history of the country.[3] Furthermore, these elections—if we do not count the sham elections of 1980[4]—were the first direct elections to take place in thirty-four years of formal independence. The 1996 Ugandan elections signified the ongoing breakdown of authoritarian rule that has swept much of Africa, Latin America, and Eastern Europe in the late twentieth century. A striking difference between this new wave of democratization and earlier ones is that for the first time, women have become an important part of the dialogue on the subject (Seidman 1993; Waylen 1994). The rhetoric of new regimes everywhere expresses a commitment to greater gender equality.[5]

Uganda is one example of an African country engaged in the process of democratization. The wheels of this process shifted into gear way back on January 26, 1986, when a bleak chapter in Ugandan politics ended with the National Resistance Movement (NRM) taking over power after almost five years of guerrilla war. The transition from years of dictatorship under Idi Amin and Milton Obote sparked considerable optimism among Ugandan women. President Yoweri Museveni emphasized the importance of gender equity to Uganda's development: "The challenges of development enjoin us to pay more than just lip service to the core issue of unequal gender relations in our society" (*New Vision*, March 9, 1988). Such political rhetoric was not new, but nobody would have predicted the concrete steps that the NRM took to follow up on this promise; not only did it defy conventional wisdom but it also cut through deepseated ideologies that stemmed from strong patriarchal forces.

President Museveni concretized his promise in the following ways: (1) Women were accorded mandatory seats at all levels of the grassroots people's resistance councils and in the National Resistance Council (NRC)—the interim national legislature; (2) the Ministry of Women in Development was created;[6] (3) the Directorate of Women's Affairs was set up within the NRM secretariat (the government mobilization body); (4) a women's studies program was instituted at Makerere University; (5) all females enrolling in government-funded tertiary institutions were granted preferential treatment;[7] and (6) women became more visible in high positions such as the cabinet and the judiciary and government commissions. All these developments set the stage for women's increased participation in formal politics and provided an avenue for their enhanced struggle for empowerment in all spheres of society. Moreover, Ugandan women have taken advantage of this recent state of restructuring, as evidenced by the mushrooming of numerous women's nongovernmental organizations (NGOs) covering a wide arena of social, economic, cultural, and political activity (Tripp 1994).

This book examines Ugandan women as new formal political actors. My research focuses on women legislators who were beneficiaries of a 1989 affirmative action policy that guaranteed women a minimum of thirty-nine seats (one from each district)[8] in Uganda's premier lawmaking institution—parliament.

The Sociopolitical History

Despite their numerical majority and the important role they played in the politics of precolonial Uganda, women are conspicuous for their absence in the literature on the political history of Uganda; most of the analyses in the standard texts have generally proceeded as if women did not exist (e.g., Morris and Read 1966; Ibingira 1973; Mittelman 1975; Karugire 1980; Uzoigwe 1982). Beginning in the late 1970s there have been attempts, mainly by Western "Africanist" scholars, to examine the role of African women in politics (e.g., Steady 1976; O'Barr 1976; Rogers 1980; Staudt 1981). Politics in precolonial Africa was far more complex that it is today, especially insofar as it fused with other aspects of social life.

Here I reexamine the precolonial role of women in the political history of Uganda by adopting a nontraditional meaning for the term "politics." In order to fully understand the political role played by women, it is imperative to challenge and redefine the boundaries of public and private life. Thus this section revisits Uganda's sociopolitical history with a difference—refocusing the historical lens to bring into vision a gendered view of Uganda's past. But what exactly is meant by the term "gender"?[9] Care must be taken not to uncritically project the Western conceptual paradigm of gender onto African cultures and societies.[10] Most importantly, the notion of gender as conceptualized in early second wave feminist writing was largely ethnocentric and generally isolated from other concepts, such as race, ethnicity, class, religion, age, and sexuality. Several feminists have criticized such an approach, arguing that gender identity cannot be separated from all the other attributes that make up an individual (Collins 1990; Spelman 1988; hooks 1984; Smith 1980; Lugones 1994). Furthermore, gender analysis in the African context must incorporate a critique of the imperialist imposition of Western notions of gender and the effect of neocolonialism on gender relations.

Concretely, a gender paradigm relevant to a peasant Catholic Sabiny woman in eastern Uganda, for example, would have to roundly address (1) elements of her indigenous culture that oppress her (e.g., clitoridectomy); (2) Catholicism, which further dominates her morality and sexuality; (3) capitalism, which places her at the very bottom of the class/gender hierarchy; (4) imperialism, which imposes alien sociocultural values, economic constraints, and political structures that dictate her existence; and (5) neocolonialism, which dehumanizes her and is reflected in policies such as structural adjustment programs (SAPs), diminishing terms of trade, and the unequal exchange of values across continents. All five systems of oppression form an integrated matrix that produces a specific social location for the Sabiny woman. Therefore, the dialectical relationship between gender, class, ethnicity, religion, imperialism, and neocolonialism is especially pertinent for an analysis of gender relations in the African context. Any analysis that lacks such a multifocal approach to gender relations in the African context can only be superficial and truncated.

The political history that follows is integrated with an analysis of the historical construction of gender, focusing on the processes through which gender relations were reshaped by extant sociopolitical conditions. By gender relations I refer to the interaction that occurs between men and women as they carry out their different roles in society. Such relations are a reflection of the roles/activities that males and females perform in society *and* the relative value/meaning attached to those roles by wider society (Brydon and Chant 1989, 1). My discussion of this political history is divided into three distinct periods: precolonial, colonial, and postindependence. The analysis of gender relations draws on Marxist feminist theories that criticize patriarchy in the wider context of imperialism, development, and underdevelopment. The Marxist dialectical method is particularly useful for this analysis because it links the "present" to material, historical, and structural forms, enabling a more elaborated elucidation of complex social phenomena.

The Precolonial Period

Uganda was declared a British protectorate in 1894 and remained so until it attained formal independence in 1962. Before colonization, the political setup in Uganda varied from *kabila* to *kabila*.[11] At least forty different *makabila* resided in the area that was mapped out and baptized "Uganda" by the stroke of the imperialist pen at the turn of the century. Broadly speaking, two types of political systems prevailed in the plurality of Uganda's social structure prior to the advent of British rule: the centrally governed kingdom states of Buganda, Ankole, Toro, and Bunyoro and the "nonstate" segmentary societies, which followed an age-set clan system, such as the Acholi, the Lugbara, and the Langi (Morris and Read 1966; Karugire 1980; Okoth 1996).[12]

To an alien observer in that era, politics in Uganda appeared to be the exclusive realm of men. This was partly because of the male dominance that prevailed in largely patriarchal societies.[13] However, the intimate inner workings of the different cultures and historically distinct arrangements between the sexes allowed for women to participate in politics, both on a formal and an informal basis (Kandiyoti 1988). The common misconception about women's political participation at this time is confounded by two important factors. The first is a misunderstanding of the meaning of "public" and "private" life in precolonial Uganda (as well as in other African societies), which leads to oversimplified cultural evaluations of the sexes based on the domestic/public divide. Because of the fluidity and interconnectedness of the two spheres, employing the public/private (or political/domestic) dichotomy as an analytic tool for conceptualizing gender relations in Uganda, as in the rest of Africa, would indeed be a pointless task (Sudarkasa 1986). In precolonial Uganda, women had never been confined to the private or domestic sphere.

Rather, multiple responsibilities between and across spheres shaped their political history, the political/juridical spheres heavily depending on personal relationships that women could (and often did) influence (Byanyima 1992).[14]

Another factor that contributes to misconceptions about women's political participation in this period stems from the male-authored, androcentric history texts. Partly influenced by the current marginalization of African women from the formal political sphere, mainstream historians tend to assume that women have never played a role in the politics of their communities (e.g., Richards 1964). As a consequence, the role of women in precolonial times is largely obscured or simply ignored. If they make reference to women at all, standard political analyses do so through images of apolitical beings at best or mere chattels at worst (e.g., Karugire 1980). Generally, women did not directly participate in political discussions, but their opinions were valued and often were sought before political decisions were taken (Lebeuf 1963). Thus women wielded social and political influence through indirect methods; physical absence did not equal political passivity (Driberg 1932; Schiller 1990).

An example of a biased historian's account of precolonial Uganda can be found in the following analysis of Buganda's history: "The acquisition of new territories gave the kings great leverage of power. . . . wars brought more material rewards—cattle, women and other prizes of war. The distribution of all these was in the hands of the kings" (Karugire 1980, 23).

Karugire's assessment develops the view earlier presented by Mahmood Mamdani, who argued that "women were a means of production, to be owned, exchanged and distributed" (Mamdani 1976, 25). Even under the broadest definition of "wealth," how could women be a source of wealth when they are not (and cannot be) products of surplus labor? (cf. Nabudere 1980, 17). The perception of women in precolonial times as "wealth" originated from ethnographies of early Western anthropologists and missionaries who fossilized African societies through a bifocal lens of sexism and Eurocentrism (e.g., Ashe 1894; Johnston 1902; Roscoe 1911, 1924). Moreover, the capture of women never ended in enslavement. John Tosh (1978, 86) suggests that women and girls were particularly targeted as war captives because "[it] allowed the ideal of polygyny to be more widely attained." Consequently, the capturing of women and girls in warfare was linked to the sociopolitical and economic growth of precolonial African societies. Nakanyike Musisi's research on Buganda elaborately demonstrates how the large-scale polygyny ("grand" or "elite" polygyny) practiced by the kings and the elite class was instrumental in the development of Buganda's political expansion and state formation (Musisi 1991).

The same gender biases continue with respect to analyses of warfare, conquest, and overall social development. How is it that mainstream historians subjectively omit from their analyses the exploits and feats performed by women, which prevail in Ugandan legends and historical tradition? Why is there no mention of Nyabingi of Kigezi, Nambi of Buganda, Nyangi of Bunyoro-Kitara, Bagaya of Toro, and the celebrated female war leader in Lango who commanded an army in battle and later established her own chieftaincy (Driberg 1932; Lebeuf 1963; Dunbar 1965; Murindwa 1994)? Why are the important political roles played by the queen mothers and the kings' classificatory sisters in the heritage of Uganda's monarchical systems often omitted from standard accounts of precolonial history?[15] Not only did these women share political power with the kings but in some cases they even exercised judicial powers, collected taxes, and condemned their own people to death (Lebeuf 1963; Schiller 1990; Jjuuko 1993). In Buganda, for example, the powers and prerogatives of the *Namasole* were tangible, superior to that of all other chiefs. On her death the office would be filled with a classificatory mother (Schiller 1990, 458–459).

In the segmentary societies of the Luo-speaking people of northern Uganda, women assumed the role of divine-mediator—the link between the living and the ancestral spirits. A divine-mediator carried considerable power and influence because she possessed the skills to heal the sick, avert evil, predict war and so forth. Because of their role in society, female mediators could (and often did) politically mobilize the populace with ease (Tosh 1978). A classic example of such influence can be found in the person of Angwen of Ngai, whose influence spread across the northern region. Such mobilization finds more recent expression in the case of the notorious mediator and warrior, Alice Lakwena. Using her traditional magical and messianic skills, Lakwena inspired and led an insurgent army that waged war against Yoweri Museveni's NRM government from 1987 to 1993. Lakwena's rebel group was finally defeated by the superior and more sophisticated government army, and she was forced into exile in Kenya.

Although during precolonial times Ugandan women were not as marginalized as they are today, their status was by no means equal to that of men. In the patriarchal societies that existed in precolonial Uganda, men dominated positions of political, economic, and social power (cf. Nzomo 1988). Kinship relations linked the two sexes within the nexus of a wider domain of structural conditions that included communities, people, and associations rooted in their working lives. Gender differences that stemmed from these relationships were (and still are) fed by belief systems embedded in inequalities of power and social behavior (Wakoko and Lobao 1996). The development of a sexual division of labor in

Uganda, as in many other African societies, preceded the colonial period (Schmidt 1991). However, and this is very important, the dynamics of such sexual division of labor at this time were somewhat different from what they became with the introduction of colonial capitalism. Ugandan society did not denigrate women's work as it does today. Gender relations at this time took on a form that was more complementary than hierarchical (Pulme 1963; Okeyo 1980). Men generally built houses, hunted, herded and milked, fished, and fought. Women cultivated, processed, and marketed crops; collected fuel and water; cared for the children, the sick, and the elderly; made pottery, cooked, cleaned, and washed.[16] There was no negative evaluation attached to these different roles. As Driberg (1932, 409) explains, "A woman carrying out her duty [was] held in just as high esteem as a man carrying out his and the nature of the occupation [was] of no moment."

Before the introduction of capitalism, most precolonial agricultural societies were divided into satellite households.[17] Each constituted a separate economic unit with agricultural produce controlled by the wife (Curley 1973).

Although customary marriages varied from *kabila* to *kabila*, they were all potentially polygynous, recognized the payment of bridewealth, and constituted a contract between the families of the bride and the groom (Obbo 1980; Tamale 1993). The institution of bridewealth that is customarily associated with marriages in Uganda played very important social roles. Bridewealth consisted of marriage gifts (e.g., livestock, goats, sheep, or some special symbol of wealth) offered by the groom to the bride's family before, at, or after the marriage. It was a means of cementing the relationship between all families concerned and of providing stability to the marriage. Driberg epitomizes the precolonial idea behind bridewealth thus:

> It is one side of a legal contract, providing for the filiation of the children and their lawful inheritance: it supplies a religious and ritual sanction, invoking the benevolent regard and interest of the ancestors, from whom the cattle were inherited: it stands as a security for the good treatment of the wife in her new home and serves as a social and political link between the clans of the contracting parties. (Driberg 1932, 413)

Traditional marriage was, therefore, *not* a commercial transaction, and the parties involved were largely free partners within the context of societies that emphasized communitarian ideals in contrast to individual autonomy.[18] Indeed, all *makabila* found in Uganda used a specific term for the marriage gift transaction distinct from that used for the payment of goods (cf. Burman 1990). A woman was free to walk out of an abusive marriage and return to her parents and relatives (and often did). Within these family/clan arrangements men and women jointly made decisions that governed the norms and ethos of their cultural, political, and juridical lives.

Several social processes were imposed by colonialism, setting in motion a set of potent factors that decidedly upset the balance of labor, sharpening the superordinate/subordinate relationship between men and women in Uganda.

The Colonial Period

Through a series of "agreements" between African chiefs/kings and the British, Uganda became a British protectorate. Retaining precolonial frameworks of political authority, albeit greatly curtailed, the colonialists used an elaborate system of indirect rule to govern the protectorate. Overall governance in Uganda was exercised by the governor, initially assisted by an executive and later by a legislative council (Legco) (Morris and Read 1966). Because of its political, economic, and numerical prominence, the kingdom of Buganda was accorded special treatment by the colonial administration—a fact that nettled non-Baganda and significantly affected the course of political developments in the country. Buganda became the hub from which the colonial power spread its stranglehold across the rest of the country, and her king, the *kabaka,* became a central figure in the political history of colonial Uganda.

With the introduction of capitalism,[19] women's relationship to men was greatly influenced by women's and men's relationship to capital. The "right" that men already had to their wives' labor was strengthened, and they gained a firmer grip on women's productive and reproductive labor. Women's subordination was further secured through their exclusion from wage employment; the power that comes with a pocketbook for the man at the end of each month was bound to restructure gender relations in the Ugandan household. Roberts provides a succinct summary of the reasons why capitalism increased the subordination of women in the noncapitalist sectors:

> The intensification of female labour in peasant economies released male labour for the production of cash crops. . . . Their [women's] productive labour was intensified to ensure the subsistence basis of labour reserve areas while their reproductive labour ensured the maintenance and reproduction of labour power at no cost to the capitalist wage. (Roberts 1984, 176)

The British introduced cash crops such as cotton, tobacco, coffee, and tea, which provided a cheap raw material supply for the factories in the metropole. Ugandan men had no choice but to engage in the production of these primary products in order to meet their tax obligations to the colonial government (Jamal 1978). Thus men cultivated economic crops while women continued to cultivate food crops as well as cash crops on a subsistence level. Under these conditions, Ugandan women became the primary producers, constituting 60 percent of the labor force in the agricultural sector and accounting for 80 percent in food production (Economic Commission for Africa 1975). The fact that women were (and are) not paid for their productive[20] and reproductive[21] labor means that they provide the chief subsidy to capitalist production. Such exploitation of women's labor markedly lowered their status relative to that of men.

When the British colonized Uganda, they transplanted their own ethnocentric version of male-dominated politics and completely ignored women's political roles. As noted by Smock:

> Colonial policies had a rather important influence on sex role definitions and opportunities for women. Christian missionaries and colonial administrators brought with them Victorian conceptions concerning the place of women in society. Generally they did not appreciate the significant contributions frequently made by women and their sense of independence. (Smock 1977, 181)

Where there had been a blurred distinction between private and public life in Uganda, British structures and policies focused on delineating a clear distinction guided by an ideology that perceived men as public actors and women as private performers. Colonialists worked hand in hand with the African patriarchs to develop inflexible customary laws, which evolved into new structures and forms of domination (Schmidt 1991; Mama 1996).

Squeezed between colonial oppression on the one hand and gender oppression on the other, women rallied together to challenge the structures of domination. The spark that lit the smoldering fire within Ugandan women came from a single event, which led to the formation of the Uganda Council of Women (UCW) in 1947. In that year the husband of Lovinsa Senkonyo, a member of the Young Wives Group (YWG—a subsidiary of YWCA), died and left her with their only daughter and the property they had jointly acquired during their twelve years of marriage. A few days after her husband's burial the widow was shocked to find that all their property, including the marital home, had been inherited by a youthful son born to her husband outside the marriage. Members of the YWG, realizing that they could face a similar fate, gathered together and stormed the bishop's house on Namirembe hill in Kampala. They demanded to know what they, as women, could get out of marriage. Asian women, who also faced serious legal and social problems (e.g., bridewealth-related "wife killings"), joined hands with their African counterparts. The UCW was soon formed as an organization to fight for women's rights.[22] This marked the watershed for the contemporary women's movement in Uganda. But women's voices continued to be excluded from national politics.

As in many other African countries, the Ugandan women's movement was closely linked to anticolonial actions and the subsequent independence movement. For example, in 1953, when the kabaka was forced into exile by the colonial power, three busloads of women clad in traditional bark cloth stormed the state house of Sir Andrew Cohen—the British governor who had ordered the kabaka's exile—demanding his return. Sir Cohen only agreed to give these women audience after they had threatened to spend the night in his compound and stage a hunger strike. In addition, women participated in demonstrations, wrote protest letters to British members of parliament, and to world leaders such as the founding prime minister of India, Jawarahal Nehru. Newspapers such as *Uganda Empya* were also used to advance the women's political cause.[23] Although the UCW was often portrayed as a useless elitist organization (Justice Minister Obwangor once described it as only good for *umalidadi*—fashion and overdressing),[24] it certainly had a political agenda. The membership of the UCW was a melting pot of multiracial women, and through it women gained political acumen. UCW members rallied around collective women's rights issues such as citizenship, civic education, and voting rights, and they actively pushed for increased female participation in national politics. In 1960 the UCW held a big conference on the status of women in relation to the laws of marriage, divorce, and inheritance. This conference was a big boost to the women's movement, serving as a vital signal to the government and the nation that women were dissatisfied with their position in society (Brown 1988).

The first African woman to enter the colonial legislative council (Legco) was UCW member Pumla Kisosonkole, who joined British-born Barbara Saben in 1957.[25] These two women, who were among the forty-nine nominated members, sat with their fifty-one male counterparts and deliberated on crucial bills and policies that were to shape the framework of an independent Uganda. The October 1958 Legco elections saw the exit of both Saben and Kisosonkole and the entry of three women, namely, Joyce Mpanga (née Masembe), Sarah Ntiro (née Nyendwoha), and Frances Akello. These women, who were nominated to the Legco by Governor Crawford, ably contributed to the lawmaking process immediately preceding independence.

Only five African women ever sat on the legislative council prior to independence, namely, Pumla Kisosonkole, Joyce Masembe, Sarah Nyendwoha, Frances Akello, and Eseza Makumbi.[26] All were nominated, as it was virtually impossible for women to be elected to this legislative body. A group called the Uganda African Women's League (UAWL) supported and endorsed African female candidates contesting for Legco. Like men, the women involved in the nationalist movement were mostly from the educated elite class and had fathers and/or husbands who were notables in Uganda's politics. Only one woman stood in the 1958 Legco elections and she lost (Apter 1967). Gender discrimination all but eliminated women from the African electoral franchise and produced practically all-male suffrage. Morris and Read explain:

> An African resident of an electoral district of 21 years of age was entitled to vote provided he was able to read and write in his own language *or* was the owner of freehold or *mailo* land *or* had occupied land for the previous two years *or* had been in regular paid employment for seven years *or* had an income of £ 100 a year *or* property worth £ 400. The vast majority of men could fulfil the minimum of these requirements. A woman, on the other hand, if illiterate would be likely to qualify as a voter only on the grounds of occupancy of land. It was a matter of local custom as to whether a woman could be held to occupy land over which her husband had occupancy rights. (Morris and Read 1966, 57 n. 1)

The year before, eight women had also stood unsuccessfully for the Buganda Lukiiko (parliament) seats. These women had campaigned hard, but the evening before polling day several *saza* (county) chiefs went on a vigorous campaigning operation around the villages and urged the exclusively male electorate not to vote for women "because," they alleged, "the kabaka had proclaimed that it was not time yet for women to get involved in politics."[27] Thus thwarted, some of these women confronted the kabaka, requesting from him chieftancy roles. However, there were no such positions for women, and the best that they could secure were peripheral positions such as board membership to municipal councils.[28]

Colonial policy on education was among the most potent factors adversely affecting the relative position of women in Africa (Graham 1971; Smock 1977; Weis 1980; Obbo 1986; Walker 1990). As in Victorian Europe, educational opportunities were disproportionately provided to males (Staudt 1981; Tamale and Oloka-Onyango 1996). Missionary education for women, such as that provided at prestigious all-girls schools like Gayaza High, Namagunga Senior, and Buloba College, was primarily geared toward providing educated men with good wives and homemakers.[29] In the words of Miss Allen, the missionary headmistress of Gayaza and later of Buloba college, "My staff will do their best to teach Domestic Science, House-wifery and Hygiene as it is taught in England" (*Uganda*

Church Review 1930, 115, quoted in Musisi 1992, 182; also see Oloka-Onyango 1992).[30] Moreover, the educated housewife was viewed by the colonizers as a potential consumer who could motivate her husband's productivity.

> She must be educated to want a better home, better furnishings, better food, better water supplies, etc. and if she wants them she will want them for her children. In short, the sustained effort from the male will only come when the woman is educated to the stage when her wants are never satisfied. (Roddan 1958; quoted in Staudt 1989, 78).

Not only did such training deny women the intellectual skills needed to participate in the Western system of politics imposed by the British but it also introduced new gender roles that in turn radically altered gender ideology (Tamale and Oloka-Onyango 1996). The impact that these modifications had on household structures in Uganda was significant. Women were relegated to a redefined, subordinated domesticity. The status of men, by contrast, was elevated and reified.

A classic example of the real constraints of participating in formal politics imposed by objective educational, social, and cultural limitations is demonstrated by the case of Rebecca Mulira. A pioneer member of the budding women's movement in colonial Uganda, Mulira was an extremely dynamic and energetic activist of national and international repute.[31] It seemed very odd indeed that a woman of Mulira's radicalism and potential never consolidated her activism by joining the highest ranks of decisionmaking. In an interview she told me, "I *really* wanted to join parliament. . . . I think that the main reason I didn't was because I did not have a university degree." Mulira was clearly ahead of her time in many respects. As a woman, however, she was constrained by the gender limitations within which she was operating.[32] Although she had overcome some of the constraints, she could not shake them off in toto. The absence of a woman of such stature from the key decisionmaking institutions in the early days of nationalist ferment clearly demonstrates the impact of the prevailing gendered context and the role that a lack of educational opportunities coupled with a political system based on educational credentials played in reproducing gender inequalities.[33] Nevertheless, numerous men who did not hold university degrees—indeed, some without significant formal educational qualifications—stood for and were elected for parliament.

While taking due note of the impediments limiting women's participation in politics, it must be remembered that, despite the gender disparities in the colonial educational system, there also existed power and class differentials among women. For instance, the historical location of women from the northern region of Uganda, coupled with colonial favoritism of the Buganda kingdom, meant that Baganda women had better opportunities, educational and otherwise, than their counterparts from the north. Almost all the prestigious girls' schools in Uganda were established in the southern region. Thus, despite the fact that missionary education for girls was relatively inferior to that for boys, it offered women the opportunity to become better exposed and more amenable to activism. The consequences of such a legacy are both class based and regionally differentiated.

The pressure and demands of Ugandan nationalists, coupled with those of multilateral imperialism in the postwar period, made it increasingly difficult and unprofitable for Britain to cling to its colonial empire (Nabudere 1980). From the late 1940s onward, Britain prepared the ground for formal independence in all its colonies. All negotiations for Uganda's independence took place between the colonizers and an elite male collection of budding indigenous politicians, with Buganda placed at center stage. Women, on the other hand, were deliberately ignored by the colonial power and the Ugandan patriarchs despite their protests and their active participation in the struggle.

By the 1950s, the colonial system had "trained" a class of elite young men who would inherit entrenched social and political power over the decades. In 1952 the first "national" political party was founded. The Uganda National Congress (UNC), like all political parties formed subsequently, was not a mass party; it closely resembled an old-boy network. Even while they agitated for democracy from the protectorate government, the parties themselves excluded specific social groups such as peasants and women (two groups with a huge overlap) from their ranks. The Progressive Party was formed in 1954 by a group of old boys from the elite Kings College Budo. It had no agenda that bore any resemblance to its name; "conspicuously conservative" is how Karugire (1980, 154) described it. Neither did the Democratic Party (DP), born in 1956, follow democratic principles by any stretch of the imagination. The Uganda Peoples Congress (UPC), born two years later, was no exception. All were ethnocentric, rallying around parochial ends that were often selfish and opportunistic—the personal acquisition of power (Karugire 1980, 168; Mittelman 1975, 71; Kabaka of Buganda 1967, 148).

The three political parties that participated in the general elections on the eve of independence were all backed by strong conservative, patriarchal institutions: UPC by the Protestant church; DP by the Roman Catholic Church; and Kabaka Yekka (KY, Kabaka alone) by the Buganda oligarchy (Karugire 1980; Okoth 1996). Uganda attained formal independence on October 9, 1962, with English as its official language and a unicameral national assembly modeled on the House of Commons replacing the colonial Legco. Milton Obote, the UPC leader who had won national elections in April 1962, ascended to the position of executive prime minister. Sir Edward Mutesa II—the kabaka of Buganda—was elected by parliament as ceremonial president and head of state in 1963.[34] Women were granted full suffrage at independence, but it meant little in reality. Not only had they been completely sidestepped in all negotiations leading up to independence but colonialism had systematically alienated them from the redefined political structure. Such alienation was maintained by the nationalist parties, with women playing only marginal roles in decisionmaking processes and in the designation of political priorities at the time.

The Postindependence Era

By the time the colonial Union Jack was lowered for good, the die of the public/private divide in Uganda had been indelibly cast. Social and political structures were in place; law, religion, and the educational system ensured that this ideology remained embedded not only in the sociopolitical strata but also within the consciousness of "independent" Ugandans. Although women continued to be excluded from formal politics, they relentlessly pressured government to consider their concerns.[35] The women's movement continued to gain momentum as new groups such as the Uganda Association of University Women (UAUW) emerged. Their activities were not confined to Uganda alone, and they reached out to the international arena. For instance, the UCW sent a delegation to the 1963 international council of women conference in Washington, D.C. The following year, Uganda was also represented at the All Africa Women's Conference held in Monrovia, Liberia.

The activities of the early prominent actors in the women's associations were initially confined to a handful of prominent women, some of whom were handpicked to attend international conferences. They nevertheless came to believe that their activities needed to reach out to the broader populace of Ugandan women. Thus in 1966 they set up the Uganda Association of Women's Organizations (UAWO) to act as an avenue through which different women shared ideas and experiences in their collective struggle for women's rights.[36] The women's movement recorded a landmark success in January 1964, when a commission was appointed to investigate the status of women.[37]

Only four years after formal independence, Milton Obote abrogated the 1962 independence constitution through a swift coup d'état. He abolished monarchies and hounded the kabaka into exile (Kabaka of Buganda 1968). From 1966, when he declared himself president with extensive executive powers (spelled out in the 1966 "pigeon-hole" constitution, tailor-made to suit his purposes),[38] Obote ruled the country under a de facto one-party state. When he announced in 1970 that parliamentary elections were scheduled for the following year, the UCW prepared to participate. At their annual meeting that year, UCW invited Felix Onama, secretary-general of UPC, to speak to them about the upcoming elections. The women requested Onama to assure them of UPC's support in speech writing, campaigning, and transportation, "since they were late starters in this type of activity." Onama responded that "it would be discriminatory to give women special aids to ensure their election because this action would emphasize the fact that they were women and de-emphasize their political competence" (minutes of UCW annual meeting; quoted in White 1973, 227). Onama's argument failed to take into account the fact that Ugandan women had been continuously excluded from the arena of formal politics and were therefore indeed handicapped in developing any such competence.

In 1971, through a bloody coup d'état, Obote was ousted by his own favored army officer, Idi Amin. The military dictator suspended the 1967 constitution and vested all executive and legislative powers in his person. Amin exercised those legislative powers with vigor and caprice throughout his nine-year rule, proclaiming decrees at whim. His desire for complete control led him to destroy or cripple all potential sources of opposition, including all women's organizations, which he banned in 1978. In their place he created a closely monitored semi-parastatal organization called the National Council of Women (NCW).[39] Operating as a bureau under the insignificant Ministry of Community Development, NCW was relegated to a very lowly status. Nevertheless, it kept the embers of women's struggles smoldering until 1986, when the government stranglehold on NGOs was removed.[40] In 1979 Amin's rule of terror ended as a joint force of exiled Ugandans and Tanzanian troops ousted him from power (Melady and Melady 1977; Jamison 1992).

Only two women out of a total number of ninety-two members sat in the first postindependence legislature (1962–1971). Both were nominees of KY. Sugra Visram, a close friend of the kabaka, was of Indian origin.[41] Florence Lubega, a daughter of former *katikiro* Samuel Wamala of Buganda, was later appointed parliamentary secretary (equivalent to deputy minister) to the Ministry of Planning and Community Development. She also served as president of the UCW. The powerful, articulate submissions of both women in the House are on record.[42] Thanks to the pressure of the women's movement, new legislation was introduced in the 1960s and early 1970s addressing some of their problems.[43]

Two women entered the House in the 1979 post-Amin interim legislature called the National Consultative Council (NCC). Rhoda Kalema was elected,[44] and Namirembe Bitamazire joined as an ex officio member, having been appointed minister of education. After a lapse of eighteen years, general elections were held in 1980.[45] Four political parties participated in the 1980 election, namely, UPC, DP, the Conservative Party (CP), and the newly formed Uganda Patriotic Movement (UPM).[46] The elections, which are believed to have been massively rigged, returned Obote to power after a nine-year hiatus. Five women competed in the 1980 elections: Cecilia Ogwal (UPC), Theresa Odongo-Oduka (UPC), Rhoda Kalema (UPM), Freda Lule (UPM), and Robinah Kasadha (UPM). Only Odongo-Oduka was successful. As the sole woman in the 145-member parliament, she also held the portfolio of deputy minister of health.[47] It is interesting to note that DP did not field any female candidates in 1980. And yet its own commission of inquiry set up to examine the reasons behind its losing the 1962 elections found, among other reasons, that it was because the party had ignored women (Muscat 1984).

Under the second Obote regime NCW struggled on against all odds. Despite the meager subsidy allotted to the organization by the government, some dedicated civil servants in the ministry of community development kept its activities alive. For example, Marjorie Ddungu, who headed the community development department, and another ministry official, Florence Nekyon, ensured that the pulse of NCW continued to be felt in the districts. In 1984, NCW prepared to hold elections for its own executive to replace the government-appointed Ministry of Community Development civil servants. The government intervened immediately to stop such elections from taking place. However, the spirit of NCW was not deflated, and in the same year it rallied to officially commemorate International Women's Day for the first time in Uganda. This was in preparation for the 1985 UN Women's Nairobi conference. The NCW wrote a cabinet memorandum after the Nairobi conference demanding that government establish a full-fledged ministry for women.[48]

Dogged by several guerrilla movements almost from the beginning of his second term of office, Obote ruled with a ruthlessness that many believe was worse than Idi Amin's (Furley 1987; Mudoola 1988; Mutibwa 1992). One of the most effective of the guerrilla groups that sprouted in 1981 was former defense minister Yoweri Kaguta Museveni's National Resistance Army/Movement (NRM/A), which operated in what became known as the Luwero Triangle, a fairly large swath of territory in northwestern Buganda. As a guerrilla movement, the NRM/A developed unique structures of governance and participation, the kernel of which was formed by the resistance councils and committees (RCs).[49] A significant advance to their operation was achieved with the mandatory inclusion of a women's representative on each committee.[50]

In the wake of growing insurgency, political instability, and internal dissension, the second Obote regime was toppled in mid-1985 by its armed forces, the Uganda National Liberation Army (UNLA). This paved the way for the NRM/A to expand its parameters of operation, eventually forcing the UNLA to sue for peace. Despite attempts at a negotiated settlement the NRM/A scuttled the peace settlement, storming Kampala and taking power in January 1986.

The NRM administration became the first postcolonial government in Uganda to take proactive measures to include women in formal politics. Between 1986, when the NRM took over power and 1989, when the policy of affirmative action for women was introduced, there were only four women in the National Resistance Council.[51] Elections to the NRC, the Constituent Assembly, and the National Assembly in 1989, 1994, and 1996, respectively, were all supposedly run on a nonpartisan basis with candidates standing on their individual merit under the aegis of the "movement" political system.[52] Thus, until the affirmative action policy was introduced, the total number of women in any given postindependence legislature never exceeded four. Figure 1.1 provides a graphic illustration of the relative improvement in women's representation in Uganda's successive parliaments during the last forty-three years. There are no figures shown for the period from 1971 to 1979 because, as earlier discussed, parliament was suspended under the regime of Idi Amin.

How can we account for the drastic changes favoring women introduced by the NRM? Were the NRM males fundamentally different from the patriarchal "old boys"? Interestingly, women did not feature at all in the NRM Ten-Point Program, which stated its original guiding philosophy.[53] Winnie Byanyima, who actively participated in the guerrilla war, sums up the general attitude of NRM/A at the time: "The NRM leadership was fully aware of the extent of women's oppression and in principle it opposed sex discrimination. However, in practice, the leadership did not openly speak against male domination" (Byanyima 1992, 140). Captain Gertrude Njuba, another guerrilla war veteran, revealed that the popular resistance army did not have a particular gender agenda.[54] It is indeed difficult to decipher the *real* reasons behind the NRM affirmative action policies for Ugandan women; the best that can be offered here is informed speculation.

Yoweri Museveni, the leader of the NRM, has been described as "a man of political shrewdness" and "an astute tactician" when it comes to foreign policy (Glickman 1992, 185). What better way to show the international community that NRM is committed to democracy than to make women more visible within the arena of decisionmaking? What better way for a regime that had ascended to power behind the barrel of the gun to gain legitimacy and to place the hitherto "sick man of Africa" back on the world map?[55] At the home front it may be that Museveni realized the potential that can be reaped from gaining the favor of a constituency

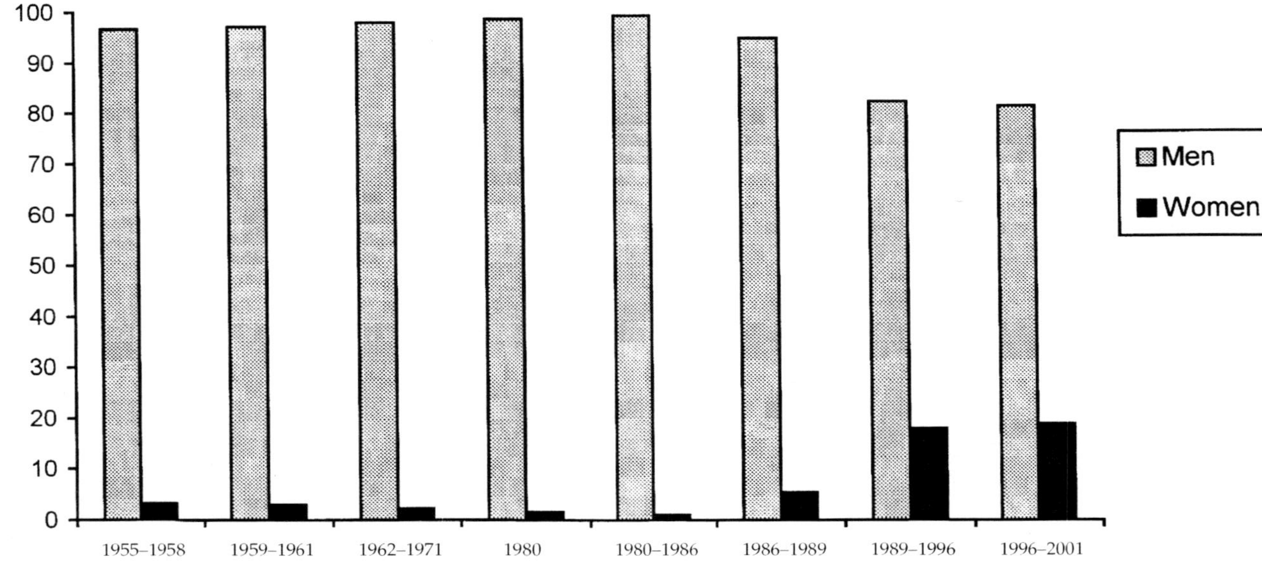

FIGURE 1.1   Percentages of Male and Female Representation in Uganda's Parliaments

that not only constituted the larger half of the population but could also exert critical influence on men as their wives, sisters, and daughters.[56] Indeed, observers have used terms such as "political expediency"[57] and "a gimmick"[58] to epitomize NRM policies on women.

But NRM policies did not emerge entirely from the blue. The period that Museveni spent in Tanzania, first as a student at the University of Dar es Salaam during the late 1960s and second as an exile in the same country during the 1970s, no doubt had a significant influence on him. During that time Tanzania with its policies of *Ujamaa* (African socialism; literally, familyhood) was the hotbed of revolutionary leftist politics which, despite its inherent contradictions, created conditions for debates and struggles over gender relations (Scott 1995). At this time, Museveni also forged connections with the Mozambiçan revolutionary party called the Front for the Liberation of Mozambique (FRELIMO) which, given its socialist aspirations, accorded women a higher profile than was normally the case in African postcolonial countries (Urdang 1989). Indeed, Tanzania and Mozambique were among the few countries in Africa to lead the way in introducing a sex quota in their parliaments.

Finally, women's significant contribution to the five-year guerrilla struggle may have added to Museveni's realization that indeed women can perform as well, if not better, than men in traditionally "male" jobs. Apart from participating in active combat, women played a significant role in the tasks of recruiting, espionage, procurement of supplies, and attending to the sick and injured. The agency of the women themselves, therefore, should not be overlooked. During and after the liberation struggle, women made their grievances known to the military high command (Byanyima 1992). Women's groups, such as ACFODE, demanded greater representation of women at all levels of decisionmaking.[59] Thus affirmative action may represent the "token reward" that NRM granted women for their role in the bush war. Museveni himself comes close to admitting this when he explains NRM's policy on women through a parable:

> A subject . . . did a distinguished service for [a king] and the king asked his subject how he could reward him. He said to the king: 'Your Majesty, I don't want any gift from you. All I want is that when we are in a public place you should just call me by my name.' The king was baffled. . . . Your Majesty, it will help me very much because if the king calls me by my name in front of so many people, everybody will wonder who I am and they will all come to me and help me (Museveni 1997, 191).

"This," Museveni concludes his story, "is what we did for the women" (Museveni 1997, 192). But the paternalism behind this parable is fairly evident. Women are not considered the equal of but merely the "subject" of men. Nor does the king "reward" the subject with full recognition of his status as an equal human being. Ultimately, the recognition given is bestowed at the "pleasure" of the king, and can, within such a conceptualization of "recognition," be just as easily removed from them. In the final analysis, the parable illustrates that the NRM's gesture toward women does not reflect a fundamental belief in their intrinsic qualities as either fellow combatants or fellow travelers in the struggle for overall emancipation.

Indeed, beyond the affirmative action policies there is very little evidence to suggest that men in the NRM leadership are fundamentally different from the pre-1986 "old boys" in showing a real commitment to women's emancipation. Examples abound to demonstrate that the policies of the NRM only pay lip service to women's emancipation. For instance, since its inception, the ministry in charge of women's affairs has always received the smallest portion of disbursements from government coffers. In the budget policy statement of the Ministry of Gender and Community Development for the financial year 1996–97, each of the eight departments within the ministry reported that their main constraint was "gross underfunding."[60] It is true that all ministries are underfunded because of the country's fledgling economy, but considering that Ugandan women constitute the mainstay of the economy, conventional wisdom would dictate that the ministry in charge of uplifting their status should be accorded priority ranking.[61] Another example to illustrate NRM's deference to male authority can be found in the post-1996 election cabinet appointments: Only six of the sixty-two members of the cabinet were female.[62] This action prompted comments such as this from female politicians:

> The president who has been a champion for the cause of equality between men and women has let us down this time. Women have contributed a lot as mothers and producers in this country; surely our president can do better. He fought for five years and women supported him. Ten years on as president, women have been in the forefront supporting him. How then can he start slipping backwards? (Byanyima, *The Crusader*, July 9–11, 1996, 2).

Such displeasure resonates with the disillusionment of Mozambiçan and Angolan women whose postrevolutionary Marxist governments accorded them affirmative action in the public sphere without demonstrating a further commitment to dismantling the male tributaries of power (Scott 1995, chap. 6).

But the issue at stake here is not in the motive that prompted government to introduce the affirmative action policy in the arena of politics.

What is more important for the women of Uganda is what they can do with such a policy. Now that women firmly have their foot in the door of national leadership, can they take full advantage and push it further to make a difference?

Not only is the Ugandan peasant woman excluded from high political office. Her right to vote for political leaders is also curtailed by the dominating husband who not only dictates whether or not she can vote but also who she should vote for. Thus, despite the fact that the constitution affords Ugandan women the full right to vote independently, gender relations shackle this freedom. This fact was clearly demonstrated in the 1996 presidential elections, as several cases of election-related domestic violence were reported. In two such cases women died for the "crime" of voting for a candidate their husbands did not support (*Monitor*, May 22–24, 1996, 9). Behind the violence that these women suffered at the hands of their abusive husbands, one can clearly discern the defiance, the challenge, and the resistance that women are putting up to male dominance. In this sense, the crowing hen metaphor relates to the wider rural female populace, which is beginning to assert the right to participate in national politics.

Beginning in the 1980s, structural adjustment policy "reforms" initiated by the World Bank and the International Monetary Fund were introduced in Uganda. The SAP package includes privatization, cutbacks in public spending, dismantling of social welfare, retrenchment of the formal labor force, and the deregulation of labor markets. These unpopular reforms have had adverse effects on the general population but most particularly on women, who are the mainstay of the production and reproduction system. They have had to shoulder the extra family responsibilities that come with the withdrawal of subsidies from their children's education, health care, food, and transportation.[63]

The economic crisis that Uganda has experienced since the late 1970s forced many women to seek innovative strategies of coping with their worsening situations (Obbo 1980, 1986; Tadria 1987; Tripp 1994; Wakoko and Lobao 1996). One such strategy was to engage in petty commodity production in the so-called informal economic sector. For these women, having access to cash provided them with some measure of economic autonomy. Sexual discrimination in the formal employment sector, coupled with the "double shift" outside and inside the home, ensures women's continued dependency and subordination. A closely related phenomenon of women-headed households is on the increase in Uganda (Obbo 1980). This fact notwithstanding, single motherhood and spinsterhood continue to be socially stigmatized. Such attitudes toward "unattached" women serve to further women's dependence on and subordination to men.[64] Finally, the new scourge of AIDS, which has hit

Ugandans with merciless brutality, killing more women than men, has also had a telling impact on gender relations (Kisekka 1990; Kaleeba 1991; ISIS 1993).[65] AIDS has served as a wake-up call for many Ugandan women to defy cultural norms and religious practices that make them vulnerable to infection, including traditional practices that require women to be submissive to their husbands' sexual advances at all times or widow inheritance, which is still practiced in some Ugandan cultures (Tamale 1993).

To conclude, the contemporary political situation of women in Uganda is affected by a host of social, cultural, and economic conditions. Those conditions have fostered a contradictory situation, on the one hand further marginalizing women and on the other forcing them to become more organized and militant in addressing their situation. These developments, as this discussion demonstrates, have had a significant impact on women's overall status. Having provided the temporal and spatial context within which Ugandan female politicians operate, I now turn to a brief analysis of some features in the relationship between gender, politics and affirmative action.

Gender, Politics, and Affirmative Action: A Precursor

Table 1.1 below provides a continentwide picture of African women's representation in national legislatures. The table reveals that no African country has reached the 1995 target of 30 percent set by the Economic and Social Council of the United Nations for the representation of women in parliament (United Nations 1992).[66] When we make comparisons across single and popular chambers regarding women's representation on the continent, Seychelles ranks highest at 27.3 percent. Ranking lowest are Djibouti and the Comoros, where the assemblies are exclusively composed of men. The mean percentage of women's representation across the continent is only 7.9. Uganda is ranked fifth (coming behind Mozambique, South Africa, and Eritrea), with a percentage of 18.1. Considering that women constitute more than half the population in Africa, the paucity of African women in decisionmaking positions is striking.

Historically, governments have attempted to redress such forms of discrimination by introducing affirmative action programs. Programs of this nature were first used in the twilight of colonialism and were termed "indigenization" or "Africanization." They sought to incorporate indigenous peoples in areas of the civil service and elsewhere from which they had been previously excluded (Adedeji 1981). The principle gained ascendance during the 1960s at the height of the civil rights and women's movement in the United States, where it has been defined thus:

> Attempts to make progress toward *substantive*, rather than merely formal, equality of opportunity for those groups, such as women or racial minorities, which are currently under-represented in significant positions in society, by explicitly taking into account the defining characteristic—sex or race—which has been the basis for discrimination. (Mullen 1988, 244, my emphasis)

Affirmative action policies in most Western countries are implemented in the spheres of employment and education, but non-Western countries are experimenting with it mostly in the sphere of politics. Ghana was one of the first African countries to introduce a quota system for women in 1960. In that year socialist-leaning president Kwame Nkrumah passed a law allowing for the nomination and election of ten women to the National Assembly by the existing members of the body (Harvey 1966, 36–37). Today other African countries having constitutions that require a quota for women's representatives in parliament include Tanzania—36 out of 274 seats; Burkina Faso—10 seats out of 178 in the Upper House; and Eritrea—10 seats out of 105.[67]

Other African countries that have experimented with affirmative action policies for women in politics include Sudan (Sadat 1987, 364) and Egypt. The Egyptian strategy, which guaranteed thirty seats for women in parliament, lasted only seven years, from 1979 to 1986. Howard-Merriam analyzed the Egyptian experiment and concluded that its failure and eventual abrogation essentially illustrated the limitations of reform from above; consequently, it also poses the problem of co-optation for underrepresented groups (Howard-Merriam 1990). This argument has been echoed by a number of feminists who are not opposed to affirmative action per se but question the liberal arguments used to support the measure. Sandra Harding, for example, criticizes the notion of "adding women and gender" to existing social and political structures without questioning their hierarchical and politically regressive agendas (Harding 1991). Iris Young is even more pointed in her criticism:

> The terms of the affirmative action debate define a set of assumptions that accept the basic structure of the division of labor and the basic process of allocating positions. . . . To the degree that the affirmative action debate limits public attention to the relatively narrow and superficial issue of the redistribution of positions within an already given framework, that debate serves the function of supporting the structural status quo. (Young 1990, 200)

Viewed from this perspective, redistributive politics, which makes use of affirmative action to increase the representation of women in legislative

TABLE 1.1 Number of Women Parliamentarians in African Countries as of January 1, 1997

	Latest Elections	Total Membership	Number of Women	% of Women
Algeria	May 1994	183	12	6.6
Angola	Sept. 1992	220	21	9.5
Benin	Mar. 1995	83	6	7.2
Botswana	Oct. 1994	47	4	8.5
Burkina Faso	May 1992	107	4	3.7
Burundi	June 1993	81	10	12.3
Cameroon	Mar. 1992	180	22	12.2
Cape Verde	Dec. 1995	72	8	11.1
Central African Republic	Sept. 1993	85	3	3.5
Chad	Apr. 1993	52	9	17.3
Comoros	Dec. 1996	43	0	0.0
Congo	Oct. 1996 (U)	60	2	3.3
	Oct. 1993 (L)	125	2	1.6
Côte d'Ivoire	Nov. 1995	168	14	8.3
Djibouti	Dec. 1992	65	0	0.0
Egypt	Nov. 1995	454	9	2.0
Equatorial Guinea	Nov. 1993	80	7	8.8
Eritrea	Feb. 1994	105	22	21.0
Ethiopia	May 1995 (U)	117	?	–
	May 1995 (L)	550	11	2.0
Gabon	Dec. 1996	120	?	–
Gambia	Oct. 1990	51	4	7.8
Ghana	Dec. 1996	200	?	–
Guina	June 1995	114	8	7.0
Guinea-Bissau	July 1994	100	10	10.0
Kenya	Dec. 1992	202	8	4.0
Lesotho	Mar. 1993 (U)	33	8	24.2
	Mar. 1993 (L)	65	3	4.6
Liberia	Mar. 1994	35	2	5.7
Libya	Jan. 1994	750	?	–
Madagascar	June 1993	134	5	3.7
Malawi	May 1994	177	10	5.6
Mali	Mar. 1992	129	3	2.3
Mauritania	Apr. 1996 (U)	56	0	0.0
	Oct. 1996 (L)	79	1	1.3
Mauritius	Dec. 1995	66	5	7.6
Morocco	Sept. 1993	333	2	0.6
Mozambique	Oct. 1994	250	63	25.2
Namibia	Dec. 1994	26	?	–
	Dec. 1994 (L)	72	13	18.1

(continues)

TABLE 1.1 *(continued)*

	Latest Elections	*Total Membership*	*Number of Women*	*% of Women*
Niger	Nov. 1996	83	?	–
Rwanda	Nov. 1994	70	12	17.1
Sao Tome and Principe	Oct. 1994	55	4	7.3
Senegal	May 1993	120	14	11.7
Seychelles	July 1993	33	9	27.3
Sierra Leone	Feb. 1996	80	5	6.3
South Africa	Apr. 1994 (U)	90	16	17.8
	Apr. 1994 (L)	400	100	25.0
Sudan	Mar. 1996	400	21	5.3
Swaziland	Oct. 1993 (U)	30	6	20.0
	Oct. 1993 (L)	65	2	3.1
Togo	Feb. 1994	81	1	1.2
Tunisia	Mar. 1994	163	11	6.7
Uganda	July 1996	276	50	18.1
U. R. Tanzania	Oct. 1995	275	48	17.5
Zaire	Apr. 1994	738	37	5.0
Zambia	Oct. 1996	155	15	9.7
Zimbabwe	Apr. 1995	150	22	14.7

U = Upper House   L = Lower House
SOURCE: Inter-Parliamentary Union, 1997. Reprinted by permission.

assemblies, would have limited value since the institution of parliament would remain rooted within a patriarchal structure (also see Bacchi 1990). Rhoda Howard views the appointment of special MPs to represent women as "a means of incorporating potential political protests into a manageable form" (Howard 1985, 293). For these feminists, therefore, a fundamental change in the social and political structure is as important as (if not more important than) increasing the numbers. Segers cautions feminists not to view affirmative action as a panacea to the problem of discrimination and oppression. She reminds them that affirmative action is "a single policy . . . a lonely policy, a voice in the wilderness" that can achieve little without the support of other policies directed at reducing disparities in wealth, status, and power (Segers 1983, 96). She concludes that at best, affirmative action co-opts talented women and minorities into the ranks of business, professional, and political elites without challenging the fundamental structural characteristics of the political economy.

A theoretical framework to guide the analysis of women's participation in Uganda's parliamentary politics can now be constructed on the basis of useful material from the preceding discussion.

The Conceptual Design

The theoretical paradigm within which I locate, view, and examine Uganda's national politics and its connection to gender is integrative and political (cf. Bashevkin 1994). The basic conceptual premise rests on a very simple argument: "When the composition of decision-making assemblies is so markedly at odds with the gender . . . make-up of the society they represent, this is clear evidence that certain voices are being silenced and suppressed" (Phillips 1992, 88). This innocuous observation rocks the conceptual boat of modern democratic theory and calls out for a reformulation of mainstream political thought and practice (Okin 1979; Pateman 1988; Mouffe 1992; Waylen 1994).

As noted earlier, the formulation of the colonial state, based on the British model, was characterized by male hegemony. At independence, Uganda inherited a structure whose ideology was designed to systematically promote male privilege and power while solidifying women's subordination. The gendered quality of the state is clearly seen in its institutions, such as cabinet, parliament, judiciary, army, and civil service. Male authority in the state is so ubiquitous that for a very long time it was taken for granted. That is, until feminist theorists started questioning the conceptual origins of the state, challenging the patriarchal relations of domination encoded therein. The artificial separation between "public" and "private" spheres was demystified, and the political linkage between the private and the political was exposed (Staudt 1989; MacKinnon 1989).

Does the gendered character of the state and its institutions mean that women face a hopeless situation whereby they can never change these institutions? Are state institutions impermeable and immune to change? In analyzing how gender shapes the character of contemporary politics, I consider the specificity of time in Uganda's politics. In other words, I perceive state institutions as a reflection of a location of history and culture, with their power sites always shifting. Even as most aspects of the patriarchal character of national politics remain intact, that character is amenable to change. Thus policies such as affirmative action provide the space for women's entry into politics and a potential for change. But the contradictions of implementing such policies under existing patriarchal structures have already been noted. Indeed, it is an unresolved chicken-and-egg conundrum. Short of an *Animal Farm*–type revolution, hens may begin crowing but they will continue to lay and hatch from eggs (the old patriarchal order).[68] The complexity of this issue is demonstrated throughout the book by showing how at some moments women empower themselves to break with their ascribed roles, only to fall back into them at other moments.

As a countervailing measure attempting to redress historical forms of gender discrimination, is affirmative action really effective? Can it ensure women equal opportunity to *substantively* influence political decisions? Scholars have argued that women's representation must reach a *critical mass* for them to achieve substantive influence in any institution (Kanter 1977; Dahlerup 1988). Such critical mass varies from 15 to 35 percent of the total numerical makeup of the institution (Dahlerup 1988; Kanter 1977). However, the premium that such scholars attach to numbers raises many conceptual questions. Numbers ultimately do not translate into substantive representation for women (Bystydzienski 1992, 15; 1995, chap. 5). If the inclusion of women in national assemblies is meant (as it should be) to foster change by incorporating a feminist policy agenda, then we need to go beyond numbers and address other important structural factors such as patterns of gender interaction that have a significant bearing on the behavior and the profile of any given institution.

Thus we need a theoretical framework that will integrate gender dynamics into the analysis of female and male legislators. As Anne Phillips (1991, 5) warns, under the seemingly innocent guise of gender neutrality, masculinity defines the terms of political theory and practice. In Uganda, as in most parts of Africa, cultural socialization experiences (transmitted through parents, schools, peers, the media, etc.) orient girls toward "feminine" mothering and wifely roles while encouraging boys into "masculine" roles that include being aggressive and ambitious and venturing into the world beyond the domestic arena (Musisi 1992; Kakwenzire 1996; Tamale 1996a).[9] Such stereotyped expectations of the sexes, which are held by men and internalized by women, help to perpetuate gender inequalities in society (Hunt 1990; Walker 1990; Hansen 1992).

Adult role socialization theorists build on childhood socialization when they hold that childhood socialization experiences are reinforced by the adult roles that women assume, especially family and work roles. Many of the tasks that women perform in the African context include unremunerated housework, childbearing and child rearing, food preparation, small-scale farming, as well as household-level production of both food and goods for the market (Mama 1996). In the wider context of our analysis of women and politics in Uganda, adult role socialization, therefore, would have a bearing on the differences between men's and women's political participation. Notions of patriarchal gender ideologies that emphasize maternal altruism and wifely duties for women and men's right to women's service and nurturance as well as to control over their reproductive capacities (Mama 1996) would all predict the performance of women and men who decide to participate in politics.

Explanations based on socialization have been criticized for ignoring the macro structural and situational impediments that stand in the way of women's participation in Western formal politics (Rinehart 1992; Mc-Glen 1980; Welch 1977; Jennings 1979). In particular, socialization/sex role theory disregards the significance of power in gender relations as well as structural and institutional factors. Moreover, this paradigm is predicated on the incorrect assumption that women are "passive subjects of a male-dominated culture [who retain], long after they have ceased physically to be children, their childlike psychological dependence upon men" (Randall 1987, 84; also see Epstein 1988, 137–140). Higher education and other extradomestic activities expose women to alternative values that can overshadow childhood socialization.

Because gender exerts a major effect on individual lives and social interactions, many feminists now view it as a social institution in and of itself. Candace West and Don Zimmerman, for example, perceive gender as an institutional and interactional enterprise whose "idiom is drawn from the institutional arena in which [social] relationships are enacted" (West and Zimmerman 1987, 137). They define gender as "the activity of managing situated conduct in light of normative conceptions of attitudes and activities appropriate for one's sex category" (West and Zimmerman 1987, 127).[70] Thus West and Zimmerman conceptualize gender as "a routine, methodical, and recurring accomplishment," which is produced through interpersonal interactions. In other words, individual women and men, as hostages to its production, "do gender."

Judith Lorber illuminates the macro structural characteristic of gender in more explicit terms when she argues:

> My concept of gender differs from previous conceptualizations in that I do not locate it in the individual or in interpersonal relations, although the construction and maintenance of gender are manifest in personal identities and in social interaction. Rather I see gender as an institution that establishes patterns of expectations for individuals, orders the social processes of everyday life, is built into the major social organizations of society, such as the economy, ideology, the family, and politics. (Lorber 1994, 1)

Although earlier theories locate gender in the individual, West and Zimmerman, as well as Lorber, locate it in the integral dynamic of social orders, outside the individual. West and Zimmerman locate gender in interpersonal interactions, but Lorber conceptualizes gender as a social institution and only views interpersonal interactions and social interaction as manifestations of its construction and maintenance (also see Laslett and Brenner 1989). These two views are not dissimilar, the only difference being that while West and Zimmerman emphasize interactions (with an idiom drawn from the institutional arena), Lorber highlights the institutional aspect (whose manifestation lies in the interactions). Lorber acknowledges this fact when she writes:

> The gendered microstructure and the gendered macrostructure reproduce and reinforce each other. The social reproduction of gender in individuals reproduces the gendered societal structure; as individuals act out gender norms and expectations in face-to-face interaction, they are constructing gendered systems of dominance and power. (Lorber 1994, 6)

Such a conceptualization is extremely useful for the analysis adopted in this book. West and Zimmerman's formulation of gender is especially useful because of its amenability to empirical research. Every time male or female legislators "do gender" by acting in a conventionally accepted manner for their sex category in the course of executing their legislative duties, they reinforce the "essentialness" of gender. For example, every time a female legislator shrinks from engaging in a showdown with her *aggressive* male colleague on the parliamentary floor, she (as well as he) is "doing gender." And every time gender is done, every time a man or a woman concedes to the structure of normative gender expectations, it serves to fortify and legitimate the gender hierarchy in society and the subordination of women by men. In doing gender, men are also doing dominance and women are doing deference (cf. Goffman 1967, 47–95). Or to put it another way, in doing gender in the male-dominated parliament, in which one of the most important social-control mechanisms—law—is formulated, women legislators simultaneously produce enactments of their "essential" femininity *and* undermine them by being actors in the legislature in the first place. This situation presents a contradiction for female legislators: Although they hold power by virtue of their positions, they are powerless by virtue of enactment. It is this very contradiction that is likely to foster further action for social change by female legislators. Drawing on Marxist and feminist theory, Brenner and Laslett (1991) argue that such inherent contradictions can lead (and have led) to women's political self-organization.

The implications of theorizing gender as an institution are significant. The institutional character of gender on the one hand, together with the gendered character of institutions on the other, facilitate my analysis in understanding its pervasiveness and the power relations in the parliamentary setting. Because such conceptualization takes into account the micro as well as the macro aspects of gender relations, it allows for a comprehensive and perspicacious examination of the material forces at work in the process of women's subordination and marginalization as well as other features such as women's capacity to organize.

Closely related to, but not quite the same as, "doing gender" is the social organization and meaning of sexuality (i.e., desire, physical intimacy, etc.). One of the ways that society builds certainty and validity about gender relations and sex differences is through the ideal of the "heterosexual matrix" (Butler 1990, chap. 2; Disch and Kane 1996). According to Judith Butler, gender coherence denotes a unity of experience, a compulsory order of sex-gender-desire. In postmodern style, she challenges the regime of presumptive heterosexuality and calls into question the cultural practices that allege a causal relationship between sex, gender, and desire. Butler further argues that the heterosexual matrix is the principal way of organizing masculinity and femininity and that a binary distinction between men and women produces and reifies hierarchical regimes of power (Butler 1990).

When Ugandan women join parliament (which in many ways symbolizes men's power), they are in effect intruding not just into the institution but into the certainties about gender relations in Ugandan society. I propose here (and will provide the evidence to illustrate this point) (1) that male legislators use certain kinds of sexual behavior to reinscribe the heterosexual matrix in their interactions with female legislators and (2) that the male power is central to it in its current form. Thus when female parliamentarians go along with or refuse to challenge the sexual harassment directed toward them by their male colleagues, they are in effect helping reinscribe the heterosexual matrix.

The above conceptualization of gender is based on Western feminist theory, and the question remains, Can gender theory be used to analyze non-Western societies? And if so, how? The assumption underlying this question is that both the philosophy and the agenda of feminism in Western societies is narrow and consequently insufficient to address the oppression of third world women (hooks 1984; Moraga and Anzaldua 1981; Joseph and Lewis 1981; Okeyo 1981; Johnson-Odim 1991). As noted earlier, the colonial process rendered a coming together of a particular kind of postcolonial state that reformulated the dynamics between patriarchy and gender in Uganda. Colonialism bureaucratized gender (and race) and institutionalized ideologies of white masculinity as normative (Mohanty 1991a). Such foreign intervention, which is manifest in ideology and the law, transformed and undercut most precolonial social values, leaving a formal structure resembling that of Western societies. In this sense, therefore, we may conclude that the *scaffolding* of Western gender theory[71] can be applicable to African societies for two reasons: first, because the general social and legal structure of most postcolonial African states is based on a Western model; second, and more important, because the division of labor in Africa, as in Western societies, has always been based on sex—a major principle of gender theory in explaining the universal oppression of women.[72] In other words, it is possible to make a *gender* analysis of non-Western societies.[73]

Hence, in an analysis of how gender affects women in politics, the realities of gender ideology in Africa today may parallel those of contemporary Western countries. *In addition*, however, the analysis of politics in Africa entails an examination of neocolonialism and imperialism, which have, in turn, left their mark on gender relations. The point is that factors other than gender figure integrally in the oppression of Third World women. Johnson-Odim writes that "gender oppression cannot be the single leg on which [Third World] feminism rests" (1991, 321). Attention must therefore be paid to the nuances of gender relations, which manifest variable factors in different societies and may in turn inform gender discourse in different contexts.

One of the realities confronting contemporary political structures is that the role of national legislatures in deciding public policy is growing more and more insignificant in the face of a powerful world economic order dominated by multilateral political and economic institutions. Although this is true for legislatures in both Western industrial democracies as well as non-Western countries of the Third World, it is most evident with respect to the latter. In order for us to understand the limitations that the new global order imposes on national decisionmaking institutions in Uganda, we need to make sense of the post cold war realities pertaining to this problem. A historiography of world politics in the post-cold war period will reveal that most state agencies are severely constrained by the straitjacket of a universal and globalizing economic order.

The formalistic nature of Uganda's independence attained in October 1962 has never been more apparent in these days of the "new world order." African countries and other states at the periphery are being pushed to the limits of underdevelopment (Chabal 1992; Ogundipe-Leslie 1994; Nabudere 1994). The global enterprise of reforming, restructuring, and privatizing the institutions of postcolonial states, no doubt, holds significant implications for social movements in general and for the African women's movement in particular (Oloka-Onyango and Tamale 1995). Already weighed down with gender oppression, Ugandan women have to carry the additional weight of increasing economic and social crises (Kyomuhendo 1992; Asowa-Okwe 1992). Moreover, insofar as the reconstruction of government institutions provides new and different kinds of dominant actors, it does not augur well for women's emancipation. Thus issues of neocolonialism and underdevelopment are integral to our conceptual framework. The work of female (and male) legislators is limited, shaped, and patterned by the interlocking forces of gender and underdevelopment, which is not to diminish other idiosyncratic characteristics of individuals.

This chapter sets the stage for an examination of women's participation in Uganda's national politics. The study investigates both macro and micro aspects of gender in the construction and reconstruction of Ugandan formal politics. Using women legislators as a case study, I demonstrate how gender and social reproduction both shape political institutions and are shaped by them.[74] Viewing the subject through a dialectical lens reveals both how politics has affected women and how it has been influenced by them.

Overview of the Book

The study is divided into nine chapters. Chapter 2 includes biographical profiles of five Ugandan female politicians. I use the profiles to demonstrate the micropolitical dynamics of gender and the role of individuality in the larger game of politics. The personal histories constitute a collective exercise in understanding the concepts of empowerment and resistance as women operate in a male-dominated arena. The complexities and contradictions facing women in politics are played out in the different strategies each woman adopts in her struggle to bring about change in the culture of Uganda's contemporary politics.

Chapter 3 investigates gender issues as they relate to the politics of parliamentary representation. Whose interests do female MPs represent? The response to this is a triple-faceted analysis of the perceptions of the female MPs themselves, those of women activists outside of parliament, and those of the grassroots women in the rural areas. The issues are framed around two theoretical types of parliamentary representation, namely, "standing for" and "acting for."

Chapter 4 examines Ugandan women in the parliamentary electoral process, particularly during the general elections of 1996. A close examination of the 1996 election campaigns reveals how politics shapes, is shaped by, and is mediated through the system of gender relations. I also tackle questions arising from the elections and their outcomes, analyzing the relationship between gender and the democratic process as revealed in its gendered institutions. The chapter ends with an analysis of issues discussed in a postelection induction workshop specially held for newly elected women parliamentarians in August 1996.

In Chapter 5, I offer a sociological/feminist analysis of the gender dynamics of intraparliamentary politics. Using the Constituent Assembly (which debated the draft constitution of 1993) as a case study, I analyze the critical implications of tokenism affecting a relatively small number of women legislators working in a male-dominated political institution, illustrating how female delegates strategized around the limitations of tokenism. Next, I discuss how male and female legislators "do gender" either through actions that conform to or differ from the socially accepted behavior for their sex category. Finally, I focus the analysis on the dialectics of sexual politics in the House. This entails a comprehensive investigation of how mechanisms of sexual harassment, discrimination, and treating women as sex objects works to further perpetuate a gender hierarchy in parliament.

Chapters 6 and 7 take a closer look at the activities of women legislators inside and outside parliament, respectively. The purpose here is to examine what women bring to politics in terms of their legislative and process concerns, as well as in their relationships with constituents. A systematic analysis of the official Hansards from the 1950s to date leads me to draw out some general trends and patterns of women's legislative activity in Chapter 6. I argue that legislative activity is molded by the institutional character of parliament as it interacts with gender. Thus I map out the general trends against a backdrop of the specialized discourse of the legislative process and procedure. My findings demonstrate that gender is central in shaping the legislative activity of men and women inside parliament.

Chapter 7 focuses on the "trench experiences" of one (nonaffirmative action) female MP—Winnie Byanyima—with the aim of exploring the relationship between legislators and their constituents. I show how gender, politics, and other social dynamics interact in determining the decisions, trends, and politicking of a woman MP when she is out in the field of her local constituency. In the last section of the chapter I move from the single case study to make some perceived distinctions between the trench activities of affirmative action women MPs and those who enter parliament through the direct route.

Chapter 8 first discusses the media in Uganda before launching into an analysis of how that media perpetuates women's subordinate status by trivializing the issues that women politicians represent and portraying them as politicians who are generally weak, indecisive, and emotional. The final and concluding chapter recaps the salient issues emerging from the study, pointing to the broader ramifications that the book brings to the issue of African women in politics. It further draws out implications for the larger body, which theorizes gender as an institution and the gendered character of patriarchal institutions such as parliament in the context of an African political economy.

Notes

1. This is by no means an isolated case. Reference to this African saying has frequently been made since women began participating in formal politics in large numbers (e.g., *Sunday Vision*, May 8, 1994, 8).

2. As I demonstrate later in this chapter, this state of affairs was accentuated with the intervention of colonialism in the latter half of the nineteenth century, when a clear distinction was marked between the "public" and the "private" spheres in the African sociopolitical setup.

3. The 1995 constitution introduced separate elections for the office of president. Prior to this, Uganda had followed the British system wherein the leader of the political party with the majority seats in parliament following a general election automatically assumes the top national executive position.

4. The multiparty parliamentary elections held in December 1980 were the first since independence in 1962. Widely believed to have been massively gerrymandered, they returned Milton Obote's Uganda Peoples Congress (UPC) to power, relegating the Democratic Party (DP) to the opposition. The leader of the Uganda Patriotic Movement (UPM), Yoweri Kaguta Museveni, decrying the elections as a fraud, departed for the "bush" soon thereafter and commenced the guerrilla struggle against the Obote regime (Karugire 1988).

5. Such rhetoric is partly on account of pressure from multilateral donor organizations such as the World Bank, which have in recent times looped "the gender question" into their mandate; the tendency now is to prevail upon debtor regimes to include women in leadership positions as a sign of their commitment to "good governance." It is also due to pressure from international feminism, which is closely monitoring state implementation of the UN Convention on the Elimination of all Forms of Discrimination Against Women (CEDAW).

6. When this ministry was set up in 1988, its full name was Ministry of Women in Development, Youth, and Culture. However, in 1994 the name was changed to Ministry of Gender, Youth, and Community Development.

7. Under this policy all women's applications for admission to government-funded institutions of higher learning are considered after adding an extra 1.5 points to their original scores in a bid to boost the aggregate number of women in this highly competitive field.

8. The number of districts in Uganda was recently increased to forty-five, thus boosting the number of women's affirmative action seats by six. By-elections are yet to be held to fill these new seats.

9. The theory of gender was introduced in the normative phases of contemporary Western feminism (so called second wave feminism) in the early 1970s. "Gender" as a concept was coined in an attempt to distinguish it from sex. Whereas "sex" is derived from biological and physiological differences between men and women, "gender" is a social and cultural construction that shapes feminine and masculine identities. (Nash and Fernandez-Kelly 1983; Burton 1985; Connel 1987; Hess and Ferree 1987). I discuss the concept of gender in greater detail under my conceptual design.

10. This is not to suggest that there exists such a thing as an essential, homogeneous African culture. Although I note the richness and the diversity of African cultures, I adopt the generic term "African" for analytical expediency to contrast it from mainstream Western principles and paradigms.

11. I deliberately use the Swahili term *Kabila* here in lieu of the more commonly used term "tribe" because of the derogatory connotations associated with the latter term. It stems from descriptions of racist European anthropologists

and missionaries of the "barbaric" and "primitive" communities of the "dark continent."

12. Although the kingdoms adopted a hierarchical system of authority, the clan remained an important basis of political, social, and economic association in both political systems; individualism as a dominant ethos of social relations was a concept alien to nearly all precolonial societies in Uganda (Karugire 1980, 15).

13. The term "patriarchy" as used in this study refers to male dominance within the specific cultural and historical arrangements of Ugandan gender relations. As this chapter will reveal, patriarchy in the Ugandan context is grounded in the institution of polygny—the practice of a man taking on multiple wives. Under this system, men are the dominant sex, having control over women and the management of gender relations. Although men are theoretically obligated to support and maintain their wives and families, in reality Ugandan women carry a considerable burden of productive and reproductive labor (albeit unwaged). This form of patriarchy offers women relative autonomy; indeed, inherent in the struggle by Ugandan women for emancipation is their attempt to maximize this relative autonomy. (Cf. Stamp 1986; Obbo 1980).

14. For a discussion and critique of the public/private distinction, see Lebeuf 1963; Rosaldo 1980; Nicholson 1986; Sudarkasa 1986; Bookman and Morgen 1988. Rosalind Petchesky blurs the distinction when she argues, "'Production' and 'reproduction,' work and the family, far from separate territories . . . are really intimately related modes that reverberate upon one another and frequently occur in the same social, physical and even psychic spaces" (1979, 376).

15. The *Namasole* (queen-mother) and *Lubuga* (Kabaka's sister) in Buganda; the *Nyina Mukama* (queen-mother) and *Mugole wa Muchwa* (king's sister) in Bunyoro; and the *Nyina Omugabe* (queen-mother) and the *Omunyana Omugabe* (king's sister) in Ankole.

16. Variations of course existed among different *makabila*. For example, among the Langi, men were potters; women milked among the Sebei, Itesot, and Karamajong; women built houses among the Karamajong; and among the Sebei, women sometimes went to battle with the men (Driberg 1932, 408; Goldschmidt 1976, 68).

17. In a polygynous arrangement each wife would often have a separate house within the homestead. A satellite household is generally composed of a wife and her unmarried offspring.

18. In the infamous case of *R v. Amkeyo* (1917) E.A.P.L.R. 14, Chief Justice Hamilton referred to bridewealth as "wife-purchasing" in total ignorance of its cultural value. He stated: "Women so obtained by a native man commonly spoken of, for want of a more precise term, as 'wives' and as 'married women,' but having regard to the vital difference in the relationship of the parties to a union by native custom from that of the parties to a legal marriage, I do not think it can be said that the native custom approximates in any way the legal idea of marriage" (Oloka-Onyango 1994). Colonial law attempted to abolish and later standardize bridewealth, which led to conceptualizing it as a purchase deal, in the process denigrating the institution with the concomitant denigration of women's status.

19. Capitalism as a concept needs to be reexamined and particularized in the concrete case of Uganda. This is important for our understanding of the way that

the capitalist economy undermined women's position (Bujra 1986). An underdeveloped form of capitalism based on precapitalist elements located in the peasantry (e.g., kinship structures and relations of production) characterized Uganda's colonial sociopolitical setup. As Stamp (1986, 30) explains, "The key to underdeveloped capitalism is that subsistence activities are more important than wages or the returns from cash crops in the reproduction of labor power."

20. As used here, the meaning of productive labor is not limited to activities that directly generate income. I adopt the Marxist-feminist definition that views unwaged domestic labor as productive because it contributes to household income in the form of saving, budgeting, or the provision of unpaid services (Brydon and Chant 1989, 11).

21. Reproductive labor includes biological reproduction, i.e., childbirth and lactation, and physical reproduction, which involves "the daily regeneration of the wage labor force through cooking, cleaning, washing, and so on" (Brydon and Chant 1989, 10).

22. From interviews with Joyce Mpanga and Rebecca Mulira, July 8 and August 2, 1996, respectively. Even though organizations such as the YWCA and Mother's Union were Western initiated and dominated by middle-class women, they served as important nodes for rallying middle class Ugandan women into action in the pursuit for their rights. For instance, although most of the activities executed in these organizations were along the line of imparting domestic skills, they provided a forum for women to learn how to speak in public and acquire leadership skills.

23. Interview with Rebecca Mulira, August 2, 1996.

24. See Official Hansard, March 9, 1965, 1287.

25. Female representation in the Legco did not happen until 1954 when Barbara Saben, together with another Briton, Alice Boase, were nominated to the council. Notably, both Saben and Boase were leading members of UCW.

26. A British woman, Barbara Saben, sat in Legco between 1958 and 1959. Eseza Makumbi replaced Joyce Mpanga in 1961 when the latter left to pursue graduate studies in the United States. She later sat on the East African Legislative Council as one of Uganda's representatives.

27. Women could stand for the Lukiiko elections but could not vote (Apter 1961, 231 n. 24).

28. Interview with Rebecca Mulira, August 9, 1996. Mulira had been one of the eight women who stood in the Lukiiko elections. Subsequently she was appointed as a councilor to the all-male municipal board of the Kampala City Council (KCC). Other women who stood for the Lukiiko polls (according to Mulira's recollection) included Sarah Ndagire, Euniya Kamanya, and Mary Nkata.

29. Gender was an important basis of the formal institutionalization of education in colonial Uganda (see Musisi 1992).

30. The fundamental direction of women's education did not change with formal independence. A commission appointed to recommend on the content and structure of education in 1963 emphasized that "while we deprecate too much differentiation of curriculum between boys and girls, definite recognition of their different objectives should be made. As most girls will eventually become wives and mothers in a largely rural community, that would be a futile education that

failed to prepare them for the duties of home making" (Uganda Government, *Report of the Uganda Education Commission*, 1963; quoted in Musisi 1992, 187).

As a graduate of Gayaza High, I can attest to the fact that despite a broadening of the curriculum following independence, home economics was an integral part of my education. The same was not true for my brother, who studied contemporaneously at the premier boys' school in Uganda, King's College Budo.

31. During our interview an enthusiastic Mulira showed me several newspaper clippings and photographs from the 1950s and 1960s, all of which documented evidence of her activism in the women's movement. She had the privilege of sharing the company of international women of prominence such as Indira Ghandi, Golda Meir, and Eleanor Roosevelt (see, e.g., *Stanford Advocate*, January 26, 1952, 10). At the 1995 fourth International Women's Conference held in Beijing, China, Mulira presented a paper entitled "Problems of Older Women in Uganda."

32. As part of the process of empowering women similar to herself, Mulira and several colleagues set up an organization called Forward Society, which was designed to conduct programs in adult education and confidence building (interview with Joyce Mpanga, March 14, 1997).

33. For further reading on the gender implications of credentialism, see Crompton (1986) and Burris (1989).

34. The 1962 independence constitution was unique in that it provided for a basically unitary state while preserving certain federal privileges to Buganda and conferring semifederal status upon the other three kingdom areas—Ankole, Bunyoro, and Toro. The kabaka was president of a country that was neither a monarchy nor a republic (Morris and Read 1966, 87). These contradictions were bound to generate conflict and came to a head in 1966, when Obote abolished monarchies, ousted the kabaka, and declared himself president of the newly established Republic of Uganda.

35. UCW wrote numerous letters and had interviews with various politicians demanding their rights. They emphasized article 16 of the Universal Declaration of Human Rights on marriage and family rights (Brown 1988).

36. Interview with Joyce Mpanga, March 14, 1998.

37. Elsewhere I discuss the limitations of the Kalema Commission. For example, all but one of the six members were male, not to mention the sample population on which the study was based, which consisted of 87.6 percent males and only 12.4 percent females (Tamale 1993, 192–193). The chairman of the commission, William Kalema, was the husband of Rhoda Kalema, whose profile is discussed in Chapter 2.

38. The coup d'ètat was "legitimized" by the "pigeon hole" constitution, thus termed because, in introducing the subject for debate in parliament on April 15, 1966, Milton Obote advised the MPs that they would find copies of the document in their respective pigeon holes—after the debate was concluded. The MPs thus discussed and passed a document they had not seen. A year later, in 1967, Obote presented a draft constitution to parliament (which had reconstituted itself into a constituent assembly) which was passed, replacing the pigeon hole one.

39. See decree no. 3 of 1973. In 1993 NCW was replaced by a semiautonomous body called the National Women's Council (NWC), which is accountable to the

Ministry of Gender and Community Development. The main objective of the NWC is "to organize women of Uganda into a unified body and engage them in activities that are of their benefit and to the nation." Creating centralized control over women's organizations was commonplace in Africa. For example, in Tanzania, President Julius Nyerere established Umoja Wa Wanawake (UWT) as an affiliate of TANU that was to serve as the overarching umbrella organization for women charged with the tasks (albeit ill equipped) of uniting, mobilizing, and liberating women (see Geiger 1982).

40. The semiparastatal status of UCW was maintained by all subsequent regimes until the NRM government took over power.

41. It is said that the Kabaka had given Visram the adoptive Kiganda name "Namubiru."

42. Following Obote's constitutional coup d'ètat of April 1966, both Sugra Visram and Florence Lubega were among the five KY MPs who declined to subscribe to the provisions of the new constitution, thus resigning their parliamentary seats. However, a year later Florence Lubega returned to parliament when the National Assembly resolved itself into a Constituent Assembly to deliberate on a new constitution for the republic of Uganda.

43. For example, the Hindu Marriage and Divorce Act (1964) and the Succession (Amendment) Decree of 1972.

44. All NCC members were elected by an electoral college of district councils.

45. The interim period between 1979 and 1980 was a very unstable one. The presidency of Yusuf Lule, who took over from Idi Amin, lasted only sixty-eight days. Godfrey Binaisa, who followed him, lasted no more than eleven months before the Military Commission led by Paulo Muwanga and deputized by Yoweri Museveni, staged a coup d'ètat. The Military Commission commandeered the sham elections on December 9, 1980 (see *Report of the Uganda Commission of Inquiry into the Violation of Human Rights*, 1994).

46. Yoweri Museveni was the leader of the newly formed UPM.

47. Odongo-Oduka was able to win the Lira south constituency largely because of her husband's popularity. He was the personal bodyguard of Milton Obote and had been very instrumental in the 1979 liberation war. However, as the sole woman in the National Assembly, she hardly ever uttered a word in the chamber (see the Hansard records of her tenure period from 1981 to 1985).

48. Interview with Joyce Mpanga, March 14, 1998.

49. "Unique" here refers to the Ugandan context, for such structures had been tested in other countries such as Mozambique and Guinea Bissau. The prototype in the context of Africa is perhaps the *ujaama* village concept developed in Julius Nyerere's Tanzania of the 1960s.

50. The RC structures were introduced in all the semiliberated zones that fell under the influence of NRA/M as the guerrilla war progressed.

51. These were Victoria Ssekitoleko, Gertrude Njuba, Betty Bigombe, and Oliva Zizinga. The original seventy-four-member NRC (which acted as the interim legislature) was primarily made up of "historicals" of NRM/A.

52. Despite the official ban on political party activity imposed by the NRM administration because of its history of divisive politics, DP, UPC, and to a smaller extent CP have continued to operate above ground, if in muted tones. These par-

ties perceive the NRM as nothing more than the UPM of old. In the first ever 1996 presidential elections UPC and DP formed an alliance in an effort to counter Museveni's candidacy.

53. For a background discussion of the ten points, see the appendix to Museveni's biography (1997, 217).

54. "The Role of Women in the NRM/NRA Protracted People's War: Its Impact on the Democratization Process in Uganda and Challenges Ahead," Keynote address delivered at an evaluation retreat for the Women's Parliamentary Caucus at Windsor Lake Victoria Hotel, Entebbe, Uganda, July 18–20, 1997.

55. When the NRM assumed power in 1986, they undertook that their interim government would be in office for a period not exceeding four years (Legal Notice no. 1, 1986). However, one year before the four-year period was to expire, the NRM decided to expand the interim legislature (NRC) through indirect elections, which also brought in affirmative action women representatives. It is this expanded NRC which, under the chairmanship of President Museveni, proclaimed a five-year extension of that period on the eve of its termination.

56. Women proved to be an indispensable part of Museveni's constituency in the May 1996 presidential elections. Although no exit poll was conducted during the elections, it is widely believed that women were largely responsible for returning Museveni to power as the first ever elected president of Uganda (see, e.g., "How Museveni and His Team Won the Big Prize," *The East African*, May 13–19, 1996, 12; "Women MPs to Petition Museveni over Cabinet Posts," *Crusader*, July 9–11, 1996, 1–2; "Women Want One Third of Cabinet," *Monitor*, July 3–4, 1996, 1).

57. Odoobo C. Bichachi, *Sunday Monitor*, December 15, 1996, 3.

58. Editorial, *Crusader*, June 25–27, 1996.

59. Caution must be taken, however, not to overstate the significance of women's "pressure" for the introduction of the affirmative action policies in Uganda. I expound on this point in Chapter 4.

60. Of the Ug.shs. 1.6 billion (US$1.6 million) approved for the recurrent budget, 93 percent was actually paid, whereas only 73 percent of the Ug.shs. 1.3 billion (US$1.3 million) approved for the development budget was disbursed.

61. Although women are the backbone of Uganda's economy, accounting for 60 percent of cash crop production and 80 percent of food production, their centrality in the economy is unacknowledged and they represent a very small percentage of the wage labor force (Economic Commission for Africa 1975; UNICEF 1994).

62. Analogously, twelve of the seventeen men who served on President Museveni's national campaign team in May 1996 were "rewarded" with big political positions whereas none of the five women who served on the same team have been similarly recognized (see Winnie Byanyima, "Times and Seasons of Ugandan Women," *Sunday Monitor*, March 30, 1997).

63. For literature on the gender implications of SAPs in sub-Saharan Africa, see Zinanga 1994; Mbilinyi 1993; Etim 1992; Aidoo 1992; and Gladwin 1991.

64. Ugandan women do not submit to such oppression complacently; Christine Obbo (1980) reports that many single women (especially in city slums) challenge the inevitability of marriage and children within wedlock. These women are in the forefront of social change.

65. The Uganda National AIDS Control Program put the death rate of women to men at 53 to 47. In Rakai district, which is thought to have the highest rate of infection, approximately 35 percent of all females between the ages of 15 and 25 are believed to be infected.

66. Only six countries had reached that level by June 1995: Sweden (40.4 percent), Norway (39.4 percent), St. Lucia (36.4 percent), Finland (33.5 percent), Netherlands (31.3 percent), and Denmark (33 percent).

67. There are other countries in which national legislation establishes mechanisms that may or can facilitate women's access to parliament, for instance, the nomination of all or some MPs. These include, Algeria (200/200), Egypt (10/454), Kenya (12/202), Lesotho (11/33 in senate), Liberia (35/35), Mauritius (4/66), Namibia (6/78), Rwanda (70/70), Swaziland 20/30 in senate), Tanzania (42/275), Zambia (8/159), and Zimbabwe (20/150) (Inter-Parliamentary Union 1997, 64).

68. Of course we know that the Orwellian revolution in *Animal Farm* eventually turned sour when the "four legs good, two legs bad" slogan turned into "some animals are more equal than others." This raises an interesting question that can hardly be ignored: Even if the possibility existed of women's effecting such a revolution, is it not possible that it could evolve into matriarchal state power and simply operate as the mirror image of the patriarchy it has replaced?

69. Empirical studies in the West show a similar trend of socialization (Maccoby and Jacklin 1975; Unger and Crawford 1992; Jacklin and Baker 1993).

70. West and Zimmerman (1987, 127) explain "sex category" to involve categorizing people through the application of a socially accepted biological criteria for classifying persons as female and male (e.g., genitalia at birth). Hence one's sex category presumes one's sex. They argue further that gender activities emerge from and bolster claims to membership in a sex category.

71. Here I talk about "the scaffolding" of Western gender theory, bearing in mind that there are several feminist theories covering a wide range of ideas. Indeed, we can only utilize Western gender theory as a general theoretical hinge because some ideas of Western feminists are based on assumptions that are inapplicable to African gender relations.

72. However, although women are oppressed worldwide, it is important to note that what constitutes the "gender division of labor" varies from society to society. Therefore it is important to ask ourselves: In which way is the gender division of labor universal and in which way is it unique to the African context? As Chandra Mohanty helpfully points out, "the concept of 'sexual division of labor' is more than just a descriptive category. It indicates the differential *value* placed on 'men's work' versus 'women's work'" (Mohanty 1991b, 68).

73. Indeed, empirical feminist studies that have been conducted in Africa rely on Western theoretical analyses while remaining careful to point out differences in the particular processes and outcomes in different African societies (e.g., Sender and Smith 1990; Stamp 1986; Seidman 1993).

74. Among the women legislators studied are included female delegates to the 1994–1995 Constituent Assembly, which discussed and promulgated the 1995 Constitution. For a detailed discussion of methodological issues, see Appendix 2.

2

Profiles of Five
Political Women

This chapter is aimed at two main objectives. First, it provides a window through which to obtain an initial peek into the world of Ugandan women politicians, raising the curtain on the larger study of the dynamics of the process of Ugandan women's engagement with formal politics. Second, and more important, it provides a starting point from which to delve into the main theoretical concepts that are analyzed in this book. The five life histories illustrate the micropolitical dynamics and the role of individuality in the contemporary politics of Uganda. They provide useful demonstrations of different styles and strategies women politicians employ to resist male dominance and to empower[1] themselves in the face of patriarchy and underdevelopment. By focusing on five individual women, I illuminate the differences among and between female politicians, highlighting the complex processes within which gender and other forms of social inequality are created, manipulated, and incorporated into individual identities (McClaurin-Allen 1990). In other words, just as with any other sector of society, women politicians are the product of class, religion, education, and ethnicity.

For varied insights into the political roles of Ugandan women, I chose the five women for their diversity in home district, socioeconomic background, personal style, and contributions to the development and operation of the women's movement in Uganda. Each woman in her own way exemplifies the manner in which women in politics empower themselves and resist gender oppression in the "male" world of politics. The narratives presented here are mostly derived from the intensive interviews I conducted with the individual women. In the concluding section of the chapter, I investigate the theoretical significance of some issues analyzed here in relation to women in politics.

Miria Matembe

During the last campaigns I stood up and said, "I am the commander of women's liberation; I'll do whatever it takes to liberate women from misery, suffering, oppression, exploitation and all that." Then one man stood up and said in a scornful voice, "Hey Matembe, which women are you talking about? Do you mean *our* women? What makes you think that our women are suffering or miserable? How dare you come here to tell us that our women are oppressed when we are living happily?" I asked this man, "Don't we have a local proverb which says that women are like cow dung: You just clean the kraal and tomorrow you get more! And how come when a man is asked the number of children he has he'll say, 'I have three children and two girls!'" (Miria Matembe)

Miria Matembe is a forty-three-year-old lawyer who was a member of the National Resistance Council (NRC) and the Constituent Assembly (CA). In 1996 she was elected to the sixth parliament. In all three legislative bodies she has represented Mbarara district on the affirmative action seat. Matembe was one of only two female commissioners on the twenty-one-member constitutional commission appointed in 1988.[2] Arguably the best-known feminist in Uganda, Matembe has earned herself the reputation of a formidable campaigner for women's rights and has come to symbolize the Ugandan women's movement. Prominent for her passionate commitment to the women's cause, she is uncompromising in the fight for women's rights. In resonant voice and dynamic style she has repeatedly called for the castration of men found guilty of rape and defilement—a prescription that has placed her in disrepute with a great number of Ugandan men who feel she attacked the core of their manhood by making such a "drastic" statement.[3]

Matembe's assertiveness started very early in life. When she was thirteen years old and had completed one year of high school, her financially strapped peasant parents decided that she should abandon her secondary school education to make way for her brothers to go to school. The young Matembe, determined to stay in school, led her illiterate mother to the office of the district education officer and personally requested a bursary, which paid for her secondary school education and gave her the opportunity to realize her childhood dreams of becoming a lawyer and eventually a parliamentarian. She never occupied leadership positions in school but was always active in debating societies and other extracurricular activities. After obtaining her law degree, she worked briefly as a law lecturer at the Kampala Institute of Bankers. In 1978 she married Nekemiya Matembe, a professional brewer, with whom she has four sons.

Matembe has been a very active founding member of Action for Development (ACFODE) and the Uganda Association of Women Lawyers (FIDA)—both of which are at the forefront in effecting radical changes in the lives of Ugandan women. A self-confessed born-again Christian, Matembe struggles for women's emancipation with a crusadelike style as she combines her call for women's justice and equality with preaching from the Bible. Although she was full of praise for the National Resistance Movement (NRM) government, she has come to the realization that women could not rely on a male-dominated government machinery to effect their full integration in critical decisionmaking positions. She was bitterly disappointed, for example, when President Museveni appointed only six women cabinet ministers out of a sixty-two-member cabinet following the mid-1996 election.

Because of her reputation, many women from all over Uganda go to Matembe, expecting her to magically solve their problems.

> Women think I can do anything; they think once you reach Matembe every problem will be solved and many times I do solve their problems. Many times I personally intervene and handle them personally but of course I can't solve each and every problem and this is a big frustration for the women who come to me expecting me to be the police, the prison warder, the arresting officer, the court, the president and the minister. In me they see everything and when she comes and I can't fulfill her expectations, maybe because a bureaucrat or some institution has got in my way, then it frustrates her and of course it hurts me.

Matembe has also been a key player in advocating for the domestic relations bill that was in the process of being streamlined by the Uganda Law Reform Commission at the time this book went to press. Thereafter, it will be formally introduced to parliament.

Perhaps the greatest advantage of Matembe's style is that it attracts public attention. Her forceful and aggressive manner of presenting women's issues leaves an indelible mark on the minds of even the most chauvinistic of men. She exemplifies the hen that has begun to crow. Her very bearing is what is normatively perceived as "masculine." For example, for most of our interview she sat with legs crossed ankle to knee—a posture traditionally associated with masculinity and power in Uganda. Almost all the male legislators interviewed conceded that Matembe's style was quite effective in selling women's issues to Ugandans, although they all expressed reservations to the effect that "sometimes she overdoes it." She is, in other words, a male chauvinist's worst nightmare. Commenting on her style, a male MP said:

> It borders on extremism; that kind of fanaticism is not good because it sends signals that women are so oppressed when they are not. . . . I would want a woman to stand up and just put the issues clearly and soberly, be cool instead of attacking and condemning men. But the way Matembe pushes she's like a revolutionary. She creates the wrong impression that men are enemies to women. Do you know that every man you see out there is working for a certain woman somewhere? (Kaweesi Ndaula, CS)[4]

Matembe's female colleagues, on the other hand, were divided on the efficacy of her style. Some felt that in the initial stages of the women's movement it was necessary to be loud and aggressive. But now that women have received the attention of government and the public, tactics must change to a more persuasive style. Although Matembe has not become less aggressive in her style, she seems to have tempered it somewhat, ironically by attempting to expose her "feminine" dimensions. In the CA she labored to display what she "treasures most" by painting an image of a gentle, loving, and considerate wife and mother: "Honorable delegates . . . I have deemed it necessary to introduce myself in that way because I would like to allay the fears of many people . . . who regard me as a rebel . . . a terrible woman who hates men." Another way that Matembe "softens" her hard-line position is by deliberately punctuating her fiery speeches with smiles, lurid jokes, and laughter.

Some women were totally opposed to Matembe's style, as indicated in the following excerpt taken from an interview transcript.

> Styles differ but what I know is that in Uganda when you want to sell a point you must find a nice way to package it. This is a world of competition. You're selling an idea and someone is buying the idea and it is a competing idea; that's the way I look at parliament and advocacy in general . . . An aggressive style in our world will not work and extremist positions do not sell. It's moderate positions which sell and we must cultivate that. (Winnie Byanyima, CS)

In spite of their criticisms many female MPs invite Matembe to address their constituencies. "I took her to my district one time but I forewarned her not to antagonize the village men; it is counterproductive for the women who look to these men as their saviors. So as long as men still hold the power we need to handle them carefully" (Mary Kamugisha, AA). These statements demonstrate the contradictions that frustrate women's political participation. On the one hand, they must be coy about embracing an activist of Matembe's leanings; on the other, they can be sure that they will get an audience to attend their rallies once she is billed as the star attraction.

Matembe can be described as a feminist on the basis of her stated positions and actions on a number of issues affecting the situation of women. However, Matembe has expressed concern about what she terms the "negative connotations" associated with the feminist label and feminism as such. Like many other women legislators, she marks distance with the "feminist" label, particularly with the radical elements that are considered intrinsic to the term. The primary reason lies in the public (read male) perception of a feminist: someone who wants to reverse sex roles, disempower the man, and place woman "on top." In other words, feminism is perceived as a subversive movement led by disgruntled women who want to radically alter the status quo and submit men to a subordinate position. Feminists are, therefore, viewed in the typical bra-burning, family-breaking mode, similar to the response to feminism in the United States back in the 1960s. Matembe prefers to describe herself as a "struglist," that is, someone struggling for the betterment of women's lives, for their human rights, and for equality between men and women. Nevertheless, she has several reservations about certain views that some feminists would take as elemental; for example, she has expressed strong objections to the description of prostitution as work, condemning the notion of sex workers: "The thought of selling one's body is so degrading to me!" she declared. Perhaps this moralistic stand on the subject of prostitution stems from her strong Christian beliefs.

Predictably, Matembe is a favorite target of the press. Most of the time Matembe simply has to open her mouth in a public forum and her words, however inconsequential, will make news in the local press the following day. She is generally portrayed as a loose cannon, an erratic eccentric who should not be taken seriously. No matter how tough she is, the media does a good job of reminding Ugandans that she is a woman. For example, on August 28, 1996, Matembe appeared for an interview on the *Guest of the Week* program featured on public television. The male interviewer asked Matembe questions that he would never ask a male politician: What do you cook at home? What is your favorite food? How many children do you have? Is your husband also born again? Although Matembe questioned the relevance of such questions, she answered all of them.

Indeed, despite (or because of) her style, Matembe the woman is still vulnerable and insecure in the field of politics. That explains why she has stood on the affirmative action district seat three times and thus far has declined to cross over to the regular county level. Almost everyone believes that Matembe should graduate to the county seat and compete directly with men. Matembe seems to be the only one who realizes that although a few women have managed to break through the numerous barriers and have successfully competed with men in mainstream politics, the majority still face persistent hurdles. Thus the time is not yet ripe for her to take on these formidable forces. But given Matembe's notoriety, it is doubtful that even with all her political experience, she would succeed on a county seat.

Rhoda Kalema

> I am not seeking reelection in June [1996] but I have identified a suitable candidate to replace me in the county and I'm vigorously campaigning and lobbying for him. Everyone keeps asking me, "Have you identified a woman?" . . . For me the issues of development and stability are more important than the gender issue. Moreover, Kiboga being a small district with only two counties . . . two of the three representatives have been women and if you're talking about gender equality then I think it's time that I gave way to a man. We women also have our limitations—physical, family responsibilities, and so on. (Rhoda Kalema)

Rhoda Kalema, a sixty-seven-year-old businesswoman, ascended the Ugandan political scene in 1979 when she joined the National Consultative Council (NCC) and served as deputy minister of culture and community development. She went on to win county seats in the NRC and the CA but chose to slip into the shadows in 1996, when she announced that she was retiring from active politics. Kalema was born into a political family, her father having served as *katikiro* (prime minister)[5] of Buganda from 1929 to 1942. Her husband, who "disappeared" in 1972 during the autocratic regime of Idi Amin, was a parliamentarian and a cabinet minister in the 1960s. The political careers of both her father and her husband doubtlessly spurred her interest in politics. Kalema bore six children and received a diploma in social studies from Edinburgh University in the United Kingdom. She unsuccessfully stood for a parliamentary seat in 1980 and shortly after that was detained for two months as a political prisoner.

Kalema's involvement in the struggle to emancipate Ugandan women goes back to the late 1950s and early 1960s, when she was involved in the activities of the Uganda Council of Women (UCW). Her mode of feminism falls into the old conservative school, which campaigns for improved rights and opportunities for women without seriously questioning the patriarchal ideology. Today, the women's organizations that Kalema most closely associates with are the Young Women's Christian Association (YWCA), Safe Motherhood, and Uganda Women's Effort to Save Orphans (UWESO)—none of which pursues radical methods of work in order to challenge the foundations of male-dominated society. Kalema strongly believes in the sanctity of marriage, with the husband being the designated head of the household and the wife having primary responsibility for running the home and caring for the children.[6] In August 1996 a women's nongovernmental organization called Forum for Women in Democracy (FOWODE) honored Kalema with a distinguished award in recognition of her role "as a transformative leader who has inspired and benefited women of all ages and backgrounds and contributed tremendously to the cause of gender equality." Although her views are relatively conservative, FOWODE understood that in the context of her generation her work in the women's movement of Uganda has indeed been "transformative."

In our interview, Kalema spoke very critically of a newly formed women's group called the Uganda Association of Second Wives and Concubines. Neither did she have kind words for female legislators who were not "properly married":

> I don't condone women leaders who live with men unmarried. It's not right . . . If one wants to become a leader, she should take enough trouble to see that she gets properly married to a man who will *allow her* [my emphasis] to perform the functions of wifehood, motherhood, and at the same time perform the functions of a parliamentarian.

Kalema does not see any real obstacles standing in the way of women parliamentarians and believes that the media gives fair coverage to women legislators. Never having stood for an affirmative action seat, Kalema does not perceive herself as a women's representative. When I asked her if she thought "women's issues" were adequately addressed in the House, she replied, "Whenever women's issues come up, I think they have been adequately addressed; in any case, if they have not, we have a representative, the women have representatives. It's up to them to fight sufficiently for these issues."

Perhaps part of Kalema's conservatism is generational. In addition, Kalema's upper-middle-class background "insulated" her from much of the double oppression that the majority of Ugandan women experience through the dialectical operation of class and gender. She broke into the political arena well before the introduction of the affirmative action policy.

A self-confessed born-again Christian, Kalema is well respected in political circles and even by the media. Male politicians especially talked very fondly of her, one of them describing her as "level-headed, democratic, and self-sufficient [i.e., does not occupy an affirmative action seat]" (Kaweesi Ndawula, CS). I asked Kalema why she had decided to end her political career, and she responded that the overwhelming reason was that she needed more time to take care of her young, orphaned grandchildren who live with her. It is very unlikely that a male legislator of her stature and popularity would have had to quit politics for a similar reason. This is an example of how gender exerts a significant influence on women's political participation. At sixty-seven, with her own children grown adults and pursuing their own careers, it is striking that Kalema is not free from child care responsibilities.

Betty Bigombe

> When I first reported for duty in Gulu, nobody—not the rebels, not the *wanainchi* (common people), nor the government troops took me seriously. Kony [the rebel leader] sent me a letter saying that it was the worst possible insult on the part of government to send a "girl" to deal with the insurgency in the area; they asked me to return to Kampala immediately or else I'd be killed. Frankly, I was quite terrified but firmly stood my ground . . . gradually everybody realized that I meant business. We then commenced serious work. (Betty Bigombe)

For Betty Bigombe to be alive today is little short of a miracle. In 1986 she was appointed a nondescript deputy minister assigned to the protocol desk of the prime minister's office. Feeling hopelessly underutilized and guilty about the perks that came with the office, she requested President Museveni to either redeploy her or accept her resignation. Little did she know that her threat was to dramatically transform her life as a woman, as a mother, as a politician, and as the most prominent negotiator in a civil war that has wracked Uganda for over a decade. Her new portfolio was minister for the pacification of the north, resident in the town of Gulu. The thirty-three-year old Bigombe assumed the challenge on December 1, 1988, after agreeing with her conscience that she would only serve for a maximum of three months. As it turned out, she remained on the battlefront for eight years.

Bigombe's father died when she was still very young, leaving her peasant mother and older siblings to raise her. Although a natural leader at school and a member of women's NGOs such as ACFODE, she had never considered politics as a career option prior to the ministerial appointment: "I always looked at politics as a dirty game and didn't want to get involved, neither did I fancy the limelight that comes with being a public figure." At Makerere University in the 1970s she received a Bachelor of Arts degree in sociology and literature and was working as a coordinator of African Development Bank projects in Nairobi, Kenya, before joining the NRM government. Bigombe was full of self-doubt when assigned the role of peace broker, a hesitance that doubtlessly stemmed from her gender and from the militaristic nature of the work that she was supposed to handle. "I had never held a gun before in my life; guns just looked so ugly and holding one filled me with a sense of violence and brutality." Constantly exposed to danger in the course of her work, Bigombe was forced to undergo military training on the job. By the time she left Gulu, the longest she ever camped in one place was two weeks. She had lived in ditches, survived on water and boiled cassava for days, waddled through guinea-worm infested rivers, carried the bullet-riddled and mutilated bodies of women and children. You name it, and Bigombe has probably endured it.

When Bigombe arrived in the northern and northeastern regions of Uganda, at least five different warring factions were fighting in the area. Over 2.5 million people had been displaced by the insurgency and the majority of the local populace supported rebel activity. Her task was enormous and was not made easier by the hostility she confronted during the first several months in office. The rebels and *wanainchi* were incensed not only by the fact that President Museveni had sent a female emissary but that he had selected someone who was not from among the "prominent" families of Acholiland. Bigombe, an Acholi from Gulu, nevertheless represented a government they were opposed to.[7] To compound the insult, Bigombe's husband was a non-Acholi from western Uganda, as is President Museveni, which the Acholi interpreted as the ultimate betrayal and disloyalty. On the government side, things were only slightly better. Military officials often failed to accord her the respect due to a minister. On several occasions, National Resistance Army (NRA) field commanders failed to notify her of major military operations. Not only was this an affront to her position as the most senior government representative in the area but, more significantly, it jeopardized her peace-seeking efforts.

Despite the odds that stood in her way, Bigombe stubbornly carried the olive branch and slowly but surely began to win the trust of many: first of the local populace, then of the NRA, and finally and most importantly of the rebel groups in the area. Her strategy was multifaceted. First, she embarked on a fact-finding tour in the region, talking to *wanainchi*, eating with them, crying with them, attending local burial ceremonies: "I wanted to know the nature of their grievances and to actively involve them in the peace process, for they are the ones who bear the brunt of the war and who are recruited into the rebel groups." Second, Bigombe reached out to women in the local population. If she could convince the women of the government's good intentions, they would in turn persuade their children and spouses to lay down their arms.

Ironically, womanhood, which had been a source of resentment for Bigombe's appointment, proved to be the most powerful tool in her attempts to pacify the northern region. For example, as a woman, she was able to win the trust of a high school student who had been abducted by the rebels.[8] For months the young girl had been forced to be Kony's "wife" but was subsequently abandoned in the bush when she was almost eight months pregnant. Bigombe "adopted" the girl, availed her of prenatal care, and provided for her after delivery. Having won the trust of this traumatized child, Bigombe was able to learn a great deal about the strengths, weaknesses, and psychology of the rebel leader.

Third, Bigombe sought out and arranged secret meetings with the rebels themselves. She always met rebel leaders on their own terms at venues they selected. Her journeys to such rendezvous, which were often in distant forests that could only be reached through thick bushes, were extremely treacherous. But her persistence paid off:

> I knew I'd won them over the first time I arrived for negotiations. I had been communicating with them via radio and all the time they thought that I was bluffing about meeting them. . . . they were also shocked to see that a *woman* had survived the tough journey which sent the message that I was very serious. . . . During these negotiations I exercised a great deal of patience and did a lot of listening. At first they were very cautious but on subsequent meetings one by one, they started pouring out their grievances while I listened. There were lots of insults towards me and towards the NRM government but never once did I lose my temper or bang tables. . . . *I graduated from being a "girl" to being a "woman" until eventually everybody started referring to me as "mother." It signified trust and respect, for they knew that a mother would never harm her child* (my emphasis).

Once the rebels had realized the tenacity, patience, and capability of Betty Bigombe, it became easy for them to trust her: As a woman, she personified a nonthreatening, safe emissary. In September 1989, Bigombe's hard work came to fruition when one rebel group after another began to put down their arms and surrender themselves to the government for reintegration into society. "At that time my main problem was with logistics." However, it took another five frustrating years of persuading, convincing, and negotiating before Bigombe convinced the leader of the Lords Resistance Army (LRA)—Joseph Kony—to make a peace agreement. Unfortunately, on the date set for signing the truce President Museveni, with the advice of male politicians and his army commanders in the north, called off the agreement. As a consequence, the insurgency continues to torment northern Uganda. Bigombe was disappointed by the reversal but remains convinced that a military strategy will never solve the insurgency.

Bigombe's story is living testimony to the heights that women can reach through resistance and empowerment. She defied the prejudices associated with womanhood while embracing its positive attributes, fought the discrimination of an institution that is traditionally male, and successfully played the role of military negotiator—normally a preserve of commissioned military men or seasoned male political actors. In the one and only public speech that Kony made in Gulu he admonished Acholi elders who were involved in political intrigue and working to sabotage Bigombe's efforts at peace:

> I don't know what you are fighting over with this lady. I don't know whether you are fighting over the right to cook in the kitchen, fighting over sub-county chieftancy or you think you should also become a minister. You only think if mummy Bigombe brings out Kony then she will have achieved what you elders failed to do. (January 11, 1994; reproduced in *Sunday Vision*, December 22, 1996, 10)

Bigombe stands out as a role model to all Ugandan women, demonstrating that it is possible to overcome patriarchal power. Her role as a consummate negotiator can be matched by very few men in the country.

Cecilia Ogwal

> NRM, like most dictatorial systems, uses women and the youth in order to promote its ideology and political philosophy. The youth and women are the soft spots usually used by authoritarian regimes because they can be easily mobilized as interest groups, right? So the movement is mobilizing women en masse and enticing them with hand-outs in the form of affirmative action. It is putting Ugandan women on a fake pedestal and making them feel big. But that's not what I want as a woman—appointing me to a post and leaving me to fumble until eventually I become a disgrace to the women's struggle. What I want is to be given the muscles to stand on my own steam, to expand the capacity of women to improve on their quality from the grassroots. . . . you know, qualitatively rather than quantitatively. (Cecilia Ogwal)

The name Cecilia Ogwal is synonymous with contemporary struggles over party politics in Uganda. In many ways, she represents the most articulate and strident voice of the opposition to the NRM government. Popularly known as the "iron lady," Ogwal served as assistant secretary-general of the Uganda People's Congress (UPC) from 1981 to 1996. Following serious controversies within the party ranks, Milton Obote—the exiled party president who lives in Lusaka, Zambia, and former head of state—sacked her from the post she had held for fifteen years. Ogwal defied Obote's dismissal and instead led a mutiny against the party president to form a splinter faction of the UPC.

The leadership squabbles in the UPC marked a much deeper malaise, which had plagued the party since its ouster from power in 1985. In the first instance, while the official party position was not to have anything to do with the NRM, several of its prominent leaders broke the ranks to join Museveni's "broad-based" regime. Second, there were considerable differences within the party over whether to participate in any of the elections held by the NRM. The divisions were also paralleled in terms of internal and external divisions that had evolved over time. The former was represented by Ogwal, who believed that being on the ground, they were in the best position to assess the political context and to design appropriate strategies to address them. The latter—in the main represented by Obote and the exiled cohort—were of the view that the NRM should be given no quarter. Many UPC supporters were beginning to perceive their exiled president as a liability, a man who had outlived his usefulness and now belonged to the political archives. I asked Ogwal if she did not think that the mutiny was disruptive of the party and played into the hands of NRM. She disagreed:

> Certain events are healthy. . . . Preventive measures had to be taken and I think anybody who loves the party would have done the same thing. Here was a situation where we felt that participation in the elections was the best strategy to sustain the struggle and somebody far away decided to dictate otherwise. This was impracticable and unacceptable to the members. So there were contradictions, a disparity between the interests of the people on the ground and those of the person living outside. . . . In such a situation I think the interests of the people should prevail.

Obote was opposed to UPC leaders and supporters participating in the 1996 general elections. He thought that UPC's participation would amount to the legitimization of the NRM dictatorship that had banned party politics in Uganda.[9] Ogwal and her followers thought otherwise. They believed that UPC's participation in the CA and the subsequent elections would not only curtail the agenda of NRM but would also provide a platform for articulating the party position and would revive their relationship with supporters on the ground. So who is this woman who dared to defy the demagogic, well-known, and (to his supporters) infallible Apollo Milton Obote, two-time president of Uganda and president of the UPC since its inception in 1960?

Cecilia Atim Ogwal was born in 1946 to Boniface and Aduk Opio in the district of Lango (also the birth district of Obote). Her father, an ex-seminarian who passed away in 1981, was a trained medical assistant and worked for government until he retired. During the 1960s Boniface Opio represented his subcounty in the Lira district council. At that time, the sectarian politics that existed in Uganda meant that Catholicism was synonymous with the Democratic Party (DP) and Protestantism, with the

UPC. Despite being a staunch Catholic, Ogwal's father steered clear of active involvement in party politics. Cecilia recalls that her father was an introvert who controlled his polygamous family of two wives and twenty-one children with an iron fist—"a disciplinarian who wanted his children to be righteous and religious."

Ogwal describes her mother as very humble and religious. She received little formal education and was a housewife who also practiced subsistence farming throughout her married life. The second child in the family, Ogwal was raised in a modest home in Adok village. However, modest as her home was, it was relatively well-to-do in the Adok community because of her father's status. While Ogwal was in the sixth grade, the local government recognized her good academic performance and offered her a scholarship. She continued to benefit from this scholarship through her O-level education at Sacred Heart secondary school, where she won the first Brook Bond Prize for the interschool English essay competition. Ogwal attended college at the University of Nairobi in neighboring Kenya and pursued a degree in commerce.[10] She was among the four pioneer women from East Africa to enlist for the course in this East African University. Her reasons for pursuing a traditionally male career are still lucid: "I wanted to prove to the prejudiced community that even girls can do commerce and become effective managers."

Armed with her commerce degree and having topped her class in business administration, Ogwal returned to Uganda in 1969 and took up a job as an assistant commercial manager in the parastatal State Trading Corporation (STC). In five short years Ogwal had climbed up the managerial ladder to reach the top: Within a year she was appointed deputy licensing officer of another parastatal, the Import and Export Corporation. In 1971 she moved on to the state-owned State Trading Corporation as operations manager and subsequently to the Advisory Board of Trade, running its subsidiary arm, Intra-African Traders (IAT). In February 1970 she married Lamek Ogwal, a civil servant working with the Ministry of Culture.

Ogwal attributes her keen interest in politics at an early age not to her upbringing but instead to the fervent political environment that she found herself steeped in during the heady years preceding formal independence.

> As we matured in the 1950s politics was extremely hectic in Uganda. You know, I was very alert and aware when different political groups were being formed in preparation for independence. So as a youth I took time to understand which party was pursuing what policy and I seriously admired the nationalistic approach of the Uganda People's Congress. Although I was brought up in a Catholic family–and if you remember many Catholics were in the Democratic Party–I chose to belong to UPC from my student days.

> . . . The degree of involvement became more and more as I got nearer and nearer to the center of politics.

While in college, Ogwal was active in student politics. For example, as a first-year college student, she was elected assistant secretary of the Uganda students' association. In her final year at Nairobi University, Ogwal was recruited as a UPC youth winger: "One of the functions in which I participated very actively and which is still vivid in my mind is the December 19, 1969, delegates' conference which ended up in the attempted assassination of Obote at Lugogo." Almost a year later, the UPC government was toppled by Idi Amin, and Obote fled into exile in Tanzania. The coup d'état led by Idi Amin found Uganda amid preparations for general elections and the countryside swarming with politicking campaigners. Among these was Ogwal's brother, Odur-Aper, a lawyer who was preparing to stand on the UPC ticket in Bombo—a town from which many of Amin's kinsfolk came.

Ogwal was part of her brother's election campaign team and first got to know Amin at this time. She was later to meet him on several occasions when he was president of Uganda. In August 1971 Ogwal's husband was arrested by Amin's men. Believing him to have been murdered, Ogwal confronted Amin and demanded to know where her husband was. Her husband was later released, in part because of Ogwal's bold act. The second time Ogwal confronted Amin was in 1974, when he invited her to take up an ambassadorial post in Germany and she declined. At the time it was almost unheard of for anyone to reject the dictator's orders. In disbelief, Amin asked Ogwal, "Don't you fear death?" She answered, "No, because for every human being there's a day of birth and there's a day of dying." Ogwal's final encounter with Amin occurred in 1975, when preparations for the Kampala Organization of African Unity (OAU) summit of heads of states were under way. As the operations commercial manager of the IAT, Ogwal was in charge of importing food supplies for the hundreds of dignitaries expected to attend the summit. Summoned by the paranoid dictator, she was accused of trying to sabotage the summit by importing poisoned rice. Finally, in 1977, Ogwal and her family fled into exile in Kenya when a confidante informed them that her name was high on Amin's hit list. They returned in 1979, after Amin's fall.

Because of her Catholic background many people in the UPC perceived Ogwal with suspicion and skepticism. When the more insightful and shrewd Obote appointed Ogwal to the party's politbureau in 1981 as assistant secretary-general, many party stalwarts were outraged. Obote was the only person who seemed to realize Ogwal's potential and her ability to reorganize the party after a decade's interruption by Idi Amin's reign of terror. Although Ogwal deputized for John Kirunda, the party secretary-general, in reality she did most of the work on the ground because the latter simultaneously held the busy cabinet portfolio of minister of internal affairs. Ogwal explained:

> The task of setting up the party secretariat and party headquarters, recruitment of staff, training of staff, and the running of the party secretariat was really my job and it wasn't easy. But I found it challenging and interesting because I'm trained in the field of management and I had a working experience in management. I knew the ins and outs of setting up an organization and putting up a good management system. . . . I know almost each and every file at the party headquarters; each and every staff there; and each and every piece of furniture there. And I thank God that even after our government was overthrown in 1985 the party remained intact. So one can say that *my* system at the secretariat has enjoyed uninterrupted activity from 1981 to date.

Ogwal was one of six women who competed for parliamentary seats in the 1980 general elections. Her decision to join the race came only three days before election day, when several elders from the Lira west constituency approached her and requested her to stand against the two male candidates with whom they were dissatisfied. She took on the challenge and lost to an incumbent cabinet minister, but only by fifteen votes. This experience offered Ogwal a new kind of self-confidence and augmented her self-assurance to build up her political career.

After the second Obote regime was ousted from power in 1985, Ogwal stayed on and ran a family business. Through her political activities she became the de facto leader of UPC in Uganda. Among the four top party executives, she was the only one in Uganda, since the vice president had died and the secretary-general, like the party president, had fled into exile. In 1992 Obote appointed Ogwal chair of the party's presidential policy commission (PPC), a body that was charged with the duty of analyzing the situation on the ground and coming up with a fresh policy structure for the party. The PPC was meant to fill the vacuum in the absence of the party president by acting as a conduit between the exiled president and the party's grassroots supporters. Ogwal disregarded the NRM clampdown on political party activities and organized party meetings at the headquarters and in the countryside. In January 1991 she was arrested together with the UPC executive members of Luwero district and underwent hours of interrogation. Such harassment and intimidation, however, did not deter Ogwal from openly continuing with party activities.

When the next opportunity to stand for political office presented itself in the form of the 1994 CA elections, Ogwal stood for the Lira municipality seat. She won the election with 90 percent of the votes, leaving the remaining 10 percent to be shared among her five male opponents. She chose to stand on the regular constituency and not the affirmative action ticket for the same reasons she decided to pursue a degree in commerce:

> I feel that time has come for women to cull their own identity. We should not be known to be leaders only because of the affirmative action policy. Some of us should prove that women in their own right can be better than men and this we can only do by competing with them and emerging winners. So while we should continue to nurture women's leadership through affirmative action, we must at the same time promote independent competition with the men.

In the CA she was one of those who prominently represented the voice of the opposition.[11] Ogwal led a group of multiparty delegates in a struggle against what were perceived as NRM-sponsored provisions in the draft constitution meant to entrench the movement system of governance. For example, they fought tooth and nail, albeit unsuccessfully, to block the (in)famous article 269, which put a clamp on political party activities.[12] In a public-address-system voice, Ogwal never minces her words and has continuously confronted Museveni and his government without fear. Her approach is earthy and direct. Among her stinging publications criticizing the NRM government are two booklets entitled *Dictatorship and Donor Policy* and *The Culture of Violent Change of Government and the Myth of Economic Miracle in Uganda.*

When the May 1996 presidential elections came around, UPC, with the endorsement of Milton Obote, decided to form a loose alliance with the Democratic Party and field a candidate to stand against Museveni. The alliance was called the Inter-Party Political Forces Cooperation (IPFC), and the candidate was to be Paul Ssemwogerere, DP president.[13] As the presidential candidates traversed the countryside on their campaign trail, it became abundantly clear that Ssemwogerere was simply a showcase, a cloak for UPC's politicking. Everywhere the IPFC candidate went, Ogwal stood beside him. Her fiery speeches, compared to his fatuous humdrum and uninspiring delivery, often stole the show. At the end of the day, the IPFC campaign trail had turned into something of a UPC revival crusade. Thus, although NRM's Museveni won the presidency, the UPC seized the opportunity to reconnect with their supporters, thanks to Ogwal.[14] Riding on the political capital she had accumulated during the May presidential campaigns, Ogwal offered her candidacy in the June parliamentary elections despite the blockade imposed by Obote. She stood against and trounced two men, one of whom was a rich business tycoon in Lira town.

Predictably, Ogwal is a favorite subject of the local media, which frequently portray her as either a rabid, irrational politician or a farcical character. For example, when public polls indicated that Museveni was ahead of Ssemwogerere (the IPFC candidate) in the weeks of the presidential campaigns, one of the FM radio stations, several times during the day, frivolously played the famous lyrics by Paul Simon and Art Garfunkel, "Oh Cecilia, you're breaking my heart, you're shaking my confidence baby,"[15] followed by nugatory comments such as, "Guess who's singing for whom?" Ogwal pays hardly any attention to such messages and reports; she believes that a thick skin capable of deflecting all manner of abuse is essential for survival in politics.

Ogwal's personal experience exemplifies a female politician for whom womanhood rarely poses an encumbrance to her political pursuits. She is quite oblivious to the fact that Ugandan women get a raw deal when it comes to participation in politics: "Ugandan men tend to give credit where credit is due. I myself rose to the upper layer of my management career at a very early age." When I asked her if she had ever encountered sexual harassment in her long political career, she burst into prolonged laughter and said, "No, in fact that's one thing I've always wondered about. I say, 'Now, how do men harass women?' And I always think, 'Why don't they harass me also?'" These facts, however, do not mean that Ogwal deliberately shuns her femininity or her wifely and motherly responsibilities. She is a self-confessed born-again Christian and a staunch believer in traditional family values.

> I want to emphasize the issue of family life. You know, the politics of a woman politician should be firmly rooted in healthy family life, otherwise her political life will ruin her family. I would hate a situation where a woman uses her femininity in exchange for political favors from men; it's disgraceful. Our husbands should be able to trust us 100 percent. So I think we need to look at our family life much more seriously than our politics and give more time to our husbands and children than to politics. . . . A woman will excel in politics if she knows how to balance her time between these two.

Indeed, Ogwal enjoys the support of her husband and twelve children.[16] However, the plight of women and girls does not feature on Ogwal's political agenda; neither does she consider herself to be a feminist: "I must admit that much as I am a woman and I really love to see women come up, but that's not really my field of expertise [laughter]. I have not pursued it as a special interest." Ogwal does not fight for women's equality; she believes in proving it.

Cecilia Ogwal has indeed proved that she can "stand on her own political steam." Her political career is living testimony to the fact that women

can, in their own right, fully participate in the game of politics. Ogwal re-
fuses to be a used as a pawn in the political maneuvers of men. She holds
her own and also attracts a flock of both male and female supporters
willing to be shepherded by her. She has combined her political, business, and domestic roles with admirable ease.

Naava Nabagesera

> I think I should have joined politics much earlier because it is unbelievable
> what I've discovered. Nothing is straightforward in this game and once you
> pursue justice you don't have many friends. There's a clique of people who
> are in power and just don't want to let go. As long as they're getting their
> own bread, they don't care what happens to the masses. We need people
> who can come out and pursue justice without fear or favor; otherwise if we
> don't do this ladies—especially women—I don't think we have much hope
> in politics. (Naava Nabagesera)

Catherine Naava Nabagesera was one of two women who contested
the Kampala district parliamentary seat—one of the hottest electoral
turfs of the 1996 general elections. Her election poster portrayed a side
profile of a strikingly attractive woman made up to the nines with a pall
of powder, scarlet lipstick, and permed hair with a neat lick fronting her
forehead. Several men and women expressed disapproval and were in
agreement over one thing: This was a candidate who simply could not
win the election. One observer commented, "She belongs in a beauty
contest, not politics."[17] To the chagrin and surprise of all the pundits
Nabagesera was beaten by a margin of just 320 votes.[18] The thirty-year-
old attorney, who runs her own legal chambers in Kampala, was a complete novice and a new personality on the Ugandan political scene. By
contrast, her opponent, Margaret Zziwa, had eight years' experience on
the Kampala district local government council[19] and had represented the
district in the Constituent Assembly.

Although Nabagesera's case represents a "loser" in the parliamentary
elections, it is of particular importance to our discussion about the empowerment and resistance experiences of women politicians in Uganda
for three main reasons. First, it clearly demonstrates women's spirit to
fight and stand for justice.[20] Second, the case exemplifies a significant
phenomenon in Third World politics, namely, the politics of patronage.
Even as Nabagesera tussled it out with Zziwa in court, larger and wider
behind-the-scenes interests were being played out. Media reports specu-
lated that Nabagesera's campaign was being underwritten by the IPFC—
the loose association of political forces that opposed the movement system of government and favored a return to multiparty politics. In other

words, it pitted the "movementists" in a direct battle with the "multipartyists." Finally, the seat for which they were competing was both strategically and politically important, not only as the nation's capital but also as a critical locale for politics. Kampala district is the heart of Uganda, and most decisions affecting the lives of Ugandans are made there. The election struggle between the two, its outcome, and the events following it provided much drama and fodder for the press, bringing several important issues concerning women in politics to the fore.

The youngest child in a family of six, Naava Nabagesera was born to a middle-class Kiganda family. The fact that her mother is the daughter of the late kabaka (king) Daudi Chwa (father of Kabaka Mutesa II) of the Buganda kingdom means that Nabagesera is of royal descent. However, since the Buganda monarchy was abolished in 1966, this aspect of her lineage carried very little significance in Nabagesera's formative years. Despite the fact that her mother was raised in the palace, she does not hold any diplomas or degree certificates. However, she has established herself as a very astute businesswoman. Nabagesera's father, who passed away in 1988, was an administrator and worked in the civil service as a district education officer.

In primary and secondary school Nabagesera held a series of responsible positions, such as prefect, school timekeeper, and head of the debating society. During her first year of law school at twenty years of age, she was married and in the same year bore a set of twins, which earned her the honorific title *Nnalongo*. Having a family to raise made it hard for Nabagesera to join campus politics, let alone pursue her law degree, and it took a lot of determination and hard work for her to complete the course. She attributes her resolute spirit to her mother:

> My mother has been a major influence in my life. She's a very vociferous woman who takes on challenges. She takes on any kind of job that can earn her a living and does not lie back and say, "I'm a lady." I've never known my mother to stay at home. She told me that if you want to go for something do it the best way you can; if you really have conviction that you can do something, just go all the way. She's a very active woman and has headed many organizations such as YWCA—she's one of the pioneers of that organization.

After obtaining her law degree and completing the bar course, Nabagesera was employed as a legal associate in a small law firm in Kampala and worked there for a year. She spent 1993 doing voluntary work as a legal adviser in a local nongovernmental organization called the Association of Women Lawyers (Federacion Internacional de Abogades, FIDA). Her work in the FIDA legal aid clinic exposed her to the realities of gender oppression and subordination suffered by Ugandan women, especially the indigent. The following year Nabagesera set up her own chambers, thus adding to the handful of female-owned law firms in Kampala.

In the first year of their marriage, Nabagesera's husband had to leave Uganda for England and has lived there ever since. For over ten years Nabagesera has virtually lived the life of a single mother, although her husband contributes to the financial well-being of the twins, who occasionally spend vacations with him in London. Nabagesera's decision to join the race for a parliamentary seat in 1996 was primarily to secure a national platform from which she could "fight for the women's cause more effectively." Her decision to join national politics was supported by a number of friends and well-wishers who provided moral and financial support during her campaign. Predictably, Nabagesera's long separation from her husband became a major issue among the electorate during the campaign period:

> The question I was asked everywhere I went was, "Are you married?" As if it is a legal qualification that an MP has to be married. This question was normally raised for female and not male candidates either as a challenge or merely as an insult. But well, I surmounted that because . . . Can you believe that I sometimes had to produce pictures of my wedding to convince the electorate? [Laughs.] Yes, I had to do it because many people couldn't believe that I was a married woman and some were saying that I wasn't even a mother; they'd say, "She doesn't look like she has kids." It was so absurd, but since I was a new figure in politics I felt the need to convince the people that I was a "credible" and "eligible" candidate by their standards.

With the restoration of the monarchies (abolished by Obote) by the NRM government in 1993, people of royal descent began to openly proclaim their ancestry. Nabagesera was no exception, especially since she was contesting for a constituency that falls within the geographical parameters of the kingdom of Buganda. The hitherto silent middle initial N suddenly crystallized as the royal name—Naava—and acquired first-name status. Everywhere she went during her campaigns, Nabagesera was introduced as "Princess Naava," attracting many royalists among the older electorate.[21]

Reactions to Nabagesera's candidacy were fraught with ambivalence. Although her campaign poster put many people off, they were at the same time attracted to her. Her campaign team consisted mostly of youth—men and women in their twenties and thirties. Generally, women seemed to be drawn to this candidate because she was a new figure in politics who promised to fight "for women's rights and development," as her campaign poster declared. Male supporters, on the other hand, were often heard making comments such as, "There is no way we can deny our vote to such a beautiful woman." Such remarks suggested that Nabagesera's physical appearance, as much as (or more than) her intellect and other credentials, was an important factor in luring a cross-section of her supporters to her campaign. She was acutely aware of this problem and explained how she minimized attention to her femininity, her looks, and her sexuality:

> First of all I don't shy away from dealing with men. By directly dealing with men all the time and exposing them to your intellectual capacity you develop some kind of "brotherhood" with them; you know, a brother/sister kind of relationship. So by working closely with men they realized that I had something upstairs (pointing to her head) to offer. . . . they begin to see me not as a vulnerable woman but as an individual.

Such a response is demonstrative of an important factor in Uganda's politics. It illustrates how female politicians often have to consciously strategize on ways to detract attention from their femininity and sexuality in order to compel the electorate to focus on and address *real* issues. This is in contrast to male politicians who are inclined to accentuate their masculinity (e.g., virility, aggressiveness, and toughness), since it is perceived as a bonus in the world of politics. But for men, intellectual capacity is presumed or at least is not questioned prima facie.

Nabagesera waged her campaign around the single issue of women's rights. She counterbalanced her inexperience in politics with two major arguments: (1) her legal training and professional experience were ideal for her to take on the job of legislating and policy formulation and (2) the years she spent in FIDA working with oppressed and abused women put her in a position to fully understand and appreciate the plight of Ugandan women. All she needed was the necessary votes to allow her do something about it. However, even though her major campaign message was the emancipation of women, Nabagesera also understood that she had to appeal to men, since they constituted the majority of the electoral college. Therefore, she was always careful to assure her listeners that her motive was not to upset the status quo, emphasizing that women must always give men the respect they deserve.[22]

Five days after the election results were declared, Nabagesera filed a petition against three parties, viz., the returning officer, the chairman of the electoral commission, and Margaret Zziwa. For a year and a half Nabagesera was entangled in a fierce legal battle in a bid to claim the Kampala district parliamentary seat, which she believed to have won had not the elections been marred with illegalities and malpractice. The grounds in her petition extended from minor matters of technical detail, such as the time period of the display of the register of voters, to the cancellation of results and switching them from the loser to the winner, and finally to the use of money and other inducements to bribe the electorate.

All the charges were denied and the respondents proceeded to make numerous preliminary objections on technical legal issues. The high court ruled in favor of Nabagesera on all preliminary objections and, as a delaying mechanism, the respondents went on to appeal each of the rulings of the preliminary objections. Nabagesera won all the appeals on the preliminary objections, allowing the case to proceed to a substantive hearing.[23] The main issues before the court were five: whether the voters' register was displayed in accordance with the law; whether voters' cards were a legal requirement; whether registered voters were stopped from voting and those not registered allowed to do so; whether valid votes were canceled; and whether voters' registers were adjusted after nominations. The same issues had been voiced by several other election losers I interviewed for this study.

The case was financially and morally debilitating for Nabagesera. Many times she thought of abandoning it altogether, as it did not appear to be worth the stress it was bringing into her life. She and her lawyers received threats from Zziwa's supporters, and one night her personal body guard was fatally shot at her residence.[24] Nabagesera told me that she did not quit at that moment because she desperately needed to see her battle for justice to the very end. Moreover, she could not bear disappointing her supporters, who kept on encouraging her to "hang in there." Another important pillar of strength for Nabagesera is her strong religious background:

> God plays a very important role in my life because I was raised in a very Christian family of what you call saved people. I myself am born-again and a devout Christian. I think everything comes from God, and I thank Him for everything that has happened to me. I have no control of what's going to happen tomorrow; I do what I can and then ask God to do the rest. I've done what I can do and I believe God must have chosen me to do something; He has a purpose for me. So I tell Him that I've done my best, I've gotten up, helped women in FIDA, I want to help them more; these are my intentions, God, help where you can.

By the time the high court got to hear the substance of the petition, almost fourteen months had lapsed and there was an enormous amount of paperwork to wade through. The final judgment on the petition, which was in Nabagesera's favor, was read on October 3, 1997. Justice Tabaro ruled that "the seat of the third respondent shall be declared vacant. This court shall forthwith certify its determination to the speaker of parliament and the electoral commission."[25] According to the law, fresh elections would have to be held within sixty days of the ruling.

Nabagesera and her supporters were ecstatic. She was carried shoulder high from the court buildings to the constitutional square in downtown Kampala in jubilation. "Justice at last, justice at last," the crowd chanted as they danced on the roads, blocking traffic (*Monitor,* October 4, 1997; *New Vision,* October 4, 1997). However, Nabagesera's days in court had not ended; the jubilation was short-lived, as all three respondents filed an appeal against the high court judgment a few weeks later. Zziwa and the other appellants had taken advantage of the loophole in the electoral law that was silent on the question of appeal. In other words, there was a gray area in the law as to what happens if the sixty days (required for conducting fresh elections) lapsed on account of a pending appeal. As it turned out, five months lapsed before the court of appeal passed its verdict. On Friday, February 13, 1998, a hushed courtroom jammed with the supporters of both Nabagesera and Zziwa listened to Justice Okello read a thirty-three-page judgment quashing the high court ruling and reinstating Zziwa as the woman representative of Kampala district. The judgment elaborated on how the learned High Court judge misdirected himself on both procedural matters and issues of substance.[26] The media captured the chance to chip in a sexist comment. One of the local newspapers carried a derogatory cartoon on the court of appeal verdict with the caption, "Well, Naava said her beauty didn't matter, now she wishes it did."[27]

Nabagesera believes that justice was not done. She considered appealing to the constitutional court but later dropped the idea. Her decision not to pursue the constitutional case was not because she did not think that she had a strong case but because the constitutional court is basically composed of the same court which had ruled against her. In the meantime, Zziwa resumed her seat in parliament amid great pomp and ceremony from her supporters. In April 1998 Nabagesera successfully stood for the affirmative action seat at the local government level and is now district councilor and deputy speaker in the Kampala city council.

Preliminary Issues Raised by the Life Histories

Regardless of the woman's socioeconomic class, religious-cultural background, ethnicity, or other personal proclivities, there is one common component—gender—that relegates all of them to a secondary status in the realm of politics. They all have to execute their political agendas within a historically entrenched male paradigm. Not only is power and privilege held by men but it is also men who define that power and its distribution. The express and subliminal privileges that men enjoy as a matter of course in a patriarchal setting are simply not available for women who wish to join this male-dominated sphere. Political activism for women, therefore, takes place within a context of tacit acceptance of the sex-gender division of labor. Highlighted is gender as an important similarity, a chain that links women across and within the specifics that define each one of them as a different and distinct individual.

Moreover, the life stories reveal that women's entry into an arena dominated by men and influenced by a masculine culture does not erase their femininity. Nor do the women eschew their traditional domestic and child care responsibilities. Rather, individual female politicians curve a space for themselves within the dominant political institutions, thus introducing fresh perspectives to politics. Their material existence as mothers, wives and homemakers, no doubt, influences the way that they "do politics." In other words, their experiences in the "private" sphere defines their lives in the "public" arena. The case of Bigombe demonstrates this point very well. For her, the stereotypic "soft" qualities of a woman, for example, compassion, nurturing, and sensitivity, proved to be very appealing to the people and to her peace negotiating work. In short, women personalize politics through the lens of a redefined culture.

None of the women discussed in this chapter could escape the pervasiveness of gender and the systematic way it is built into political institutions. Whether it is Matembe facing the hostile and sexist media, Kalema mothering her orphaned grandchildren, Bigombe struggling for recognition in a male-dominated insurgency situation, Ogwal taking on the dominant pillars of a major political party, or Nabagesera clarifying issues of her sexuality to the prejudiced public, all were forced to confront an ideology of domination and/or bargain with long-established gendered structures of power. Even though Nabagesera's case, on the face of it, was between two women contesting for an affirmative action legislative seat, the forces of male patronage were ever present. Each one of the five personal lives and their different selves articulates the wider patriarchal organization of Ugandan society.

What is significant about Matembe's personal style? The aggressive, radical method of advocating for women's rights has its pros and cons. On the positive side it strengthens the bargaining position of moderates such as Kalema. Herbert Haines (1984) describes this phenomenon as the *positive radical flank effect* and explains that it can happen in either of two ways. First, the radicals provide a militant edge against which moderates' strategies and demands are regarded as "reasonable." Second, radicals can create crises that are resolved to the advantage of the moderates.[28] Matembe's style and activities illustrate the potential power of the women's movement for delivering the feminist message to *wanainchi*. Moreover, it makes it difficult for women to become ensnared into the cooptative web of the dominant group.

However, a *negative radical flank effect* may manifest itself through a general backlash whereby the goals and activities of the movement are discredited and the position of the moderates is thus undermined (Haines 1984, 32). A radical approach also has the tendency to alienate not only men but also would-be liberal female converts. It is sometimes counterproductive to radically attempt changing the thinking of people whose values are deeply rooted in history, politics, society, religion, and the institutional structures patriarchy has created. In comparison, the less radical, reformist style, although highly susceptible to cooptation, stands to gain a great deal from working within the polity to bring about change. The women's movement in Uganda may indeed be perpetuated by cooptation if one looks at it as "exploiting the institutional environment of scarce resources" (Martin 1990). Accessing preexisting political infrastructures to achieve feminist goals, for example, may be viewed as co-opting government and not vice versa. In sum, a diversity in methods should not be viewed in a purely negative way because ultimately, the women's movement stands to gain from each of them.

Religion seems to be an important force in influencing the belief systems of Ugandans, as all the examples of the showcased women show (except one). Historically, religion has always played a powerful role in shaping cultural patterns, delimiting social roles and ultimately defining the status of women in Ugandan society. Here, we see yet another role that it plays in women's engagement with politics. Diverse women politicians find solace in religion as a way of easily dealing with the patriarchal political structures. Perceiving their "deviant" role in politics as "a call from God" somehow provides them with the mantle to resist all odds. Despite its conservatism, inasmuch as it serves as a link between personal, social, and cultural conditions of women, religion presents a potential avenue for dynamism for women politicians.[29] Obviously, religion itself is not an uncontested arena of action, but feminists are able to utilize its humanizing values, such as equality and nondiscrimination, as avenues for broader gender struggles. Indeed, Matembe is famous for taking biblical stories, such as the story of Eve's creation, and turning them on their head.[30] Linda Thomas (1994) illuminates the symbolic way that religion constructed an integral form of political resistance for black Africans in South Africa, whereas Fredrick Harris (1994) documents the pivotal role that religion played in the history of African-American political activism in the United States.

To conclude, the five profiles presented here exemplify commonalties within diversity. Each woman is unique and different from the others but shares certain similarities with them. It is these commonalties, located mostly outside the individual women, that speak to the overarching conceptual framework of this book. When we move beyond these distinct women, we begin to see the bigger picture, grasp the contradictions, and comprehend "what's going on." We see the different ways that the complex, multifaceted institution of gender interacts with women's political participation. In the rest of the book, I elaborate on how that dynamic contributes to shaping the character of Uganda's politics.

Notes

1. "Empowerment" as used in this study does not connote the conventional notion of dominance or "power over"; rather, I adopt a feminist meaning of empowerment, which perceives the concept as a process involving the use of power as competence or a "power to" (Carroll 1972, 604; Bystydzienski 1992, introduction). Hence, as part of the oppressed group, Ugandan women who participate in formal politics devise ways of gaining some control over their personal and interpersonal lives as they participate in a movement for social change.

2. A constitutional commission was set up in 1988 to solicit the public's views on a new constitution. Under the chairmanship of Justice Benjamin Odoki, the commission prepared the draft constitution and submitted it to government in December 1992. This draft constitution formed the basis for the debates of the Constituent Assembly (May 1994 through August 1995), which was responsible for passing the 1995 constitution.

3. A male legislator I interviewed told me that a lot of men in parliament refer to Matembe by a "secret nickname," *Maama Kelele* (a loud, clattery woman).

4. The acronyms AA and CS that follow respondents' names indicate whether the respondent held an affirmative action seat or a county seat, respectively, at the conclusion of my study.

5. All African terms used in this thesis with their English equivalents are listed in Appendix 1.

6. When Kalema discovered that I did not adopt my husband's name, she reprimanded me for "setting a bad example for our young girls in society."

7. This fact seemed to hang around Bigombe's neck like a millstone, for in both the 1994 and the 1996 polls she lost to her male opponents in the county races.

8. Joseph Kony's LRA systematically abducts children and turns them into soldiers or wives for the rebels.

9. On June 17, 1996, Obote sent a press release from his exile home in Lusaka, Zambia, outlining his reasons for sacking the assistant secretary-general (*New Vision* June 28, 1996).

10. At that time Nairobi was one of the three constituent colleges of the University of East Africa (the other two being Makerere and Dar es Salaam). Under this arrangement, each of the colleges specialized in a particular professional discipline. Thus East African students who wished to pursue studies in commerce would go to Nairobi; Makerere covered medicine and Dar es Salaam specialized in Law.

11. See "Ogwal Spits Fire in CA," *Daily Topic,* July 29, 1994; "Cissy Ogwal Floors Four, Carries CA," *Monitor,* July 29, 1994.

12. When the new constitution was finally promulgated in September 1995, Cecilia Ogwal refused to append her signature to the document, arguing that she

could not be party to a law that entrenches a monolithic and dictatorial system (see "Ogwal Walks Out of CA," *New Vision*, September 23, 1995).

13. Such an alliance was indeed a twist in the history of Ugandan politics, for in 1961 the same UPC had engaged in a "marriage of convenience" with Kabaka Yekka (KY) against DP. UPC understood that the party could not win, given its blood-stained history, and that they needed to garner DP support, especially in the central region of Buganda.

14. Indeed, the IPFC candidate was able to garner over 90 percent of the votes cast in the northern region of Uganda.

15. The version of the song that Capital radio played was the latest one by artist Suggs.

16. Seven of the twelve are Ogwal's biological children; five are adopted.

17. Interview with Naava Nabagesera, December 5, 1997.

18. Margaret Zziwa polled 4,332 votes while Naava Nabagesera secured 4,012 votes.

19. Zziwa had over the years risen through the LC hierarchy to become the Kampala City Council general-secretary and also chairperson of the Kampala district women's council. Indeed, she used this background as a tool to campaign against her relatively inexperienced opponent.

20. As soon as the electoral results were announced, Nabagesera alleged fraud and filed a petition in the high court seeking the nullification of the results.

21. She strategically informed Baganda readers of the vernacular newspaper *Ngabo* (June 18, 1996) of her lineage by stating that her mother is "Lovisa Nakimbugwe Birabwa, daughter of Ssekabaka (king of kings) Daudi Chwa."

22. See, for example, Nabagesera's newspaper advertisement in the vernacular daily *Ngabo* (June 18, 1996).

23. See "Zziwa Case Sets Precedent," *New Vision*, November 26, 1996.

24. See "Candidate's Home Guard Murdered," *New Vision*, June 5, 1996.

25. See *Catherine Naava Nabagesera v. Gordon Mwesigye, Stephen Akabway, and Margaret Zziwa*, Election Petition no. 11 (1996).

26. See *The Returning Officer, Kampala; Chairman, Electoral Commission; and Margaret Zziwa v. Catherine Naava Nabagesera*, Civil Appeal no. 39 (1997).

27. *Monitor*, February 14, 1998, 1.

28. During the late 1960s and early 1970s the appearance of radical feminists within the U.S. women's movement had the effect of "normalizing" mainstream reformist women's organizations by not appearing "too far-out," which improved the bargaining position of the latter (Freeman 1975).

29. My focus on "religion" here is not on sets of institutions (e.g., the church or the mosque) but rather on a belief system/ontology to which people adhere, one that gives meaning to their lives.

30. For example, Matembe tells the story of how, after creating man, God was dissatisfied; subsequently, he decided to *improve* on his creation in the form of woman.

3

Gender and the Politics of
Parliamentary Representation

A defining moment in the political history of Uganda occurred in 1989. In
that year the profile of its parliament altered significantly as the first cohort of female beneficiaries of an affirmative action policy took their seats
in the National Resistance Council. A veteran male parliamentarian re-
marked:

> Women are no longer regarded as eccentrics in the political field and more
> and more women are coming out to participate as a matter of course. Their
> mere presence in the House, I think, caused men to contribute in a more cau-
> tious manner . . . to censor themselves in whatever they said, that it was not
> offensive to women. And of course now there's far more emphasis on
> women's issues, gender matters. . . . They're given more prominence. (Kizza
> Besigye, AR)

After two more "affirmative action elections" the presence of women
in Uganda's premier lawmaking body, though still relatively small, has
become something of an ordinary occurrence. Tight races for affirmative
action seats in the Constituent Assembly elections of 1994 marked an increase in women's political awareness relative to the 1989 race. The June
1996 parliamentary race for the National Assembly was even more competitive, with more women than ever before standing for the affirmative
action seats. In that race 106 women competed for the thirty-nine seats reserved for women,[1] and 28 tussled it out with men for the county seats.
This chapter examines the complex issue of parliamentary representation
as it relates to affirmative action women legislators in the specific context
of Uganda. Because women who fill the affirmative action seats are
elected by an electoral college, I begin the discussion in this chapter with
a brief explanation of the complex political structure within which these
elections took place.[2]

Popular Democracy in Uganda

When Museveni's National Resistance Army (NRA) took over power in January 1986, the guerrilla liberators introduced a novel form of popular democracy under which civil society was to exercise power in a five-tiered system of local councils (LCs).[3] At the base of the LC hierarchical structure is the village council (LC I), with all adult residents of the village as ex officio members; the hierarchy ascends through parish council (LC II), subcounty council (LC III), county council (LC IV) and finally to the district council (LC V).[4] Each LC elects an executive committee of nine members, who are responsible for implementing policies and decisions made at that level.[5] Only LC I committee members are elected directly by all village residents; the rest of the committees are elected by an electoral college comprising councilors at the level immediately below.[6] As the pyramid in Figure 3.1 suggests, the electorate shrinks progressively at each rung in the hierarchical ladder of the LC system—an important fact that is discussed later in this chapter. Executive committee members are elected from the pool of councilors at each level; the seats that fall vacant after each set of elections to a higher level are filled through by-elections.

Parallel to the LC system is an arrangement of women's councils (WCs) introduced in 1993. The broad objective of the WCs is to mobilize women for social, political, and cultural activities.[7] Figure 3.2 shows that the hierarchical structure and election process of women's councils and committees is similar to that of the LC system, with two major differences. First, the electorate is exclusively female and, second, there are five committee members instead of nine.[8]

Thus far each of the three cohorts of affirmative action female legislators has been elected indirectly by electoral colleges. In 1989, all legislators were elected to the expanded National Resistance Council (NRC) by an electoral college; county MPs, by executive committees at the LC III level and district affirmative action MPs, by executive committees at the LC V level. In the two subsequent elections, however, county representatives were elected through universal adult suffrage, whereas women district representatives were elected by expanded electoral colleges. The Constituent Assembly (CA) district women delegates were elected in 1994 by an electoral college comprising all councilors at the subcounty (LC III) level within the district as well as all members of the subcounty women's councils within the district. The National Women's Council statute was hurriedly passed by the NRC to ensure that women's councils participated in the CA elections. In fact, other than taking part in elections, the WCs have been in limbo since their inception in 1993. In some parts of the country women's councils did not exist and were only filled on the eve of

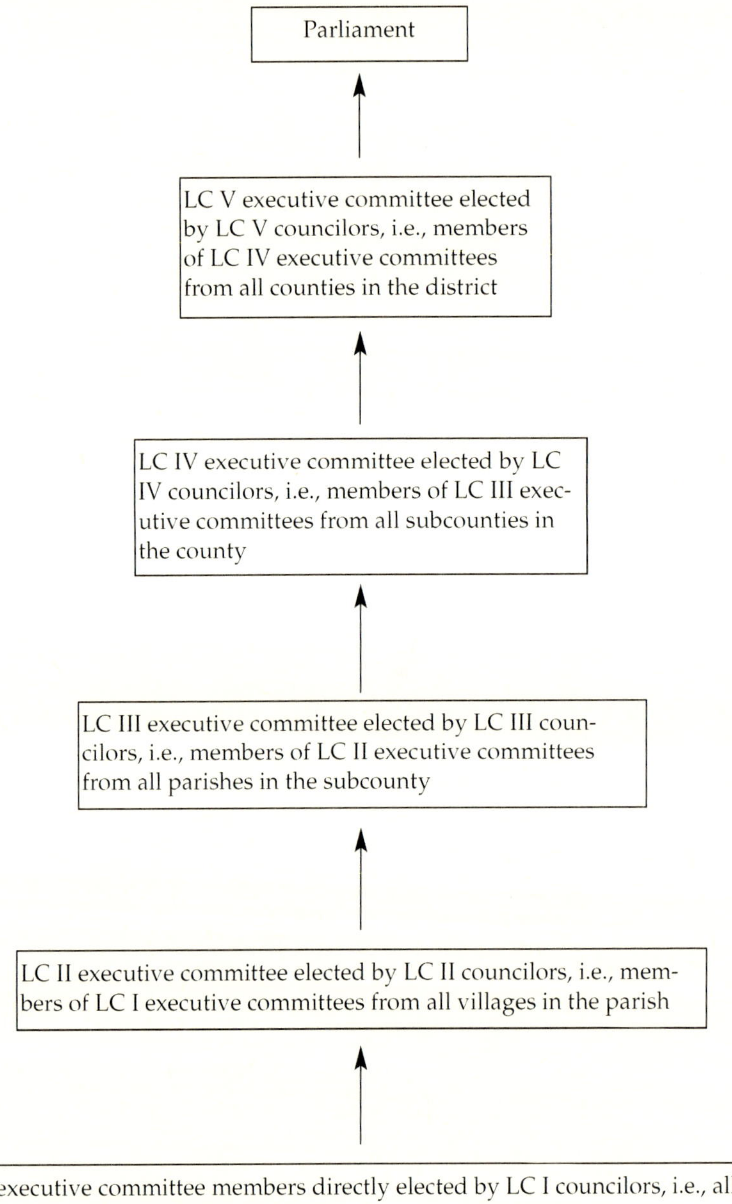

FIGURE 3.1   The Hierarchical Structure of Local Councils and Committees

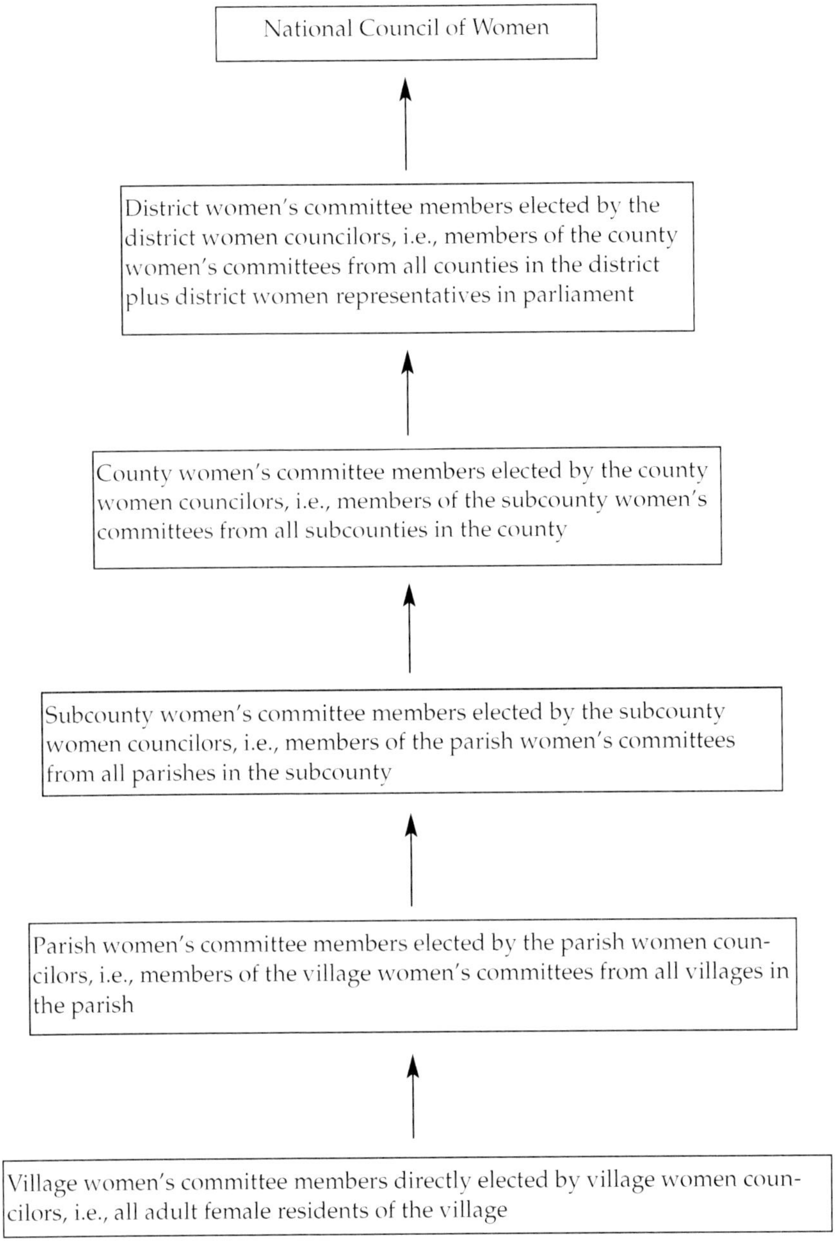

National Council of Women

↑

District women's committee members elected by the district women councilors, i.e., members of the county women's committees from all counties in the district plus district women representatives in parliament

↑

County women's committee members elected by the county women councilors, i.e., members of the subcounty women's committees from all subcounties in the county

↑

Subcounty women's committee members elected by the subcounty women councilors, i.e., members of the parish women's committees from all parishes in the subcounty

↑

Parish women's committee members elected by the parish women councilors, i.e., members of the village women's committees from all villages in the parish

↑

Village women's committee members directly elected by village women councilors, i.e., all adult female residents of the village

FIGURE 3.2   The Hierarchical Structure of Women's Councils and Committees

the June 1996 elections (*Monitor*, June 26, 1996, 1). Lack of facilitation from government and conflict between the role of the WC chairperson and the secretary for women in the LC system are just two of the problems that afflict this institution.[9] District women representatives to the current National Assembly were elected by an even larger electoral college comprising all councilors at parish (LC II) and subcounty (LC III) levels within the district, plus all members of parish women councils within the district. Candidates for the affirmative action seats need not be part of the electoral college.

Although the notion of representation in Uganda is practiced at all levels (village, parish, subcounty, county, and district), the institution of parliament exemplifies its manifestation par excellence. But what exactly constitutes the representative*ness* of representatives? And for the purposes of the present study, do women in Uganda regard female MPs as their representatives? Do women parliamentarians perceive themselves primarily as *women's* representatives?[10] If so, can they purport to speak for other women? Are they always representative to the same degree? If not, what factors explain the difference? There are several ways of thinking about representation, and many scholars have conceptualized the notion. Such theories, although not developed with Uganda's unique features in mind, provide useful grounding for our analysis.

In her classic book *The Concept of Representation* (1967) Hanna Pitkin defines representation simply as making something present in some sense that is nevertheless not present literally or in fact (Pitkin 1967, 144). In political terms she narrows it down to the relationship through which the people of a nation are present in the actions of government (Pitkin 1967, 232). She identifies two major types of representation: (1) "standing for" representation and (2) "acting for" representation.[11]

"Standing for" Representation

During the second half of the nineteenth century several political theorists realized that democracy as commonly practiced favored dominant groups in society while practically disfranchising the minorities. The voices of those who were disadvantaged on the basis of gender, race, ethnicity, class, age, and so forth, were essentially absent from "representative governments" (Mill 1861; Hare 1873; Sterne 1871; Swabey 1939). Arguing for a representative body that is truly reflective of the wider society it purports to represent, a case was made for proportional representation. To capture the meaning of proportional representation, figurative terms such as "exact portrait in miniature" (Adams 1852–1865), "microcosm" (Tussman 1960), "reduced photograph" (Forney 1900), "map drawn to scale" (Mirabeau 1834), and "sample" (Swabey 1939) were used. The essence of proportional representation is to have an accurate part-by-part mirror image of the society it represents (Pitkin 1967, 61–66). Following the proportionists' recommendation literally would mean that Ugandan women would constitute approximately 51 percent of the national assembly. But these proportional notions of representation are not tenable in the real world, since the economically and politically dominant groups always dominate in representative bodies while the "minorities" are left out.

Marie Swabey adopts a technical view of proportional representation. Swabey compares it to mathematical random sampling following the rules of probability: "The principle of sampling in democratic theory is that a smaller group, selected impartially or at random from a larger group, tends to have the character of the larger group" (Swabey 1939, 25). Swabey's theory is based on the underlying assumption that the opinion of those who vote at elections is a "fair, trustworthy sample of what the opinion of the general public would be if they expressed it" (Swabey 1939, 25). But even the most sanguine observer would not describe the electoral process of political representatives as impartial. Eligibility qualifications of potential aspirants close the political door to a large segment of the population. For example, a minimum educational qualification of an advanced-level high school certificate (or its equivalent) effectively blocks more than 90 percent of the female population from participating in Ugandan parliamentary politics.[12]

Goran Hyden (1995) makes a case for proportional representation as the best system for Uganda in this postchaos era of its political history.[13] He argues that the plurality/majority[14] electoral system inherited from the British colonialists works to reinforce the existing fissures within Ugandan society, fostering "cultural but not political pluralism" (1995, 182). In a bid to "delocalize" the vote and facilitate the transition to a multiparty democracy, Hyden recommends the list system version of proportional representation. In this case the parties nominate lists of candidates in multimember constituencies and voters cast their ballots for one party list or the other; the seats are allocated to the party lists in proportion to the number of votes they have collected (1995, 184). Despite the promise that Hyden's scheme holds for marginalized social groups, it is difficult to see how, without affirmative action within parties, women would find an edge in a system in which male-dominated party organizations have considerable influence over the nominations of candidates whose names initially make it to the lists. Indeed, Lindeke and Wanzala (1994) found that during the 1992 Namibian general elections, proportional representation did not necessarily translate into higher representation for women in the national legislature.[15] Moreover, female legislators who find their way to parliament through proportional representation often face the dilemma of pursuing feminist goals while toeing the party line (which may clash with the former) at the same time. This, in part, explains why many women MPs in South Africa have a sense of frustration and burnout.[16]

By introducing positive action to increase the proportion of women in the National Assembly, the National Resistance Movement (NRM) government intended only to create "descriptive representatives" who "stood for" women. When the principle was enshrined in the 1995 constitution, the language was carefully crafted to ensure that these women were not perceived as representatives *of* women as a special group. Article 33 provides that "women shall have the right to affirmative action for the purpose of redressing the imbalances created by history, tradition or custom." However, the tone becomes more subdued in article 78, which describes an affirmative action female parliamentarian as a "woman representative *for* every district" (my emphasis). This is in stark contrast to other categories of affirmative action parliamentarians, who are said to represent special interest groups and are described as "representatives *of* the army, youth, workers, persons with disabilities" (my emphasis).[17] By emphasizing the descriptive nature of women representatives the constitution creates what Byanyima calls "status quo" representatives and not "emancipationists."[18] The NRM "allows" women to partake of the political cake: to participate in decisionmaking but not to represent women as an interest group; not to carry special responsibility for women.

Arguments against interest-defined groups prevail in contemporary writings of mainstream political thinkers. Augmenting Edmund Burke's notion of "objective interests," theorists like Bobbio (1987) and Arblaster (1987) denounce interest-defined groups in national politics and instead advocate a democracy that views people as citizens, not bearers of interests (Pitkin 1967; Phillips 1991, 1995). Opposition to group interests emanates from liberal democratic thinking, which emphasizes individualism. But such thinking is incompatible with African societies in which democratic philosophy is underpinned by the notion of plurality. It is also inconsistent with the principle that lies behind affirmative action. By introducing a measure that guarantees women's greater representation, the NRM was in effect acknowledging the political relevance of sexual difference. Then it had to go the whole distance and recognize women as a group.

Feminists have also shied away from speaking of "women's interests" for fear of falling into the trap of essentializing an obviously heterogeneous group of people (Moraga and Anzaldua 1981; AAWORD 1982; Savane 1982; Mohanty et al. 1991). Ugandan women obviously are not a faceless monolith with respect to class, religion, ethnicity, age, and so forth. Although these differences must be acknowledged, dwelling on them and sidelining the common oppression and subordination that women suffer as a group, in my view, will only spell doom for the women's movement. Focusing on such differences derails political activism that seeks to change the status quo (cf. Reagon 1983; Young 1994; Oloka-Onyango and Tamale 1995).[19]

Phillips (1995) points out that the variety of women's interests does not refute the claim that interests are gendered. Women as a group can make claims for special interests and concerns that are distinct from men's because of their materially different position in society. For example, experiences of inequality regarding pregnancy and property inheritance directly affect Ugandan women but not Ugandan men. Moreover, ideas, interests, and concerns in Uganda's politics have already been clearly demarcated by patriarchal orthodoxies that rendered alternatives invisible. Thus there is a need to introduce new people (women) who will represent and develop alternative ideas (cf. Phillips 1995, chap. 3).

The professional backgrounds of women MPs generally tend to follow traditional female jobs such as teaching, nursing, clerking, and social work, whereas those of men gravitate toward the legal, business, and science-based professions. But the profile of a typical Ugandan woman remains totally absent from the House.[20] More than 90 percent of the women in Uganda are illiterate or semiliterate rural peasants engaged in subsistence farming. The incongruity that exists between their position and the Westminster-type politics that is practiced in Uganda is stark. Many women MPs told me how intimidated they felt the first time they entered the assembly chamber for business. In contrast, from what the men told me, it was apparent that most of them slipped into the parliamentary setup with relative ease and naturalness.

House ritual, with its exclusive use of the English language and intricate rules of procedure, is not in consonance with the society outside the House. I myself was quite taken aback the first time I attended a parliamentary session during my study. The sergeant at arms, meticulously garbed in a starched uniform and white gloves and carrying a molded gold-plated mace, pompously announces the arrival of the Speaker before leading him into the assembly chamber. A colonial prayer is uttered in old English dialect before members can take their seats.[21] Preservation of both symbolic and real vestiges of colonialism (e.g., insistence on the exclusive use of English in the House) serves to perpetuate the patriarchal structure and to alienate the greater majority of the population.

The severest criticism leveled against proportionists is that they overemphasize the notion of composition while neglecting the actions of the representatives (see, e.g., Hermens 1941). Pitkin faults the proportionists' view for providing a partial perspective of representation and criticizes it for emphasizing the aspect of "being like you" rather than "acting for you" (Pitkin 1967, 89). For her, representation must mean more than being typical or resembling. Thus if the image of Ugandan women legislators does not "mirror" that of the majority of women in the wider population, can it be argued that they nevertheless represent their interests in parliament? Does womanhood provide them with a license for "acting for" Ugandan women? Proportionists need to go beyond seeking ways of a proper institutionalization of representative government and think about the activity of representation.

"Acting for" Representation

> The performance of a woman representative should be measured by her record of gender sensitivity and [the] equal opportunity legislation she has moved or actively supported. And also by the programs she has initiated or contributed to enhance the status of women. (Winnie Byanyima, MP, *Monitor*, January 26–29, 1996)

The litmus test proposed above is predicated on two underlying assumptions. First, it assumes "substantive acting for" on the part of women parliamentarians. Second, it takes the female political elite as an interest-based group that represents the interests of Ugandan women. Pitkin believes that the view of representation as "acting for" (as opposed to symbolic "standing for") is the one that makes representation truly political. Conceiving of representation as a human activity, Pitkin defines it thus:

> Representing here means acting in the interest of the represented, in a manner responsive to them. The representative must act independently; his action must involve discretion and judgment; he must be the one who acts. The represented must also be capable of independent action and judgment—and, despite the resulting potential for conflict between [them] about what is to be done, that conflict must not normally take place—or if it occurs an explanation must be possible in terms of the interest of the represented. (Pitkin 1967, 209).

Pitkin further argues that rationality is not a guarantee in the field of politics, since people may be dogmatically committed to certain issues. Therefore she concedes that substantive representation entails a combination of bargaining and compromise that include conflicting commitments (Pitkin 1967, 212).

Minority groups, especially those that suffer gender and racial oppression, have called for an alternative politics of representation. A prominent voice in this quarter belongs to black feminist theorist bell hooks, who challenges systems of domination based on racism, sexism, and class elitism.[22] Likewise, Lani Guinier has attacked commentators such as Abigail Thernstrom (1987), who have revived the doctrine of "virtual" representation in order to justify "monochromatic legislatures on the premise that whites can represent blacks" (Guinier 1994, 36). The doctrine of virtual representation, which is rooted in eighteenth-century political discourse, assumes surrogate representation based on common interest.[23] Michelman defines virtual representation as a doctrine which "asserts that one can be represented in a political regime in which one has no actual participatory rule, not even as an elector, through the participation of another who is one's likeness" (Michelman 1986, 51). Guinier urges minority groups to never settle for virtual representation but to demand "actual" representation.

Affirmative action women legislators in Uganda, like no other representatives, exemplify the contradictions resulting from conflicting commitments. Scholars such as Stephen Carter (1991) lament the view that perceives affirmative action as a means for assuring substantive representation of a special group. He points to the danger of conflating the ideals of affirmative action with the proposition that all beneficiaries of affirmative action should become representatives of their people. Talking about the rhetoric of representation among black people in the United States, Carter writes:

> Black people who have attained a measure of success in the white world are assumed—and, indeed, expected—always and everywhere to represent the race, not in the traditional and still important senses of serving as role models for those who will come later or opening doors by proving their worth, but in a strange new sense of bringing excluded voices into the corridors of power, thereby articulating the interests of a constituency. (Carter 1991, 32–33)

This view holds that the reason for inclusive politics is to "bring that voice [which has hitherto been excluded] inside" (Carter 1991, 36). In the context of women and politics, it would mean that gender is a good proxy for a particular viewpoint (perhaps a feminist one) for female legislators who are beneficiaries of affirmative action. But in reality we know that each woman "on the inside" holds personal values and parochial interests that do not necessarily represent the views of their constituents, let alone feminist views. Not all female MPs can represent or are willing to represent the interests and concerns of women in the legislature. Indeed, there are some male legislators whose views are more representative of women's interests than those of some women. One female legislator, who did not stand on the affirmative action ticket, minced no words about not being a women's representative:

> I am a woman on the outside with a man's heart inside! I am not a feminist.
> Although I come from an all-girls family and I would like to protect them, I
> didn't come to parliament to represent women's issues. I think the biggest
> enemy of women is women! Men are my partners. (Salaamu Musumba, CS)

For this legislator, "womanhood" does not require a "feminine" viewpoint. On the contrary, she identifies with "masculine" values and assim-
ilates into patriarchal structures, norms, and biases. Most female county
representatives perceive of themselves as representing men and women
and emphasize that they are not in parliament to pursue "the women
question." But not all women who enter the House through the direct
route hold such views; one of them stated that her primary role is to ensure that all laws passed "take into account the gender dimension and
contribute towards achievement of equality of opportunity" (Winnie
Byanyima, CS).

Instituting an affirmative action policy in Ugandan politics introduced
the phenomenon of double representation. Every constituent in the country has at least two representatives in parliament—the affirmative action
district woman representative and the regular county representative. The
phenomenon of double representation is significant in two fundamental
ways. First, it raises the potential for a clash between the two representatives, particularly given the fact that the affirmative action legislator does
not (despite the prevailing belief) represent women alone. In other
words, affirmative action representatives lay claim to representing *everybody* in their district. Potentially and in fact the issues addressed by the
two representatives are the same, requiring the affirmative action representative to tread cautiously in order to avoid offending the county representatives. Often the county representatives expect affirmative action
MPs to concentrate on women's issues in the district and only obliquely
deal with other issues concerning county constituencies within the district.[24]

Second, double representation has an impact on the "facilitation" of
MPs whereby the women district representatives demand more facilitation in terms of allowances because of the relatively larger size of their
constituencies. As two affirmative action MPs put it:

> After placing us in charge of a whole district, government did not facilitate
> us as such. Do you know that we are given the same allowance as the ordi-
> nary county representatives? A person who is in charge of three subcoun-
> ties receives the same allowance as me who has forty-six subcounties.
> Now, is government really serious about affirmative action? I've tried to
> pursue this matter in parliament but I was booed down. (Miria Matembe,
> AA)

> It is preposterous for me to get the same amount of allowance for facilitating
> a whole district of four counties as the MP who only has to work in one of
> these counties. Time and again we have appealed to government to increase
> our allowances but we haven't even got the support of our colleagues who
> represent counties. I don't know why, but they don't feel we should receive
> extra facilitation. They argue that after all they cover these areas and yet
> when women constituents approach them for guidance they always tell
> them, "That problem you should present to the woman MP, she's responsi-
> ble for your issues." (Sarah Namusoke, AA)

The basic question that any woman who occupies the affirmative action seat is immediately confronted with is whether she represents
women or the district. The answer to this question poses a particular
dilemma to affirmative action MPs for a number of reasons. First, because sex is the raison d'être for their very presence in the House, issues
of gender cannot easily be ignored. Second, the unique feature of affirmative action constituencies being districts (as opposed to counties for the
regular seats) means that these women have a larger area of operation
than other MPs. Finally, and perhaps most important, the issue of representation for affirmative action MPs is closely tied to the fact that they,
unlike regular members, are elected into office not by universal suffrage
but by an electoral college that is predominantly male.[25] This raises questions of allegiance and accountability.

Of the female parliamentarians who participated in this study, 67 percent recognized that they held a special mandate to represent women because of the history of gender discrimination leveled against them. For
the remaining 33 percent, it was difficult to discern whether their response to this particular question was colored by the official position or
whether it stemmed from their personal belief. The comment of one
member was quite revealing:

> MUTAGAMBA: At first we had the impression . . . I considered
> myself as somebody representing women and I thought . . . in
> fact I went a long way to organize women. But then we were
> made to understand that we actually don't represent women
> alone; we represent the entire district. You are the woman repre-
> sentative for the entire district, so it took on a wider scope—men,
> women, children, and the rivers [laughter] are all represented by
> a woman, so you had to be an all-rounder in the district affairs.
>
> SYLVIA: You said you were made to realize, by who?
>
> MUTAGAMBA: We had a number of . . . some seminars trying to
> tell us exactly what was expected of us, as pioneers of women in
> affirmative action. But we argued a long time whether we were

women's representatives or a woman district representative, so finally the NRM secretariat came in to officially describe our position. They told us that we are women representatives, representing the entire district, not necessarily representing women alone.

Further evidence that many of the pioneer affirmative action parliamentarians initially regarded themselves as women's representatives can be gleaned from the words of a former minister of Women in Development, Gertrude Byekwaso, in her maiden speech as an affirmative action representative:

> I wish to congratulate my colleagues here—the honorable members, particularly the women because this is the first time to see women in a bigger number [sic] than before. First of all, I wish to extend . . . in fact *I will be cheating the women of Masaka whom I represent here and the entire population of the women of Uganda if I do not say anything on their behalf.* So permit me to extend my sincere gratitude to the NRM government and its leaders for having come out of the bush with clear cut policies which favour women. (Official Hansard, April 25, 1989, 40; my emphasis)

After several years of walking the affirmative action road, many who regarded "acting for" women as their primary role in parliament were put back in line by colleagues who reminded them that they represent *everybody* in the district. For example, at an induction workshop organized for the newly elected women legislators in July 1996, a young and enthusiastic newcomer proudly announced that she was representing the women of her district. An older veteran MP immediately reproached her for misconstruing her representative role: "I want all of us to get this very clear; we are not elected to represent only women. We represent all men, women, and children in the district" (Joyce Mpaga, AA). In our interview a few weeks later, the same newcomer's response to the question fell within the 33 percent category mentioned above.

The self-descriptor "people's representative" used by some women was more formal than real, as shown on the floor of the parliamentary chamber. No matter who it is that female MPs purport to represent, my observations in the House revealed that seven times out of ten, when a woman stood up to contribute to any debate on the floor, the interjection touched upon women's specific needs or concerns, especially as they relate to (under)development;[26] their practice, at least in the House, generally pointed to their "acting for" women. It also underlines the notion that for African women, issues other than gender figure integrally in their oppression; gender cannot be extracted from the crippling wider context of underdevelopment.

Another reason that may lie behind some female legislators' perceiving their representative role in gender-neutral terms is that declaring themselves to be women's representatives will lead to their being perceived as narrow-minded and unable to measure up to their male colleagues.[27] As one member put it:

> The women's cause cannot be isolated from the wider perspective of the district. That is my outlook because when you try to push the women's cause too far there's that resentment which naturally comes with it. So to be successful you have to show all the people that you care for their sentiments too. So when I am working on water, although it's the women who suffer most in the face of water shortage, I solved it as a district problem. So I made myself project the image of caring for the district. . . . So as long as I wrapped an issue with a district backdrop then the district council would support it. It doesn't mean that I am not interested in the women's cause. (Esther Opoti, CS)

Notably, none of the male representatives interviewed for this study claimed a primary agenda of representing men. This is not surprising, since men as a gender group are not marginalized in Ugandan society. Thus male MPs do not need to address "men's issues" as such. Moreover, in this era of interest group politics, it would not be "politically correct" for male MPs to speak out directly for a group that has historically enjoyed dominance and privilege.

Pitkin perceives representation not as a one-moment affair but as a *process*. This means that fair representation hinges on creating and maintaining linkages between the representative and the represented (also see Kim et al. 1984). Do Ugandan female parliamentarians foster any linkages with women outside parliament? My study demonstrated that the relationship between women MPs and women's networks outside parliament was tenuous at best. Every official of a women's organization with whom I talked shared a common regret that effective links did not exist between female politicians and women's networks within Uganda. The chairperson of the Ugandan Association of Women Lawyers (FIDA) summed up the position of these women when she said:

> Women expect so much from their representatives; the women representatives, on the other hand, feel that they are in parliament in their individual capacities and they deserve to be there because they've worked hard for it. So when the two agendas don't meet you can never come together to help one another. We don't know how to lobby them; they don't know how to appeal downwards. So they operate in a sort of ivory tower—up there and nobody really cares about them. Yet they should be using us to promote their careers. It's only towards election time . . . now everybody is fumbling

around FIDA, "Please come and bring your program to the women in my district" [laughter].

The president of the Uganda Association of University Women (UAUW) thought that there was a lot of informal interaction between parliamentarians and individuals within her organization because many female legislators were peers of UAUW members; but there was less official contact with the organization itself. "Otherwise we're all in our different cocoons, the NGOs doing their own thing and the parliamentarians doing their own thing. If there is any interaction, it's very intermittent."

Of the women parliamentarians I interviewed, 72 percent held memberships in women's organizations directly involved in pursuing women's rights, but only 17 percent of them were active members. These active members also happened to be the most vocal in pursuing women's issues in the House. This finding was in line with earlier research showing that women's organizations serve as an important linkage mechanism connecting women legislators to other women and to women's interests as a whole (Førde and Hernes 1988; Carroll 1992).

Interestingly enough, almost everyone outside parliament seems to think that female parliamentarians have a special role in representing women. Media, professionals, and, most importantly, grassroots women in the rural areas generally perceive women MPs (regardless of their mode of entering the House) as representatives of women as a special group. The peasant women I interviewed were disillusioned with politicians generally, but especially with women MPs whom they look up to for leadership and guidance:

> All women representatives, starting from LC I to MPs, seek office for their personal gains; they don't care about us. I don't even know the name of my woman MP. Where does she live anyway? They come down to the [community] center only at campaign time, pretending to love us; but we never see them again. (Nassozi)

> She [the district MP] did *absolutely* nothing for us women in this village . . . And you know it's not monetary support that we are asking for but guidance, mobilization, practical skills, maybe introduce some flower seeds here so that we embark on a commercial flower project. There are so many possibilities. (Aida)

> I think I saw our representative here once, in church for someone's burial service. I've also heard her voice on the radio but that's it. I hear that the new one used to be a minister in yesteryears but what good is that for us here? (Nnalongo Kiwanuka)

> I didn't even know that we had a woman's representative in parliament.
> . . . The local LC I secretary for women? No, I don't know her either. The
> other day I saw a big gathering at the school grounds which I mistook for an
> LC court meeting but later learnt that FIDA had been teaching women . . .
> My husband won't let me attend women's meetings. He thinks that "bad"
> ideas will be planted into my head. (Yiga)

But if women legislators do not network with women's organizations and grassroots women, they have a close working relationship with the Ministry of Gender and Community Development. In spite of the ministry's underfunded budget, it maintains formal and informal links with female legislators through activities such as conferences at the district, the national, and even the international level. The ministry official reported that "women MPs are interested in and enthusiastic about our activities. But it is difficult for them to follow them up individually because they are financially handicapped." It is not very surprising that female politicians are closer to the ministry—a government machinery—than to nongovernmental organizations. As politicians, they have greater personal stakes in the Ministry of Gender than they do in the women's voluntary organizations. The potential that the Ministry of Gender holds in opening political doors for women politicians is not lost on many.

Ironically, male constituents, more than female constituents, run to female MPs for help and assistance. This phenomenon relates to the role of a parliamentarian in underdeveloped economies, which is fundamentally different from that of his or her counterpart in the industrialized democracies. Whereas the latter is primarily concerned with legislation, the former is also expected to play the role of developer, which entails initiating projects to introduce basic amenities such as running water, electricity, paved roads, schools, hospitals, and so forth to the constituency. In his state of the nation speech at the opening of the Sixth Parliament in 1996, President Museveni implored parliamentarians to develop their areas, to "make a fresh contract by which we shall have eliminated poverty from all constituencies by the end of the five years of this Parliament." This matter is complicated further by the distorted sense held by *wanainchi* of what an MP should do. Many MPs related stories of constituents showing up at the doorsteps of their residences and offices literally begging for alms. The sight of dust-covered *wanainchi* waiting to talk to their MPs in the main lobby of the National Assembly is not unusual. Their demands range from money for food, medicine, or school fees to arbitration of domestic violence disputes. One member made the following detailed observations:

> Incidentally, one thing I found out is that *wanainchi* don't seem to know . . .
> they actually don't know the role of a member of parliament; that is the worst

part about being a member of parliament in the so-called developing countries. Your electorate doesn't know your role. And in fact when you are even contesting elections they don't care about you making law; what matters is whether the roads are made, whether the wells are dug, whether even the pit latrines in the houses are okay. These people expect you to even pay fees for their children. They have wrong expectations out of you as a member of parliament. . . . People seem to expect you to go even in their houses everyday, sit and drink with them and do all these things with them. Your electorate doesn't know where you begin and where you end. It doesn't know your role therefore they are not in the position to appreciate your work even when you spend all your life and energy doing work. (Miria Matembe, AA)

Of the total number of interviewees (men and women), 82 percent said that the worst aspect of being a parliamentarian was the unreasonable demands of the *wanainchi*. However, the majority (68 percent) of women reported that the best thing that they got out of their roles as representatives was the personal gratification that they felt as a result of assisting people and solving their problems.[28] The problem of the misconstrued role of a parliamentarian is exacerbated by the complication of "clientalism," which Allen (1991) defines as the exchange of political support for individual or collective material benefits. Many constituents perceive these requests for alms as a logical extension of the culture of clientalism.

Since the majority of Ugandan women cannot possibly send "one of their own" to parliament, at the very least they should be permitted to have a direct say in who represents them there. The existing electoral process of affirmative action female representatives denotes virtual representation. Ironically, during the debate over the parliamentary elections bill in 1995, the majority of female NRC legislators vehemently opposed a male-sponsored motion that sought to amend the mode of their elections from electoral college to universal suffrage.[29] Their primary justification for opposing the amendment was that campaigning to a universal electorate in a district would be too cumbersome compared to mainstream candidates, who only have to traverse much smaller counties.[30] However, most of the women who had argued for the electoral college were seriously rethinking their original positions after going through the 1996 election exercise:

Actually we became victims of our own law. We thought it would be very easy to go through an electoral college. In the long run we have realized that it is very disadvantageous, very dangerous, and something that is very easily manipulated. So I would recommend for an amendment to remove electoral colleges for the next elections. (Ida Bikorwenda, AA)

I was in parliament which decided on the electoral college; we thought that because of the district size it would be the best alternative. We also thought that the LCs, being an educated group, would be in a better position to elect capable women than the wider uneducated electorate. But experience has taught me otherwise; I also realized that by the way, most of the lower parish LC officials are also illiterate. They use their thumb marks for signatures. So with this experience of the last elections behind me I would not like to see the electoral college voting for women again. They are very manipulative; the registers especially were doctored and abused. (Ruth Aliu, AA)

Yeah, right now, after participating and after seeing really what happened I wouldn't side with the electoral college. Because we were moving throughout the whole district. You could spend the same time and money as the person meeting everybody yet you only meet fourteen people, the local council—the nine executives and five women from the women's council. And yet if you could go and meet the whole village I think it would have saved . . . So I think it's high time parliament passes a law and we go in for adult suffrage. (Juliet Bintu, AA)

I think I'd have preferred the universal adult suffrage in electing women. In any case whether you go college or universal you still have to traverse the whole district because these representatives are scattered all over the district. In effect it becomes more difficult because you have to look for them in their houses. So the argument that you don't have to move so much for electoral college does not hold water. We had to go parish by parish; mine were 118 parishes so if I had gone and addressed people per parish like I did visiting one or two individuals, it would be much better for my standing. Because when you meet a group of people, say 100 and address them you can leave them without leaving a coin but when you visit someone in their home, he knows you need his vote and you actually kneel down for him. He's so arrogant knowing that you're at his mercy so you must "cough" something. Do you see the difference? (Okullo Aketch, AA)

When I suggested the possibility of women alone voting for affirmative action female MPs, most members opposed it for fear of being branded narrowly as "women's representatives" and being prevented from contributing to wider debates on account of this fact.

A different but closely related debate concerned the number of times an individual woman was eligible to stand for an affirmative action seat; an amendment was proposed to limit the number to one or two terms. The argument was that the affirmative action seat should be regarded as a training ground for preparing women to enter mainstream politics, ultimately initiating as many women as possible and in the process empowering more women to participate in formal politics. The counterargument contended that it was dangerous to compromise quality and capacity building with quantity and that Ugandan society was not yet ready to objectively accept women into "malestream" politics. Indeed, in the 1996 elections, women lost several powerful MPs who ventured into the county contests after having been on the affirmative action seat.[31]

The above discussion reveals the complexity inherent in the notion of representation. The theoretical and historical controversies surrounding this concept are further complicated in the specific case of Ugandan female parliamentarians because of their unique status. Their sex may offer them space to view politics through a different prism, colored by a long history of gender oppression and marginalization and hence regarding themselves primarily as representatives of women. Yet the heterogeneity among Ugandan women places significant limits to such group representations.

Furthermore, the election procedure, with its male-dominated electoral college, doubtlessly factors into the representative role of women holding affirmative action seats. Women legislators find themselves between a rock and a hard place—forced to find a balance between the dictates of their sex and the gendered context in which they operate. What seems clear is that a fresh approach to representation is needed in Ugandan politics; one that does not stem from existing political structures, which are enmeshed in patriarchal, Eurocentric-liberal paradigms. The entire structure of governance needs to be restructured and transformed before the interests of the female sector of *wanainchi* is truly represented at the national level.

Notes

1. Three candidates were returned unopposed.

2. By legislation passed in 1997, the composition of local councils and the process of electing councilors were amended. Most significant in relation to women's representation was the increase in affirmative action women's seats from one to one-third of the LC executive council. Furthermore, the new law did away with electoral colleges so that female councilors from LC I to LC V are presently elected by adult universal suffrage (see Local Governments Act 1997).

3. Until 1995, the local councils were known as resistance councils (RCs). However, I avoid the term "RC" in this book to avoid confusion. Many scholars have criticized the institution of LCs as not constituting "popular democracy," since its organizational structure did not originate from below but rather it was forced on the masses from above with its powers and goals being delineated by the state (e.g., Mamdani 1986; Salyaga 1987; Ddungu 1989; Oloka-Onyango 1991).

4. Note that in the urban centers parishes are designated as "wards" and subcounties as "divisions."

5. The nine portfolios as outlined in section 10(1) of Resistance Council statute no. 9 of 1987 are (1) chairman, (2) vice chairman, (3) secretary, (4) secretary for youth, (5) secretary for information, (6) secretary for women, (7) secretary for secu-

rity, (8) secretary for finance, and (9) secretary for mass mobilization and education. The LC committees have quasi-legislative and administrative powers; LC I, LC II, and LC III also have limited judicial powers (see Oloka-Onyango 1991, 1993).

6. The 1997 Local Governments Act, which aimed at greater decentralization of Uganda's system of administration, introduced substantive changes regarding the constitution, election, and powers of LCs. However, I describe the operations of the pre-1997 LC system because it is under that system that the electoral colleges, which elected affirmative action women in 1989, 1994, and 1996, emanated.

7. The primary actor in establishing WCs was the department of women's affairs in the NRM secretariat. In its proposal document, the department envisaged that "with women nationally organized through this unitary structure the work of mobilizing women and ultimate emancipation will be made easy. . . . The women's councils will have a crucial role [to play] in fostering the horizontal relationship between Ugandan women and the Ministry of Women in Development" (Undated document on file, NRM Secretariat, Kampala).

8. The five portfolios on the women's committees as established by the National Women's Council Statute, 1993, are as follows: (1) chairperson, (2) vice chairperson, (3) secretary, (4) publicity secretary, and (5) secretary for finance.

9. The conflict that arose from the duplicity of the two roles was recently resolved by merging the offices of the WC chairperson and LC secretary for women at the village and parish levels (see section 48(2) of the Local Governments Act 1997). Many Ugandan feminists have questioned the necessity of women's councils, arguing that their role is at best diversionary because they hold no real power. It has been proposed that these councils be scrapped so that women can concentrate their energy on influencing political decisions within the LC structures, wherein the real power lies.

10. Of course the same question is rarely asked of male parliamentarians, that is, "Do male parliamentarians primarily perceive themselves as men's representatives?" As people who have historically dominated political institutions, the actors themselves, as well as the general public, usually take it for granted that male MPs are *"people's* representatives." But because the number of women legislators is still relatively small and because they are considered to be an aberration in national assemblies, the assumption is that women's presence there is/should be for a limited special interest constituency. It was, therefore, crucial for me to address this assumption in my study.

11. "Standing for" representation is also referred to as "descriptive representation," whereas "acting for" representation is sometimes called "substantive representation." These terms were coined by Griffiths (1960) and adopted by Pitkin. Jerry Perkins and Diane Fowlkes (1980) have characterized "standing for" as social representation and "acting for" as opinion representation.

12. See article 80 of the constitution of Uganda, 1995. In Uganda, women make up a small percentage of the total number of students at the advanced high school level (Kwesiga 1993). In 1967, out of the total number of students at this level, males constituted 78 percent and females made up 22 percent. Almost three decades later, in 1995, the statistics at the same educational level had shifted only slightly, males constituting 70 percent compared to 30 percent for females (Planning Unit, Ministry of Education Headquarters, Kampala).

13. Namibia, Mozambique, and South Africa are examples of African countries that have adopted proportional representation in their electoral structures.

14. Under the majoritarian electoral system, voters in a constituency choose a single candidate to represent them in parliament, and there is more emphasis on individual candidates than on parties (Norris 1985, 98–99).

15. In the Nordic countries a party list electoral system operates sex quotas (thanks to the self-conscious political engineering of the women's movement) implemented within particular political parties. These have significantly boosted women's election to the national legislatures. By 1995, women had taken 40 percent of the parliamentary seats in Sweden; 39 percent in Norway, 34 percent in Finland, and 25 percent in Iceland (Inter-parliamentary Union 1995; Phillips 1995).

16. In her recent study of women parliamentarians in South Africa, Hannah Britton found that more than half of her respondents did not plan to return to parliament after their terms of office because they felt there was no room for their voices to be heard; they believed that they would be more effective in their community work ("Women Have the Numbers but Not the Power," *Parliamentary Whip*, April 18, 1997).

17. Indeed, unlike women district representatives, all these interest groups are elected exclusively by their own kind.

18. See Winnie Byanyima, "A Fresh Vision for Women MPs," *Monitor*, January 26–29, 1996.

19. Iris Young provides a key to the dilemma posed by essentialism versus pragmatic politics within feminist theory. She draws on Jean-Paul Sartre's phenomenon of serial collectivity and suggests a reconceptualization of women "as a collective without identifying common attributes that all women have or implying that all women have a common identity" (Young 1994, 714). Woman as series is not associated with personal or group identity, rather it is a "passive unity," a "background" or "anonymous" condition. "Gender, like class, is a vast, multifaceted, layered, complex, and overlapping set of structures and objects. *Women* are the individuals who are positioned as feminine by the activities surrounding those structures and objects" (Young 1994, 728).

20. In this regard, Uganda is similar to most countries around the world in which parliaments are dominated by a class of men and women belonging to the professional elite.

21. In July 1996, when the new parliament discussed their rules of procedure, the issue of abolishing the prayer came up; proponents of this proposal argued that the prayer was anachronistic and nobody ever paid attention to it anyway. However, those in favor of the prayer won, only conceding that the text of the prayer be replaced with a modern English dialect.

22. Although bell hooks's (1994) main focus is cultural representation, her arguments have wider implications for political representation too.

23. For a detailed discussion of virtual representation, see Pitkin (1967, 171–180), who discusses Burke's theory of the representation of interests.

24. In Chapter 7 this issue is discussed in more detail.

25. Typically, LC committees at all levels are entirely male save the portfolio of secretary for women (Mamdani 1994; also see Florence Alaro, "Electoral Colleges

Weaken Democracy," *New Vision*, April 10, 1996, 24; Patrick Luganda, "Must Men Forever Supervise Women?" *New Vision*, June 21, 1996, 4).

26. To cite just one example, during the discussion of a bill on water, women pointed out that its provisions were too metropolitan and neglected the needs of that section of Uganda's population who faced the brunt of scarcity of clean water—women in the rural areas.

27. Rosemary Whip (1991) found that Australian women parliamentarians harbored similar fears. Many thought that being labeled a "women's issues" parliamentarian might be detrimental to their careers (also see Vallance 1979).

28. In contrast, when I asked the male legislators what the best thing was for them, most (69 percent) responses suggested that the finest thing was the power and prestige that come with the office: "It's the feeling of conquest, the respect"; "being at center stage"; "making history for the country." A few women also indicated that power and status were important to them.

29. See George Lugalambi, "Women's Mandate Is Dilute," *Crusader*, February 2–9, 1996, 4; Florence Alaro, "Electoral Colleges Weaken Democracy," *New Vision*, April 10, 1996, 24; Winnie Byanyima, "A Fresh Vision for Women MPs," *Monitor*, January 26–29, 1996.

30. The number of counties in a district depends on the district size and may vary from two, as in Bundibugyo, Kalangala, Kiboga, and Hoima districts, to eleven, as in Iganga, Masaka, and Mpigi districts.

31. Victoria Sebagereka, Esther Mugarura, Esther Opoti, Betty Bigombe, Irene Wekiya, and Beatrice Bakojja are the incumbents who faced the public axe when they ran on the open ticket. All four affirmative action MPs who attempted to compete for county seats during the CA elections in 1994 but lost returned to the affirmative action race in 1996 and won: Joan Rwabyomere, Joyce Mpanga, Rebecca Kadaga, and Gertrude Byekwaso-Lubega.

4

Women in the Parliamentary Electoral Process

Campaigns and Gender Identities

Taking the June 1996 elections as a reference point, this chapter analyzes Ugandan women as political actors in the formal electoral process. It focuses on issues of election campaigns and their outcomes. The 1996 parliamentary campaigns were a classic example of the different ways that gender conditions the culture of politics in Uganda. Before analyzing the campaigns, I briefly examine some of the reasons why women legislators decide to stand for office.

The general circumstances under which the majority of women legislators run for office must be well appreciated before their given reasons for joining politics are analyzed. When the affirmative action policy was introduced in 1989, the Ugandan women's movement, although more than four decades old, was not a formidable force. The tempo of women's activism had been drastically affected by a generation of civil strife and the centralized control over civil society wielded by successive dictatorial regimes. Indeed, the women's movement was not fully resuscitated until the mid-eighties. As noted by Aili Tripp (1994), the proliferation of women's groups in Uganda occurred after the NRM (National Resistance Movement) assumed power in 1986. Women entered into informal and formal associations mainly as a response to the deepening social and economic crises, the relative security ushered in by the NRM government serving as a catalyst to their blossoming. Women's organizations at the time were thus preoccupied with matters such as economic survival and legal rights awareness campaigns. Although women demanded greater political participation at every opportunity, no significant pressure group had crystallized within the women's movement to pursue this agenda exclusively.[1] Thus the affirmative action policy did not evolve directly from the struggle and demands of women's grassroots organizations.[2] Rather, it was imposed from above for reasons having more to do with political maneuvering than a genuine commitment to women's rights. After having been consistently left out of national decisionmaking, women suddenly found the doors flung open for them to enter and participate. Obviously, women were as ill prepared for this new task as men would be if asked overnight to tend homes.

Yet because the space into which women were being pushed was both compositionally and institutionally a male one and because of the absence of a concerted effort on the part of women to mobilize politically, men immediately became self-appointed hunters of "appropriate" women to fill the newly created seats. Over 90 percent of the women who joined the NRC (National Resistance Council) in 1989 reported that they had been approached by male "elders" from their districts who requested them to stand for the affirmative action seat. The following anecdote is fairly typical of most women's introduction into the world of politics:

> I used to be active in students' politics at Makerere [University] but then when I got out to work I forgot about it. . . . It happened that the same week that government announced the affirmative action policy I went to see [a cabinet minister from her district]. So as we were talking, the minister told me that our district had failed to identify a woman representative. He asked me, "Would you be interested?" I said, "No, I don't want to get involved in politics." So I let it rest, but then he went and met with his colleagues and after some time they telephoned me. Again I said no. Then the third time he called and said, "We are leaving for Soroti [district] today. If you change your mind, please follow us there." I said, "I don't think so." Then he sent another message saying, "Ruth, we're stuck. We have failed to identify a suitable woman; the only one we have is not up to the standard we want." I told the messenger to go back and tell him that I don't even have money for the bus fare. So the man came back at about 8:00 P.M. with 10,000 shillings. He said that I should leave very early the following morning if I was serious. So that's how I came to be involved in politics. (Ruth Aliu, AA)

This NRC member easily beat her sole opponent, who lived and worked in the district but was not of the *kabila* found in Soroti district, thus "not meeting the standards" of the elders.

But if most women MPs were approached, cajoled, or nudged to join politics in 1989, the significance of such methods faded in subsequent elections. Although men continued to undertake the self-appointed role of recruiting suitable (read quiescent) female candidates for the affirmative action seats, more and more women began to take the initiative in deciding to run for the legislature. For example, one woman told me how she left her family and job in Europe to join the Constituent Assembly (CA) race in 1994:

> The political turbulence that hit Teso in the mid-eighties brought a lot of suf-
> fering to the people in the region, and when I looked . . . I was of course very
> far away safe and secure in a very well-paying job in London. But when I
> looked at the suffering of the people—I know it sounds really stupid and al-
> truistic to say this—but when I looked at the suffering of the people I
> thought that as long as I had any blood in me which was Itesot I really had
> to come and try and help them to get out of that mess. I could see that there
> was likely to be no end unless there was a different approach to settling, re-
> solving that conflict in Teso. It was clear to me that the problem in Teso was
> really basically one of leadership and the type of leadership that was neces-
> sary to take that part of the country into the twenty-first century. And I felt
> very strongly that talking to my people, seeing their suffering, identifying
> with their needs, and looking at the leadership which was then in Teso . . .
> that I could perhaps join in the ranks of leadership, and that if I did, it would
> be in the best interest of my people so I left my job in London and every-
> thing . . . basically abandoned my job until eventually they had to sack me. I
> also left my family in Britain and came and worked. (Grace Akello, AA)

Many from the original cohort of 1989 female legislators have rerun in
all subsequent elections. For instance, in the 1996 elections, thirty-eight of
the original cohort of fifty (76 percent) competed—ten for the county
seats and twenty-eight for the district seats. Once they were on the trail,
the political magnet continued to pull them. "You know it gets addictive;
once you get into it you can't get out despite the problems" (Rebecca
Kadaga, AA). Today, women's reasons for running are as varied as their
number. Some joined politics because they thought it was their responsibility "to serve the people"; others, because they wanted "to change the
culture of politics." Still others felt that it was "a calling from God." A
few simply regarded it as "a job like any other." Only five of the female
MPs said that they had nourished long-standing ambitions to join politics. The absence of any institutional framework to support politically
ambitious women was significant. Most women's NGO leaders I interviewed told me that the women's movement is yet to achieve the organizational and financial resources to influence or back the crop of women
who run for office.[3] Indeed, none of my interviewees pointed to the
movement as being a factor in influencing their choice to run. However,
one of the strategies that the Forum for Women in Democracy
(FOWODE) has lined up for the medium term is to identify and support
potential female candidates in future elections.[4]

What about the few women who competed against men for the county
seats without the benefit of affirmative action or a previous nomination?[5]
These women either had a long partisan political history or they simply
did not feel that their femininity made them vulnerable to losing the race.
They held strong convictions that they could easily unseat the male in-

cumbents and took on the challenge. A few Ugandan women have made the quantum leap from affirmative action seats to county seats.[6] Occupying high positions of power, such as a cabinet post, especially, creates significant electoral rewards for women in this sense. For example, it was relatively easy for cabinet minister and vice president Specioza Kazibwe to graduate from her 1989 affirmative action seat and rout her male opponents in both the 1994 CA elections and the 1996 general elections.[7]

It is noteworthy that for eleven of the fifteen men interviewed in this study, formal politics had clearly been a career option that they had kept open, even prepared for. I quote one example:

> I have had a long-standing interest in politics. I think ever since my school days at Budo, I was president of the political society at Budo. When I was in the USA, I was the president of the East African Students' Union for two terms, a student of political science, and also one who participated in all the wars that have been here ever since 1979. (Israel Mayengo, CS)

Four other male interviewees reported that they decided to run for political office when elders in their counties called on them to do so. But they required less persuading than the women did. For the men, invitations from the elders seemed to have served simply as a cue, a blessing that they had long been anticipating. Whereas formal politics was far from the minds of most Ugandan women due to a long history of systematic exclusion, for men it was not incongruent with the positions of power that society already accorded them.

The Campaigns

Whether the race was between women and women or between women and men, femininity and gender identity assumed center stage on the campaign podium.[8] Women spent a great deal of campaign time convincing the electorate of their moral aptness to stand for political office instead of articulating political issues. In fact, the campaign trail for female candidates resembled a court martial wherein they had to defend their sexual morality.[9] Whereas the hallmark of the 1996 parliamentary race was mud slinging, its character took on sex-specific dimensions. The "mud" for most men constituted issues concerning corruption, political ineptitude, and affiliations that have come to be viewed as pejorative, for example, "multipartyist."[10] Women, on the other hand, encountered slurs regarding their marital status, sexuality, and (in)fidelity. A married woman was penalized for neglecting her husband and family. A woman who was "unattached" was put to task to prove that she was not a *malaya* (prostitute)[11]:

They [the electorate] always remembered to point out that I'm single; I may get married and disappear with their constituency! Or that I'll get married and disappear with their constitution, taking it to my husband's district [laughter]. . . . so many other insults. (Esther Opoti, CS)

They said, "Oh, this woman, she is very pretty, she is young, she is a widow, soon she will get married." So, you shouldn't give her your votes because she is going to be like Stella—you know, there is a lady who stood in my late husband's place and she got married to somebody from Rwanda or something like that. So that was a big plot against me during my campaigns. (Victoria Sebagereka, CS)

The problem is when men start feeding your husband with poisonous stories. You know, men to men. They say, "Now you have let the woman free, she is going to become a wife to all the men in parliament. You better forget about her." (Mary Kamugisha, AA)

During the campaigns my opponents tried to attack me from a woman angle and culture and to use family values or to question my morality—being single and not having children—and even trying to delve in my previous relationships, personal relationships. (Winnie Byanyima, CS)

We women who decide to join politics have to develop a very thick skin. Otherwise you can actually easily be discouraged by the world. In fact the men know very well that if you want to scare away a woman talk about her. . . . Do you know that they accused me of being a murderer? That I killed my late husband? That I'm a prostitute? All sorts of things came up. (Margaret Zziwa, AA)

My opponent was married and she made my spinsterhood an issue. Oh, it was the talk of the campaign. First of all she spread a rumor that I had plans to get married to a man from another district. She said that I'd postponed the wedding because of the elections. So she asked the electorate, "How can you give your vote to someone who is going to run away from you?" (Naome Kabasharira, AA)

There were six of us in the race for the county . . . I was surprised because during the campaigns I could easily talk to the four men but this one woman didn't even want to sit next to me, let alone talk to me. She was always on my neck. . . . One time she called a consultative meeting with the voters and she started abusing me; she called me an illiterate and things like that. And she created so many stories just to damage my reputation but I wouldn't react. She tried to use newspapers but I never said anything. In the end I

> trounced her badly. She came out third with 4,100 and something votes
> whereas I got 8,555. (Tezira Jamwa, CS)

Marital status is a target commonly used for penalizing women in politics worldwide. American senator Barbara Mikulski commented that women who run for office can never win on this issue, "If you were married, you were neglecting him. If you were widowed, you killed him. If you were divorced, you didn't keep him. And if you were single, you couldn't get a husband anyway" (quoted in Braden 1996, 7). Surprisingly, even the women contestants themselves used the "morality card" against each other. In neck-and-neck races women took advantage of such "sexist barometers" to outmaneuver their opponents. They understood exactly what the male-dominated electorate wanted to hear and took advantage of it.

Most women had to emphasize their femininity in order to win over the electorate. Particularly for the affirmative action candidates, appearing and acting feminine augured well with an electorate that was dominated by traditional, chauvinist men. For example, the standard attire for most women on the campaign trail was the traditional *busuti* or *shuuka*, both of which accentuated their femininity. Many had to bring their husbands to campaign rallies to prove that they were "attached." In one case a candidate had to promise the electorate that finding herself a husband would be her number one priority if elected. All these apparent acts of deference were tactical strategies that women candidates employed to circumvent patriarchal authority.

Again, because almost three-fourths of their electorate is male, women in the race for district seats had to be very careful not to antagonize them by appearing to threaten their position of dominance and power. As a *New Vision* reporter analyzing women's campaigns put it:

> The ladies have touched lightly on matters that could draw the wrath of the males for obvious reasons. It is not politically expedient to harp on a theme that annoys the largest proportion of the electoral college that is scheduled to elect a candidate. (*New Vision,* June 21, 1996, 4)

Margaret Zziwa, for instance, whose campaign poster promised her constituents "unity, development, and women's empowerment," had been actively involved in sensitizing grassroots women about their rights within the LC (local councils) system for several years. Nevertheless, she painted quite a different picture when it came to campaigning. "Don't get me wrong," she told her electorate, "I am not advocating for *omwenkanonkano* (equality) for women in the home; only equality in the workplace." In a bid to outdo her opponent, Naava Nabagesera, the only other contender and also an active advocate of women's rights, replied, "I am not for women's equality either. . . . I always serve meals to my husband kneeling down! I know how to give men the respect they deserve."[12]

Both candidates were saying what was "politically correct" to the audience of conservative LC male officials whose votes they were competing for. It did not seem to matter that they went down on record misrepresenting their beliefs and ideals as long as the strategy guaranteed their entry into parliament. Once they got there, it would be a different story all together.

But women in the race for county seats consciously deemphasized their female identities by, for example, deliberately choosing not to wear makeup. They refused to be derailed, sticking to the issues no matter what.

> I presented myself as an anticorruption candidate and they tried, first of all, to tarnish my credentials as someone who is corrupt. They tried to make corruption a nonissue. I focused on it and said it is an issue. Then he changed tactics and said, "But you're not credible; you're corrupt yourself." He planted a story in a local magazine and circulated it, but I sued him and then he kept quiet. So he tried to attack me. There I was attacked as somebody who is aggressive and who is uncompromising [laughter] simply because I had been fighting the local government, which really was not just corrupt but it was really oppressing people, particularly women, widows, old men, the most vulnerable people. So I pushed them into a corner and they were saying that I was not compromising. (Winnie Byanyima, CS)

But while the county female candidates soft-peddled their female identity, it seemed that they could not escape from it in other contexts. For example, in all but three county races in which women competed, their opponents were exclusively male. Both women I interviewed who had faced other women at the county races strongly believed that their opponents had been "planted" by men in their counties to divide their votes. If this was in fact true, it is evidence of attempts by the dominant group to prevent women from gathering women's votes at the county level. It also suggests that these female candidates perceived the presence of the other women as somehow encroaching on "turf" they felt was theirs alone (by referring to their female competitors as "plants" they are marginalizing them). At any rate, the system of gender was so pervasive and so dominant in these women's electoral lives that they had to "frame" the issue as male-female.

The campaign trail inducted almost all of the women in this study into the world of machination, shrewdness, deceit, and aggressiveness—characteristics that Ugandan society does not associate with femininity. For example, women, like men, needed to use money and gifts in exchange for votes. This practice was in clear contravention of section 98(1) of the parliamentary elections (interim provisions) statute 1996, which provides:

> Any person who, either before or during an election with intent, either directly or indirectly, to influence another person to vote or refrain from voting for any candidate, gives or provides or causes to be given or provided any money, gift or other consideration to that other person, commits the offense of bribery and is liable on conviction to a fine not exceeding two hundred thousand shillings or imprisonment not exceeding two years or both.

Several women admitted using one type of inducement or the other, as illustrated in the following vivid experience related by one candidate:

> There were three of us, but somewhere in the middle of the campaigns the money element increased because my opponents started stepping up their money. So what I did—which is public knowledge—I just bought soap. . . . Yeah, everyone in the electoral college got a bar of soap; that was very expensive and it was about eight days before the election. As the election day approached, I had to give out cash—2,000 shillings each and my opponent offered 5,000. (Kyohairwe, AA)[13]

Another woman who contested with six men was reported to have distributed underpants to male and female voters in her county (*Crusader*, July 2–4, 1996, 3). Such bribes might seem inconsequential in a secret-ballot voting system. However, as another member enlightened me, that is not the case:

> SYLVIA: It's a secret ballot, right? I don't see why the electorate won't take X's money and then vote for Y.
>
> OKULLO: You have to understand that this is an illiterate society. People are told that we have recorded your name and when you go to vote, the computer inside the ballot box will tell us who you have voted for! They believe it. Democracy will never go with poverty and illiteracy. It's only education and knowledge which will make people vote wisely.

Almost three quarters of the women parliamentarians I interviewed expressed a concern with what they sensed to be a hostile attitude from other women during the campaign period. Indeed, "women are women's worst enemy" was a theme that recurred throughout my study. Somehow, women, more than men, were perceived as posing the biggest threat to their political advancement.

> Mind you some of us women are our own worst enemies. We really go out of our way to destroy each other. (Grace Akello, AA)

> You know women. . . . we are fighting the same cause but many times women forget this. Instead they think that they're fighting a personal selfish cause. Their personal interests come before everything else. Women are so divided and it is very difficult to go back and unite them. (Esther Opoti, CS)

> You know women are jealous by nature. . . . they think that politics means getting rich and they don't like seeing you better off really than they are. (Mary Kamugisha, AA)

> As women we have a problem. . . . what I have come to realize is that women are . . . you know we destroy ourselves because of this prestige . . . you know, big position and all that. And you find that at the end of the day we have not achieved much and even those people who are aspiring . . . who are making progress, we have pulled them down. I think we've got to keep, you know, to have more interactions among ourselves and really redefine our objectives, why we are in politics, because if we lose track of that, it will be very sad; then the idea of having women in parliament will have been lost. (Mary Mutagamba, AA)

> Women everywhere in Uganda should always throw their full support behind women politicians. . . . I think that the reason why most women undermine fellow women is because of tradition. . . . you know, traditionally, we grew up feeling jealous and envious of each other. But there's a trend that things are changing and I hope that women will be able to strengthen that change. (Jeninah Ntabgoba, AA)

> We women have not exploited the goodwill of our fellow women. This is mainly because there's a lot of infighting between women. Particularly within the middle cadre; they fight a lot for leadership. So you find a lot of conflicts and what not, someone wants to be recognized and so on. That's my observation, and it has lived with us for a very long time. But it's not good for the struggle; we should always take time to consult with one another, to link up with one another regardless of our political views. (Cecilia Ogwal, CS)

It would not be accurate to stereotype Ugandan women as a polarized group; feelings of resentment and suspicion toward other women who seek to join the political arena may be explained sociologically as stemming from the existing gender structures in Ugandan society. It is symptomatic of the normative operations of patriarchy (cf. Breitenberg 1993). The basic ideology underpinning the public/private divide is part and parcel of the sociopolitical strata, and it makes up a significant part of popular consciousness. Although women are active in social and economic activities, they have come to accept the notion that public life, which society (read patriarchy) rewards with more privileges, status, and prestige, is a realm to be enjoyed exclusively by men. When a woman decides to cross into the privileged, powerful world of politics, most women (and men) will see her as enjoying privileges that she does not deserve. This illuminates the contradiction inherent in a patriarchal political system: It simultaneously enables and constrains women's political participation and leads to the notion that "women are women's worst enemy." At best it is just one of the numerous patriarchal myths that perpetuate the status quo.

A related myth is the "queen bee syndrome," which refers to a woman who acquires a powerful position in a traditionally male-run workplace and does not feel any allegiance toward other women or any desire to help them (Caplan 1983, 59). More than 50 percent of the female MPs I interviewed felt that the majority of women appointed to cabinet posts and other high positions of power alienated themselves from their female colleagues in parliament. These MPs believed that such women suffered from the queen bee syndrome. Two members expressed it this way:

> Women, once they get in high positions, they become very selfish. They seem to be afraid of any woman coming near their level. They feel threatened by other women. I think it's a survival instinct. And this is not my personal feeling. . . . all the women in parliament feel the same way. I mean they don't want us near them. The vice president is a good case in point. Being gender-sensitive and all you'd think that she'd be the first person to lobby for women. But once they get there they forget the cause which took them there and really become very, very difficult and unapproachable. This is very discouraging you know for us who are up-and-coming. (Rossette Ikote, AA)

> It is surprising, but the reality is that when women climb up and they are beyond a certain level they begin to start fighting the ones below. In fact they don't want them to reach their level, which is very sad because being so few in decisionmaking positions we should be trying to pull others to come up but no, they fear to be overshadowed. . . . This is the problem with us women. (Esther Opoti, CS)

A number of points need to be made about the origin, the content, and implications of the queen bee syndrome in the context of Ugandan society. First, the phenomenon has direct links to the patriarchal structures that exist in Ugandan society. Vice President Kazibwe and other women cabinet ministers owe their positions to a man or a group of men in power. If such women try to help other women gain access to similar positions, then they face the danger of losing the special status they enjoy.[14] Because women in such positions are rare, there is no real incentive among the men who control the distribution of those positions to increase their numbers. If men did not dominate these top decisionmaking positions and a female cabinet minister were not a unique phenomenon, then women appointed to these positions would not be in danger of becoming queen bees. But women are not the only ones who protect their position of power in high government positions. The male dictators and their protégés who have clung to power for decades in African states are never described as "king bees." The double standard and sexist connotations underlying this phenomenon have a lot to do with the gross underrepresentation of women in the sphere of politics. Until political power ceases to be the exclusive domain of men and the numbers of women in high political positions correspond to their numerical dominance in the general population, the queen bee syndrome will persist.

The sum of the analysis above is that gender had a significant influence on the entire election campaigns process. Regardless of whether the race was between women and women or between men and women, patriarchal ideology infused the rhetoric and discourse of all female campaigners. The issues became lost in the quest to be elected by any means necessary. Clearly, therefore, patriarchal ideology is so deeply ingrained in the yarn of Uganda's social fabric that campaigners are left with little choice but to use it as a means to an end; it matters little whether one believes in its underlying tenets. Politicking is thus predetermined and shaped by forces beyond the control of male and female candidates. The rules of the political game have long been set by the men who have dominated the field. As in a four-hundred-meter race, they dictate that candidates compete and that the first to cross the finish line wins. It is a zero-sum game: Between the starting and finish lines, the runners do whatever is in their power to prevail over other competitors: manipulate, "blow their own horn," assert, even lie—all of which belie the stereotypic characteristics of women in Uganda. To go against the grain would amount to political suicide and spell instant loss of the race.

Elections and Outcomes: A Taste of "Engendered Democracy"?

In the 1996 race for parliament eight women beat men at the polls to join their affirmative action sisters who had won the thirty-nine district seats. In addition, two women represent people with disabilities and one repre-

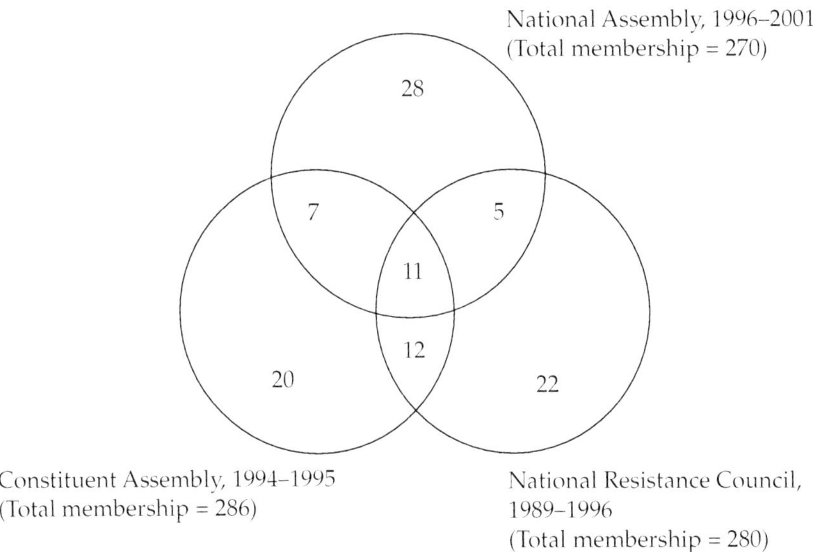

FIGURE 4.1   Female Membership in Three Legislative Bodies

sents the army. The minister of state in charge of economic monitoring is an ex-officio member of parliament by virtue of her cabinet position. This brings the overall total to fifty-one female representatives, accounting for 18.8 percent of the total membership of the legislature.[15] As Figure 4.1 shows, at least eleven women who were members of the NRC and the CA are also in the current national assembly; seven served in both the NRC and the CA; five served in the NRC and the present assembly; and twelve former constituent assembly delegates (CADs) were reelected as parliamentary representatives. Thus at least twenty-eight of the fifty-one (55 percent) women who were voted into parliament in 1996 had some prior experience with lawmaking. It is these women (especially the eleven who have been in all three parliaments) who possess the greatest potential for creating women's political space and building political autonomy within the female cadre of politicians. Eventually, with the benefits that come with political experience, incumbency, and greater visibility, these women are likely to graduate to the county seats and thus leave room for more women to enter the field through affirmative action.

Of the women legislators in the study 25 percent hailed from "political families," and only 10 percent described themselves as feminists.[16] However, 90 percent made a correlation between childhood upbringing and their entering politics, citing examples such as growing up in homes that treated boys and girls similarly (or in the case of all-daughter families, being raised as surrogate sons), having mothers who were strong and opinionated, and playing leadership roles in schools. But there is no discernible common thread that weaves together the life histories of Ugandan women who end up in parliament.

The overall composition of women in the National Assembly (NA), as with the NRC and the CA, still demonstrates skewed representation. The fact that most women shy away from the county seat and very few of those who pursue it succeed points to two important factors. First, the obstacles that stand in the way of women's right to compete freely in formal politics remain intact. Political structures remain sexually segregated, exhibiting a high degree of gender discrimination. Second, a quota system that only ensures skewed representation may actually be regressive to the women's objective of achieving fair representation. The prevailing attitude may be summed up as follows: NRM has given women so much. What else can they possibly want? When a woman contests for a county seat, the issue boils down to: She's a woman trying to steal a seat from a man—a man who has a family to look after; what does she want it for? This attitude prevents making further gains in the quest for gender parity in politics, and it also reinforces the notion that the NRM "gave" women something that they did not earn. If the NRM so chose, it could repossess that "gift." Ugandan women, therefore, need to take Seger's caution[17] very seriously and view affirmative action simply as one policy that in and of itself cannot solve the problem of discrimination and oppression.

Having taken note of the not-so-affirmative effects of affirmative action, I must add a rejoinder. The mere participation of Ugandan women in the electoral process—boosted by the affirmative action policy—has somewhat tempered the more crass and virulently hostile response of men to the presence of women in the political arena. Neighboring Kenya, where no such policy exists, presents a contrast. In the December 1997 presidential, parliamentary, and civic elections, women candidates were vilified and intimidated on a scale that is not conceivable in the postaffirmative action Ugandan political scene, despite the fact that the Kenyan election produced the first women presidential candidates in the history of East African electoral politics.[18] Vigilante groups of male youths made it extremely difficult for female candidates to even campaign peacefully, let alone get over the first hurdle of nomination. Such groups took to threatening women candidates with all kinds of harm, including sexual assault, "if they continued campaigning against men."[19] One of the parliamentary candidates, Margaret Owegi, stated, "It is very disturbing, I can't even campaign. Youths keep round-the-clock watch on me. They tell me a woman has no leadership role in the constituency."[20] Another civic electoral candidate, Jane Achieng, revealed, "During the nominations conducted through queue voting, young men carrying whips forced people out of my queue to that of my rival. Women, the majority of whom had lined behind me, got terrified and abandoned me. I lost a contest I would have won."[21] Indeed, when the final election results were declared, the number of successful women MPs was only four (out of 202), compared to eight in the previous parliament.[22]

In Uganda, during the 1996 elections, state patronage played a significant role in influencing both the campaigns and the voting results of candidates, regardless of sex. Van de Walle (1994) points out that in many postcolonial African countries, opportunities in terms of access, economic wealth, and political power are almost exclusively controlled by the state. Therefore, the accumulation of personal wealth and the establishment of a political machine depend on access to or linkage with state power. In his analysis of the CA elections, Nelson Kasfir (1995) found that patronage indeed played an important role in Ugandan politics. Describing patronage as a "lop-sided arrangement" that benefits patrons (politicians) more than clients (electorate), Kasfir argues that the latter can often make small but effective claims on politicians (Kasfir 1995, 172). Elections are often viewed as one such opportunity for clients to benefit from the patronage of the respective candidates. But clients are invariably making an investment that extends beyond the handouts that accompany the election campaigns. The investment for both client and patron is the office to be won and the perks that will come with it, some of which, it is hoped, will trickle down from the patron to the clients.

To the extent that Ugandan politics had been dominated by men who matured in a system that was heavily influenced by patronage, how much political space was available for women to succeed in similar regard? Did the NRM government consider women important enough and critical enough as a cog in the wheel of power to extend state patronage to them? My interviews revealed that a good number of women politicians, like men, run for office on account of the opportunities for personal wealth and access to state power. For example, more than half of the women who won the June 1996 race had served earlier that year in one capacity or another on President Museveni's campaign team in their districts. By closely identifying themselves with the NRM government, these women set themselves up for state favors during and after their own individual races for office. Furthermore, at least two women MPs intimated to me that a high-ranking state official (in control of patronage) had "promised" them a "big government post" if they won the elections. Another woman was offered a post if she stood down for a better favored candidate in her district. Perhaps the most telling "payback" that affirmative action women extended to government was to constitute the core of the parliamentary NRM caucus that lobbies for and pushes government policies through parliament. Thus these women MPs, all of whom are simultaneously members of the parliamentary women's caucus, are exposed to a potential conflict of loyalties. Supposing the NRM caucus whip is urging its members to support an inherently gender-insensitive bill: Should female members toe the NRM line? Or should they challenge it?[23] Supposing they challenged it, would not their actions be perceived as a breach of confidence?

The attitude that NRM is a benevolent savior of women was abundantly clear among female parliamentarians. Most women MPs view the affirmative action policy as a favor (as opposed to a right) and view the NRM as a critical factor in not only the initial enactment of the policy but also its continuation. In other words, without the NRM, women would not be where they are. Such attitudes can be extrapolated from the following comments made by different affirmative action members:

> You know we would not be talking about all these things if we didn't have the exclusive support of government. Since independence—even from time immemorial, really—there was no government which expressed a bias towards women's emancipation. But the National Resistance Movement government came out very clearly and supported the women's cause and it is because of the NRM government as our biggest ally that we have been able to do all these things. . . . So really I would like to pay tribute to the National Resistance Movement for its support. (Joan Rwabyomere, AA)

> I feel that we, as women MPs do not need to be aggressive because we have already been invited to come to the political table. . . . now that government has invited us to the table I think we should now be women and remain women and we will be heard even if we don't shout. (Benigna Mukiibi, AA)

> Yes, I must say that I'm grateful for the openness of this government regarding the position of women in this society. We have been exposed and I hope that we shall continue to be exposed. But there's one area that I'm always sad about: We women, especially the educated few, contribute to our oppression. (Loi Nkwasibwe, AA)

> We should use this chance; it's God's grace that we have this chance. We should use it to consolidate our position so that . . . you never know, next time, the next government might be antiwomen. If we don't do it now, we would have missed the chance. (Mary Kamugisha, AA)

Reactions such as those expressed above are not atypical of top-down initiatives that have generally turned out to be ineffective (Ogunleye 1990, 1993). It is not difficult for the women who make such comments to consider the NRM as their "savior." The government was not necessarily wrong in introducing affirmative action, but such top-down initiatives, in which government "invites" marginalized groups to participate, form an insecure foundation for creating radical change. The official from the Ministry of Gender made a similar observation:

R :   Affirmative action is good but it raises the question of loyalty on the part of women MPs.

S :   What do you mean?

R :   They owe their allegiance to government—the National Resistance Movement government—which is responsible for their presence there. This was very apparent during CA debates in which women would support NRM interests en masse without much debate. That's my problem with affirmative action; it's not empowering because when you listen to most female politicians you'll find that they still relate their presence in the House to NRM instead of thinking about their presence there as contributing to decisionmaking, standing for certain positions and things like that. . . . I seriously believe that we must take on affirmative action with a new dimension.

Had the affirmative action program been implemented as a result of pressure exerted by the Ugandan women's movement (i.e., bottom-up grassroots movement), perhaps the rules for participation would have been devised by women themselves. The beneficiaries of such a policy would hardly regard it as a favor. Neither would the NRM hold women psychologically hostage, engendering the kind of complacency and self-satisfaction that is sometimes exhibited by some women parliamentarians.[24]

A related factor that directly points to the handicapping effects of the top-down affirmative action policy was that several "affirmative action legislators" who lost the 1996 elections felt hopelessly at sea and felt that government owed it to them to "fix" them in another high political office.

I get so concerned to see that I and many of my colleagues who were in parliament are just roaming around without being employed. We're wasted because we're a resource; we should be counselors to some of the women just starting out in parliament. . . . *We should be catered for* in some way either by getting us employment or bringing us together if we want the women's cause to be championed. (Juliet Bintu, AA, my emphasis)

Such attitudes, which cannot envision life beyond government handouts and pampering, illustrate the limitations of the affirmative action policy. Some women politicians feel dependent on the government even after their stints in office have come to an end.

Many candidates cried foul after the parliamentary elections, and several petitions were filed challenging the results.[25] The charges ranged from voter intimidation to blatant ballot stuffing. In the case of women's elections, electoral college registers were a source of controversy. But six disgruntled candidates I interviewed either had opted not to file petitions or were contemplating dropping all charges. Even though these candidates claimed to have overwhelming evidence of fraud, they had little hope of winning in court against an opponent who had already proved that she or he would go to all lengths to win; there was no guarantee, for example, that witnesses would not be intimidated, let alone bribed out of testifying. Moreover, the budgets of many candidates were already in the red after the stiff campaign exercise, and the prospect of incurring additional expenses in legal costs was not very appealing.

> Yeah, I consulted my lawyer who tried to petition but eventually . . . as I told you some of these government machinery were involved in the malpractice so my friends advised me that if the RDC [Resident District Commissioner] participated you shouldn't pursue it. I spent a lot of money facilitating my campaign agents and I wasn't sure that I'd succeed in court and I'd end up spending more money, including costs for the other party. So I decided to withdraw the petition. I'd given it considerable thought and I'd started the process, but then I called it off. I know there was massive fraud, but it's up to government to see that this doesn't happen again in 2001. (Juliet Bintu, AA)

The few who pursued their petitions to the end were largely disappointed as courts dismissed one petition after the other in a fashion that provoked raised eyebrows in many quarters.[26]

Women who lost in the 1996 race point to a number of benefits that they gained from the experience, the most commonly cited being a feeling of empowerment and self-confidence. Mary Mugyenyi, for example, a university lecturer who competed for a county seat, said:

> Needless to say, I was the first woman from the constituency ever to contest parliamentary elections. While I did not achieve the first objective, I feel a sense of accomplishment. . . . I tested the ground and opened the field for the women in the constituency to enter politics. No one would deny the stiffness of the competition. I gave the two male candidates [such a hard time] to the extent that they had to make a behind-the-scenes coalition in order for one of them to go through. This sets an encouraging example for other women in the future. (*Voices*, November 1996, 7)

The Bahima people where Mugyenyi sought votes are among the most conservative traditionalists in Uganda. For her to have given her two male contestants a run for their money by putting up such a stiff race was therefore a major breakthrough in the gender politics of the Bahima. To this extent, the achievements that women got out of the elections were both quantitative and qualitative. The experience that female candidates obtained from the elections and the increased visibility of women in the electoral process both marked significant strides for Uganda's future politics.

The FOWODE Workshop

I conclude this chapter by turning to the FOWODE meeting organized for women legislators in the wake of the 1996 parliamentary elections. The two-day induction workshop was attended by three-fourths of the women in the present assembly.[27] The session included the following topics: interpersonal relations and the image of a woman parliamentarian; building confidence; the art of speaking, strategizing, and lobbying; parliamentary procedures; working with the print media; before the camera; and agenda setting and parliamentary research. The meeting was a curious one, swinging from a very conservative traditional mind-set to a progressive feminist one. The pendulumlike swings occurring during the workshop bring into bold relief the contradiction that women parliamentarians are confronted with: as *people* they hold power and at the same time as powerless *women* they operate in a context of a patriarchal society and institution.

Female MPs find themselves in a position in which they can work to change the status quo; yet to do so, not only do they have to lobby the support of their male colleagues (for they are numerically disadvantaged) but they also have to negotiate around traditional roles and expectations. It is a complex and difficult road that they are trekking. An illustration of such contradiction can be found in the working hours of legislators. The rules of procedure of the present assembly provide that parliament officially meets up to 6:00 P.M. That time was arrived at as a compromise after female legislators argued that 8:00 P.M. (which had been proposed by the men) was "too late for women who had family duties of looking after children." Men's caustic response, which illuminated the contradiction, was, "But you are fighting for equal rights."

In the safety of their private space, women candidly discussed a range of important topics that directly affect them as female politicians. "We must seek the support of our spouses. Share your experiences with him; don't rub it in by perpetually reminding him that you're an 'honorable' and he is not," one member opined while the rest nodded in unison.[28] "To avoid embarrassing situations, always do your research before standing up to contribute on any issue being debated on the floor," said another. The issue of "women pulling each other down" was discussed at length. All women present promised to work toward collaboration in the five years of parliamentary work ahead. They acknowledged that by "pulling each other down" they played into the hands of stereotypical images, provoking comments from men such as, "look at women at their best."

Part of the discussion seemed to be geared toward finding ways of neatly fitting into the male world of politics:

- "Dress like a parliamentarian but don't overdo it; the lipstick and perfume you wear shouldn't act as a constant reminder to the man sitting next to you that he is sitting next to a beautiful woman."
- "In doing your work be careful not to step on the toes of men who represent counties in your district or they will think that you want to unseat them," one resource person lectured.
- "Learn the tricks of men and strike a balance between being a woman in parliament and saying no when the relationship is not a working relationship."
- "Reading newspapers is a must for women MPs, including the sports page so that you can fit in any conversation."

None of the women present challenged the rationale behind this counsel. But this does not mean that women parliamentarians are one big happy family that holds consensus views on most issues. Several women I spoke to during breaks sneered at some of the conservative outlooks that colored the general mood of the workshop. As in any other human organization, there are bound to be differences in opinion and beliefs. The important issue, which many seemed to recognize, is the need to respect these differences without allowing them to distract members from the wider common struggle.

When it got to concrete strategizing, the women MPs embarked on a feminist agenda. They drew clear distinctions between the "practical needs" and "strategic needs" of women in Uganda. Noting that politicians in the past have concentrated on practical needs such as clean water, health services, and credit facilities, they asserted that such strategies were not sufficient for solving systematic gender discrimination. Thus they also resolved to address the strategic needs that entail eliminating institutional sexism and promoting equal opportunity and women's access to decisionmaking organs.[29] Adopting post-Beijing terminology, they spoke of endorsing "gender mainstreaming" by ensuring that a gender perspective is integrated into all laws, policies, programs, and projects. "It is our duty; discrimination doesn't end just because a woman is in place." To facilitate their short-term plan, they designed a tripartite working framework. At the pinnacle was the need to organize future gender-awareness seminars for themselves. Next was the need to follow the Australian and the South African examples, wherein female politicians make a gender-impact analysis of all ministerial budgets. They do this by desegregating budgetary allocations along gender lines, for example, by determining how much money in the ministry of agriculture will benefit women.[30] Finally they resolved to work on a checklist including several questions by which all upcoming government bills and policies would be run to test for gender sensitivity.

Needless to say, the task that women MPs set for themselves in the FOWODE workshop is a very daunting one and cannot easily be achieved. It might take a revolution to eliminate all the underlying problems of the systematic discrimination within the neocolonial, paternalistic socioeconomic structures that exist in Uganda. However, the fact that the women political elite are beginning to discuss these issues is a far cry from the NRC years, when female MPs floundered through the unfamiliar world of politics. It became very clear in the FOWODE workshop that female legislators had gone beyond asserting the importance of numerical equity and were now embracing the notion of a "women's perspective," which they sought to incorporate into institutional politics.[31] Moreover, women legislators had brilliantly demonstrated their ability to make a difference in the CA. Assembly chairman and current Speaker of the National Assembly, James Wapakhabulo, told me:

> I can speak particularly from my experience as chairman of the CA. At first when women came in they were sort of . . . they didn't know each other really. Maybe a few knew each other but not even politically. Yeah, but as time went on, they began forming into a caucus and I dare say that that caucus achieved a lot of things. If one reads the constitution in areas of property, when it comes to divorce or death of partners, in areas of establishing affirmative action institutions like the equal opportunities commission, that really was something that came straight from the pressure of women. The area of children, and generally in pushing for more effective representation in constitutional arrangements today. If you remember the Odoki Commission had recommended fifteen parliamentary seats for women [in the draft constitution] but this group lobbied quite effectively and it was reinstated to thirty-nine—one woman from each district. And they even went beyond that and insisted on having a predetermined share of seats in local councils so that from the word go one-third of seats in a district council is reserved for women, which I think is no small achievement.

Indeed, it was from the womb of the CA women's caucus that FOWODE was born. Details of this caucus and its impact on deliberations in the CA and gender politics in general will be discussed in the next chapter.

Overall, despite the travails of the electoral process, which manifested politics at its most tumultuous and basic, the experience must be regarded as an edifying one for women politicians. Clearly, several steps remain to be taken, both in terms of the caliber and the consciousness of those who fought in and eventually succeeded in the election and in relation to the population they sought to convince, the issues that were articulated, and the public and media response to them. Nevertheless, an important first step has been made through the creation of affirmative action seats—a first step that can be built upon in the overall process of enhancing the profile of women's participation in the formal political process. This point gains in perspective once we have examined the actions of these representatives in the House, that is, the process of actually engaging in parliamentary politics.

Notes

1. In contrast, the post-1989 period, with more women joining the political ranks, spurred the birth of women's organizations such as FOWODE, whose exclusive agenda was to pursue women's rights in the arena of politics.

2. In this respect I differ from Tripp, who, without providing cogent evidence, places a great deal of responsibility for NRM's liberal agenda for women on the women's movement (see Tripp 1994: 115–116). This will especially become clear later in this chapter from the stories women tell about how they became politically involved. In other African countries, such as Nigeria and Kenya, where strong women's movements have put pressure on their governments to enhance women's political participation, women's representation in formal politics remains dismal. Indeed, many of these governments simply dismiss women's issues as being of no concern to their political schemes. For example, following the December 1997 Kenyan parliamentary and presidential elections, President arap Moi created the portfolio of minister of women and youth affairs; not only was the post given to a male but barely a month after its creation it was unceremoniously scrapped and the holder of the position was transferred (*Daily Nation*, February 18, 1998; *The East African* February 23–March 1, 1998).

3. For example, in April 1996 an organization that connects several women's groups, Women's Network (UWONET), met for the purpose of "putting women's issues on the election agenda." A strongly worded manifesto was composed and distributed to the media. However, as one UWONET member told me, the task force on governance and politics within their organization was incapacitated to go beyond this document in following up their mandate on the ground.

4. In January–February 1998, for instance, FOWODE set up a candidates' advisory desk (CAD) for women who wished to stand in the local council elections. Many women from all corners of Uganda took advantage of this facility to learn campaigning skills, prepare political manifestos, and so forth.

5. Those who have done so successfully include Rhoda Kalema, (1979, 1989, 1994), Winnie Byanyima (1994, 1996), Cecilia Ogwal (1994, 1996), Veronica Nakyanzi (1994), Salaamu Musumba (1996), and Juliet Kafire (1996).

6. Only six women so far have crossed from affirmative action or nominee status to county representatives. These are Specioza Kazibwe (1994, 1996), Janat Mukwaya (1994, 1996), Victoria Ssekitoleko (1994), Esther Opoti (1994), Tezira Jamwa (1996), and Fiona Egunyu (1996).

7. Kazibwe was appointed vice president in November 1994, thus becoming the first woman vice president in the history of Uganda. She was a perfect choice for President Museveni in a country where intricate power balancing on the basis of ethnicity, religion, political ideology, and (more recently) gender are of crucial importance. As a Protestant from western Uganda, President Museveni needed his second in command to represent alternative attributes and inclination. Kazibwe, being a female Catholic from eastern Uganda and a former DP, fitted such a profile.

8. Campaigns for all parliamentarians were legally restricted to "joint candidates' meetings" at which all contestants as a group faced voters in different parishes and addressed them for a maximum of twenty minutes each, followed by a question-answer session (see S.48 of the Parliamentary Elections (Interim Provisions) Statute, 1996).

9. The "morality" weapon for keeping Ugandan women "under control" has a long history. In 1972, for example, Idi Amin passed a law to "prohibit the wearing of certain dresses which outrage decency and are injurious to public morals" (see the Penal Code Act (Amendment) decree no. 9 (1972); also see Obbo 1980, 87). Audrey Wipper also found this method to be prevalent elsewhere in Africa, e.g., Ethiopia, Kenya, Tanzania, Malawi, and Zambia (Wipper 1972).

10. The term "multipartyist," which refers to one who supports multiparty politics, has acquired derogatory attributes because of the violence, civil strife, and dictatorship associated with divisive party politics in Uganda's history. During the 1996 elections many campaign rallies centered around multiparty versus movement politics.

11. See, for example, "LC IV Chairman Flees Women's Rally," *Monitor*, June 17, 1996, 6; "Kulany Says Rivals Made Up Love Story," *New Vision*, May 27, 1996, 48; "Women on the Frontline," *New Vision*, April 30, 1996, 15; "Want to Be a Woman Leader? You Have Got to Tell Lies," *Sunday Vision*, May 8, 1994, 8; "I'm Married to Col. Besigye-Byanyima," *Crusader*, June 18–20, 1996, 1.

12. June 17, 1996, at 8:00 P.M., Radio Uganda Station.

13. I use a pseudonym to protect the identity of the interviewee.

14. In this connection also, Kazibwe has, of late, publicly downplayed her background as an "affirmative action baby" and has emphasized the notion of meritocracy (see, e.g., an official press release, "Kazibwe Not Affirmative Action

Product," *Monitor*, December 14, 1996, 4; also see Onyango-Obbo, "When the Chickens Come to Roost," *East African*, January 27–February 2, 1997, 9).

15. At the time of writing this book elections for youth representatives were still awaiting passage of the relevant law. It is most likely that some women will be elected among the five representatives.

16. "Political family" here means that one or both of their parents were involved in politics as a parliamentarian, a chief, or a political party official. This number was very close to that of the male parliamentarians (26 percent) who hailed from political families. Most of the female legislators did not want to use the label "feminist" to describe themselves, not necessarily because they did not embrace feminist ideals but because the term is grossly misunderstood in the context of Uganda to stand for a radicalism (of white Western imperialist import), which they were less willing to associate with.

17. See introduction, chapter 1.

18. Charity Kaluki Ngilu of the Social Democratic Party (SDP) was one of the key opposing candidates to the incumbent, Daniel arap Moi. Also among the fourteen candidates who contested for the presidential seat in the December 1997 elections was another woman—Professor Wangari Maathai of the Liberal Party of Kenya.

19. See John Jabatiso, "Women Candidates Fall on Gender Biases," *Sunday Nation*, December 28, 1997.

20. Ibid.

21. Ibid.

22. An additional four nominated members brought the total number of women MPs in the new parliament to eight.

23. Examples of NRM bills that sailed through parliament and were later found to adversely affect women include the statutes on privatization, value added tax (VAT), and income tax.

24. An example of the efficacy of a bottom-up grassroots initiative is the Nigerian development agency known as Country Women's Association of Nigeria (COWAN). As a rural women's nongovernmental community development organization, COWAN has exerted sufficient pressure on the Nigerian government to turn much of its action agenda into national policies, for example, the establishment of people's and community banks (Ogunleye 1993). These in turn have effectively empowered groups of rural women by assisting them to be responsible for their own development.

25. See *New Vision*, June 24, 1996, 3.

26. Nabagesera's petition (discussed in Chapter 2) is a case in point. Also see *Crusader*, October 7–17, 1996, 7.

27. FOWODE extended invitations to all MPs who represent other marginalized groups, and hence there were four male MPs in attendance. Miria Matembe (AA) told me that she was not too enthusiastic about FOWODE activities because she believed that it usurped the role of the Uganda Women Parliamentarians Association (UWOPA)—an organization established by NRC women MPs and one that many respondents reported has "yet to take off" in achieving its objective. Another MP said that she did not attend FOWODE workshops because "these FOWODE people were not very transparent when they initiated the idea because

I believe that some of us who have been around [in politics] for long should have been consulted when that kind of thing is being set up. But when they just invite you to attend a workshop sometimes you feel that, 'Well, if I'm not needed let them go ahead without me.'" (Cecilia Ogwal, CS).

28. In connection with this point, one member shared the following views with me in an interview: "You have to understand the nature of a man and being a woman politician when he is not . . . There are tense moments in our household sometimes. Sometimes he feels I'm becoming "too political," so then I avoid political discussions simply because I know that he may not take it well. You see, I personally appreciate that politics is a field that women are only beginning to break through and as pioneers of the process, we have to sacrifice and compromise in many ways so that the next generation have it easier. (Benigna Mukiibi, AA)

29. Molyneux (1985) explains that strategic interests are derived deductively from the analysis of women's subordination. Examples of such interests include abolition of the sexual division of labor; alleviation of the burden of domestic labor and child care; and removal of institutionalized forms of discrimination. However, the dichotomization of strategic and practical gender needs has been criticized by some feminists as being problematic because of its elitist underpinnings which are based on the wrong assumption—that struggles for practical gender needs cannot transform into struggles for strategic needs. Moreover, the distinction degrades practical needs and removes them from the wider political and legal context of women's struggles (e.g., Lind 1992; Schreiner 1996).

30. This goal was followed up in July 1997, when FOWODE organized a workshop for women parliamentarians to which experts from South Africa were invited to share their own experience in implementing the gender budget initiative.

31. Throughout my study, it struck me how far removed academia was from the real world. In the pragmatic lives of politicians, theoretical issues such as "essentialism" do not seem to matter; women legislators had no time to entangle themselves in such hair-splitting theoretical concepts, and they talked of "women's interests" with a refreshing focus on praxis for social change. *Whose* social change? That is a question for academics to ponder.

5

The Gender Dynamics of Intraparliamentary Politics

In Chapter 1 I discussed gender relations in Uganda, highlighting the historical evolution of gender as a social construction that engendered an asymmetrical valuation between the sexes that valorized masculinity and devalued femininity. The relations of power, resources, and personalities between Ugandan men and women, no doubt, reflects their respective performance in the political arena. The dialectics of tokenism, power, socialization, the institution of gender, and underdevelopment operate together in shaping the political activities of Ugandan men and women. In this chapter, I first analyze the potential for women, as autonomous political actors, to influence the decisions of a skewed institution—the Constituent Assembly (CA)—wherein the 1995 Ugandan constitution was debated and promulgated. Second, I investigate the complex ways that gender inhibits, empowers, and influences legislators in the Ugandan parliament, thus highlighting its prominence and pervasiveness in this sphere of society. Finally, I examine the way sexuality is used to perpetuate women's oppression and subordination in the august House.

Patriarchy as a force is so powerful that it permeates and dictates much of what goes on in Uganda's legislatures. However, the institution of patriarchy is not without cracks. The work of female constituent assembly delegates (CADs), which is examined in the first section, demonstrates how these cracks can be penetrated to the advantage of Ugandan women. But like all success stories recorded in history, the gains made by women politicians come at a cost. Compromises, concessions, and trade-offs are all part of the game that Ugandan women legislators are forced to play. Further discussion sheds some light on the difficult and circuitous road that female politicians negotiate on a daily basis in the political process. The styles they adopt and the decisions they make, even their options in personal matters, all reflect women's interrogation with and negotiation around patriarchy.

Tokenism and Women's Caucusing

A general review of the media in Western countries suggests that a pot-bellied, fly-covered African child has greater chances of hitting the front page of any Western newspaper than an African leader (Crawford 1996). It was thus somewhat surprising to find a flattering headline story on Ugandan women politicians in the WomaNews section of the *Chicago Tribune* of December 1, 1996. The article included two pictures of women legislators.[1] The world is beginning to take note of the significant strides that Ugandan women have made in national decisionmaking, and there is no denying the extraordinary record that they are making in the annals of the nation's political history. The *Chicago Tribune* story highlighted the progressive gender provisions in the 1995 constitution; quoting from what it termed a "Women's Constitution," it reproduced the following provisions of the document:

National Objectives:

vi. The state shall ensure gender balance and fair representation of marginalized groups on all constitutional and other bodies.

xv. The state shall recognize the significant role that women play in society.

Fundamental Human Rights and Freedoms:

33. (1) Women shall be accorded full and equal dignity of the person with men.

(2) The state shall provide the facilities and opportunities necessary to enhance the welfare of women to enable them to realize their full potential and advancement.

(3) The state shall protect women and their rights, taking into account their unique status and natural maternal functions in society.

(4) Women shall have the right to equal treatment with men and that right shall include equal opportunities in political, economic and social activities.

(5) Women shall have the right to affirmative action for the purpose of redressing the imbalances created by history, tradition or custom.

(6) Laws, cultures, customs or traditions which are against the dignity, welfare or interest of women or which undermine their status are prohibited by this Constitution.

40. (4) The employer of every woman shall accord her protection during pregnancy and after birth, in accordance with the law.

The Legislature:

78. (1)(b)   One woman representative for every district;

Local Government:

180 (1)(b)   One third of the membership of each local government
council shall be reserved for women

The above articles are but a sample of the "feminist" provisions included in the 1995 constitution.[2] These provisions form a solid foundation for the Ugandan women's movement to challenge all forms of gender discrimination and oppression.

The progressive nature of this document can only be appreciated in relation to its predecessor—the 1967 constitution—and the draft constitution that constituted the basic document for the CA debates. Under the
1967 constitution discrimination on the grounds of sex was not prohibited, just as personal laws relating to marriage, divorce, adoption, burial,
and devolution of property on death were exempt from the provision
that prohibited discrimination.[3] Furthermore, entitlement to Ugandan
citizenship flowed exclusively from the male lineage, and the language
of the entire document adopted the masculine gender.[4] The proposed
draft constitution, although it scrapped all the discriminatory provisions
of the 1967 document and squarely addressed issues of gender, was not
quite as liberal as the present document. For example, the draft had only
proposed a fifteen-person quota for women in parliament and had not
proposed any sex quota at the local government level.[5] Neither had it
provided for an equal-opportunities commission nor was it written in
gender-neutral language.

How were the token female CADs able to make such monumental
achievements in an assembly as skewed as the CA? How did they fight
patriarchy, chauvinism, and powerlessness to secure one of the most
"women-friendly" constitutions worldwide? The answer is caucusing.

The strategy was to draw as many sympathetic and moderate male
CADs to their side as possible in order to augment their numbers. Facilitated by the National Association of Women's Organizations in Uganda
(NAWOU)[6] and with financial assistance from the Friedrich Ebert Foundation, the women's caucus formed "gender dialogues" that facilitated
consensus building and created an exclusive environment for exchang-
ing views among women CADs.[7] A full-fledged support facility known
as the Gender Information Center was set up within the conference center complex in which the Constituent Assembly was located. It provided
women delegates with facilities for research, consultancy, meeting, lob-

bying, and secretarial assistance. In addition, the center ran a weekly radio program geared toward educating *wananchi* on constitutional issues being discussed in the CA, particularly those directly affecting women (NAWOU 1995).

The kind of support that the women's movement lent to female CADs had never before been seen in the NRC (National Resistance Council) and the present assembly. The explanation for this is, first, women could have perceived the role of the Constituent Assembly not only as being transitory but also as being fundamentally important in that the constitutional framework shaped women's future democratic and human rights. Second, there was a "donor element" behind the unprecedented support of female politicians from the women's movement. Foreign donors seized on the issue of constitution making as one that met their own objectives and injected money into the exercise to facilitate women's organizations in their collaboration with the CA women's caucus.

The women's caucus in the CA was determined to make a difference to the constitution-making process in Uganda. Several workshops were organized in the sixteen months of the CA deliberations to increase women's effectiveness on the floor. Female political experts were invited from all over the world to share their experiences with the women CADs. For example, Congresswomen Patricia Saiki and Charlene Drew Jarvis, as well as political consultants Daryl Glenney and Dorrit Marks, were invited from the United States to address the women's caucus in April 1995 (*New Vision*, April 25, 1995). Professor Akande from the University of Lagos and Ludgera Klemp from Dar es Salaam also led delegations from Nigeria and Tanzania, respectively, which exchanged views with the female CADs. Under another program called LINK, feminists from Zimbabwe, Zambia, and Canada were invited to share their skills with Ugandan women politicians.

Women delegates used different strategies at different times to achieve their goals. For example, in order to win over as many male CADs as possible, women delegates realized that sometimes they had to tone down the language of their demands. During such debates, they would urge "notoriously" outspoken feminists, who were likely to put off most men by what men considered to be "their usual clamoring," to remain in the shadows. Then a soft-spoken woman or even a man would be selected to present the women's case in a moderate manner acceptable to most men. This kind of pragmatism is sometimes a necessary compromise in any kind of negotiations between unequal parties. Another common technique that women legislators adopted was to couch their arguments in statements that appealed to basic logic. For instance, on many occasions female representatives reminded their offensively sexist male colleagues that by insulting women in general they were effectively insulting their own mothers, sisters, and daughters. Female delegates constantly reminded their male colleagues that they did not seek to reverse the gender hierarchy: "Since the male delegates here are our fathers, husbands, sons, neighbours, let us negotiate skillfully for their support. Our cause is developmental; it is not a displacement of men by women" (Loyce Bwambale, *Proceedings of the Constituent Assembly,* July 14, 1994, 852).

Sometimes, for strategic reasons, female delegates chose to compromise with patriarchy rather than confront it. For instance, when it came to very controversial issues such as the right to abortion, pro-choice female delegates strategically "used" two male colleagues from the medical profession to sponsor the amendment in the hope that it would quell outright antagonism. Furthermore, the debate on the assembly floor was largely left to male participants. The end result was a middle-of-the-road position: "No person has the right to terminate the life of an unborn child except as may be authorized by law" (article 22 (2) of the 1995 constitution). Although this fell short of the aspirations of abortion rights activists, it was an improvement on the previous position, which criminalized all types of abortion in Uganda.

But structural and other limitations stand in the way of women's successful caucusing in parliament. The biggest obstacle lies in the men's club character of parliament, which often treats women as intruders. As the CA experience illustrates, men rallied together to defend their position no matter how much lobbying women did when it came to legislating on crucial matters that directly impinge on men's power over women. This mechanism came into play when female CADs made an unsuccessful constitutional attempt to eliminate the gross injustice that millions of Ugandan women suffered in the dissolution of marriage. The proposed clause (one of whose three sponsors was a man) was as follows: "On dissolution of marriage men and women shall have the right to equitably share all property jointly acquired during the marriage." Despite the careful strategizing and intensive lobbying in support of this amendment, the women lost to a majority of male CADs who were threatened by the implications of the amendment.[8] Attacks against the amendment were shrouded in hollow arguments that such a provision would lead to increased family breakups, promote self-seeking women, serve only the interests of elite women, or would be very problematic to implement. The *real* reasons of course are located in the power attached to property ownership, which customary law has jealously guarded for Ugandan men. One male delegate argued that "when marriages are contracted . . . the young man getting married pays dowry. Now, if that marriage is dissolved, who will benefit if the property he will have acquired during the marriage is to be shared?" (Ben Etonu, *Proceedings of the Constituent Assembly,* September 8, 1994, 1987).

Nevertheless, the CA experience in Uganda proved that token women in a skewed parliament can in fact influence the culture of the institution, albeit with limitations imposed by patriarchy. A number of other points emerge from the CA experience. First, making strategic alliances with progressive men, despite the potential for co-optation by way of a compromising quid pro quo, is expected in order for women to achieve their objectives. Second, tokenism can pay off if there is a clear perception of the objectives the group struggles for. Such commitment means a willingness to allocate personal time, energy, finances, and other necessary resources to the realization of the goals of the cause. Finally, successes achieved in such struggles must be considered incrementally. Although the full impact of the struggles of the women's caucus are yet to manifest themselves in concrete benefits for the Ugandan woman, the normative provisions of the 1995 constitution cannot be underestimated.

Against the backdrop of the progressive constitution that I have painted here, I move on to show the contradictions, tensions, and complexities that operate in a relatively conservative and traditional framework of parliament.

"Doing Gender" in the House

A casual observer sitting in the public gallery of the National Assembly on a typical business day would probably use adjectives such as "modest," "reticent," and "diffident" to describe the general character of the honorable female members seated there. Press reports that constantly portray women parliamentarians as passive adornments to the august House reinforce such perceptions. Such descriptions were especially true for the NRC and may have been less common for women in the CA or for the present national assembly with the entry of a core of more dynamic, vocal, and articulate women.

Several reasons may account for the apparent passiveness of women representatives, such as, first, their relative inexperience in lawmaking. This is further exacerbated by the nature of the assembly, which lacks an effective opposition side to facilitate the debate of bills; as beneficiaries of an NRM-sponsored affirmative action policy, most female legislators feel that they owe their allegiance to the government and will not oppose most of its proposed legislation. Another reason may be that their conspicuousness as token women prompts them to deflect attention from themselves by keeping a low profile.[9] Moreover, the fact that parliamentarians in Uganda lack basic facilities such as office space, research assistants, and a library is bound to reflect on their effectiveness as legislators. One member summed it up in the following fashion:

> We were going to parliament for the first time while many of our male colleagues had been there before at different stages of Uganda's political life and are skilled orators, you know. Their lives are a kind of big bank of knowledge and information and what have you. Now, you get the newer people who don't really have the basic skills of debating. There is no facility for research . . . and I think it would be ideal to give us office space or a desk to work from . . . So you find that actually the quality of the debate which goes on in the House is lacking. And with women it's even worse. (Rosette Ikote, AA)

The above explanations notwithstanding, I suggest that the legislative activities of women representatives are best explained in terms of gender. Gender as a structure is so pervasive that it orders the social interaction between female and male legislators and infiltrates the parliamentary institution itself. Like builders constructing a skyscraper, female and male parliamentarians (re)construct gendered systems of dominance and power by acting out gender norms and expectations in the House. As the premier body responsible for enacting laws—social control mechanisms—parliament's role in maintaining power relations is obvious. In this political context gender is used as a mechanism for maintaining power relations. In this section I describe and analyze the lawmaking process, examining how men and women "do gender" in the House. I will show how doing gender reproduces and reinforces the gender hierarchy in Ugandan society. At other times, however, it may challenge it.

My observations in the National Assembly clearly revealed patterns of behavior and action that reinforced the gender asymmetry. The entire institution exudes what might normatively be called masculinity, beginning with the physical setting of the main chamber: the massive granite structure of towering piers and heavy grilled entryways, the sergeant at arms, the Speaker's mace, the predominance of dark colors—all suggest virility. The ambiance is intimidating and alienating. All of this is mediated by a highly rigidified protocol and hierarchy. Carved above the main chamber entrance is an elaborate dark mahogany mural depicting the fruits of independence. The imposing steel doors of the chamber open onto the Speaker's dais, which is draped with a tawny velvet canopy, on the other end of the large room. The clerk's table of dark, polished wood sits in the middle of the hall a few meters below the Speaker's platform. On either side of the forest-green-carpeted room run five tiers of green leather-upholstered benches, each row having a seating capacity of approximately thirty people. Five microphones, which debaters must speak through when contributing to floor discussions, serve each row. The walls, paneled in varnished hardwood, rise up to high vaulted ceilings and the second floor, which accommodates gallery benches reserved for the press and the public. Above the main entrance and directly facing the Speaker's dais peers a large black clock reminding honorable members of the rigidity and calibration of the parliamentary system. In the four corners of the chamber are auxiliary entrances, each equipped with high-tech security cameras.

As explained in Chapter 4, in Uganda the parliament retains vestiges of colonial rule, which stemmed from models synonymous with male hegemony. The language used in the House not only follows a strict formal code but is largely androcentric. Male parliamentarians, consciously or subconsciously, address the House with remarks such as "look at the bill, gentlemen" and may add facetiously "oh, and gentlewomen." When the woman deputy Speaker is presiding over a sitting, many MPs (male and female) address the chair as "Mr. Speaker, sir" simply because historically that chair has been occupied by men. The dress code is very formal, with men being required to wear suits and ties of the Western style. One time a male MP who arrived at parliament for business smartly clad in a West African type of shirt was requested to leave immediately and dress himself "appropriately." Women usually dress up smartly in cotton dresses, often adorned with a jacket, scarf, or such other accessories to add a touch of formality to their appearance. The rules also require the MPs to bow before the Speaker's chair each time they enter or leave the chamber. All these formalities collectively serve to alienate women, who have been largely relegated to the informal, private sphere of Ugandan society.[10]

Men dominate House debates and are picked on to speak more often than women. When a woman is on her feet, she is more likely to be met with noise and inattention in the House than a man is. Scoffs, jeers, and other boorish behavior, although directed at both female and male members, almost always emanate from the men. I noted that men tended to interrupt female members with points of information, order, and clarification more than they did fellow men. Although women legislators also interjected when men were contributing, they did so less frequently than their male counterparts. Most of their interjections were either defensive points of information directed at sexist provocation from their male colleagues or pleas to the chair to rule an offensive member out of order. Interrupting is one of the ways people in power maintain the status quo; it is a gesture of dominance.[11]

My observations included specific examples of how men and women reinforced the "essentialness" of gender in the course of executing their legislative duties. For instance, when the House was debating the children's bill in October 1995, a concern was raised about the increasing number of Ugandan men who neglect to support and maintain their children. A female member informed the assembly that there were some culprits among the male MPs, alleging that she had received a number of complaints from the wives of several "respectable" parliamentarians. Her comments created a commotion in the House as the male parliamentarians requested her to substantiate her allegations. But before the female member could name any names, a female colleague sitting near her begged her to stop by pulling on her sleeve and whispering into her ear. Thus the female member's point was crushed. The women's response to the challenge is, however, not unambiguous. It could be argued that they did gender in sparing the faces of the culprits and thus defending the grand edifice of male power. That fear to face down the daring men may have exhibited timidity on the part of the women and victory for all Ugandan men. However, it is also possible that these women spared the culprits out of political pragmatism, as a strategic concession not to antagonize those in power (at least for the time being). Indeed, for women legislators, the line distinguishing "doing gender" and "political pragmatism" can at times become very blurred.

During the debate on the children's bill I observed male parliamentarians turning a serious debate on children's issues into loud banter. A Muslim MP stood up and said, "Increasing the age of minority to eighteen years is unrealistic and unscientific; the prophet Mohammed married Aisha when she was nine years old." Loud laughter ensued. On the question of female genital mutilation, another male MP responded to a female member's submission on the evils of the practice of clitoridectomy: "Stitching women is not new; chastity belts existed in medieval Europe where women were locked by their husbands and unlocked before use." Again, loud laughter ensued. On a point of clarification another male member asked, "Can the honorable member holding the floor enlighten the House on the various mechanics of locking and unlocking?" More laughter. At that point a female member stood up and asked the chair if it was in order for members to digress from the bill on the floor. "Yes," held the chair amid more laughter, "they are merely seeking clarification." Another male MP defending female genital mutilation argued that the growth of keloids in the private parts of some young girls was "not caused by the circumcision but was a direct result of the sensitivity of women's skins." More loud laughter. After that session ended, a woman MP, Jeninah Ntabgoba, stopped me in the hallway and said, "You see how these men make fun of serious issues affecting women and children? I hope that you include this in your report."

The views of one male parliamentarian I interviewed also exemplified the terms under which men would like women to participate in a field they have long considered as their exclusive domain:

> Yeah, women in politics, I am impressed they have come up but I would like to caution them on one thing. When they come to parliament *they should behave in a motherly manner.* It's embarrassing sometimes when a lady is in parliament and she conducts herself in a manner which is unbecoming. It's not good for her moral turpitude and it affects her performance in her constituency. I've heard some of my male colleagues saying this. . . . We need mature ladies in the House because those ones are more motherly and know how to respect themselves. . . . Another thing is that some ladies should avoid being arrogant to the opposite sex; they have not been arrogant to me as such but you hear stories. (Jackson Bambalira, CS, my emphasis)

The caution for "more motherliness" and "less arrogance" highlights the intersection of power, gender, and dominance in parliamentary politics. It stems directly from the notion of maternal altruism inherent in African gender ideology. By feminizing the role of women MPs in this way, men are setting the political parameters: Women will be accepted in the "men's club" only as nurturing, deferential caretakers. It is an illustration of the regulatory agenda behind gender identity.

Analysis of the interviews I conducted corroborates the conclusions reached above. A female parliamentarian, a member of NRC who serves in the Sixth Assembly, shared her views on why women generally do not contribute as much as men to House debates.

> First of all, it's a daunting task to stand up in that House and contribute something. Women are afraid to speak up, which is not the case for men. I personally listen to some of the contributions the men make and I can't believe a mature, grown-up person with 100 percent of all their mental faculties working can say some of the things they say; they are so insane. But men just get up and say it and don't think twice about it. But a woman, you know, will not just get up and talk such rubbish. And then there are so many debating skills that women are not equipped with. But men will use it to get noticed, okay? So you find a man is always raising points of information without making any substantive contribution. And also you have to be very aggressive and forceful to get the attention of the Speaker; women are not like that. I sit back a lot and I don't say what I want to say but it's going through my mind. I reason out really what is going on the floor and what I would have said but then I don't say it. Then a man gets up and says it and gets a standing ovation and [laughter] I say to myself, "Why didn't you stand and say that?" . . . I don't consider myself to be shy but sometimes I hold back. Men just pop up and

down as you know. . . . it's much easier for them to talk, to expose themselves. A lot of time they expose themselves to ridicule but a woman will be very afraid to stand up and be ridiculed. (Rosette Ikote, AA)

Of the female legislators I interviewed, 92 percent shared the sentiments and logic expressed above. Clearly, gender (i.e., cultural ideas about appropriate male and female behavior) has overriding implications for the quality and quantity of contributions made by women legislators in the Ugandan parliament. The posturing and pontificating exhibited by male legislators is "doing dominance." By the same token, women's self-doubt and reserved manner amounts to "doing deference" in the House (West and Zimmerman 1987). The general performance of male and female legislators in Uganda reflects their respective cultural dispositions.

The leadership of any organization has a significant influence on the general culture of that particular organization. The fact that in the NRC both the chairman (Kigongo) and his deputy (Adyebo) were men proved important to the general contribution of female legislators in that body. Both men were extremely insensitive to gender issues, and the deputy chairman was notorious for his bias against female members when it came to picking members who wished to contribute to debates on the chamber floor. Several times the chair would let male legislators get away with sexist and even offensive utterances, as evidenced in the following example, taken from the records of a second reading of a bill to reinforce protection for victims of rape, sexual abuse, and exploitation:

ONESMUS TURYAHABWA: The Ministry of Women in Development, sir, should also make programmes to defend African culture. We would like to see our Ugandan women beautiful and attractive in the context of Africa. We do not like to see our women jump out of our African culture, try to imitate the cultures outside Africa. To be admired by who? Maybe by the Whites! But I want us to see our African women, a Ugandan woman beautiful for a Ugandan man [laughter]. So, Mr. Chairman, sir, the Ministry for Women in Development should come out with a fashion of dressing, a fashion of hair treating, a fashion of finger treating, lips treating, these other things which make us look at our women should be a policy for [the] good of Ugandan man [laughter].

JOYCE MPANGA: Point of order! Thank you, Mr. Chairman. Is the honourable member on the floor in order to presume that the woman in Uganda exists for the pleasure of a man?

CHAIRMAN: This is his own opinion.

JOY MUGARURA: Point of information! Thank you, Mr. Chairman. May I inform the member on the floor that we are human beings with human rights . . . and so giving us a uniform and a way of life would be interfering with our rights.
CHAIRMAN: (to Turyahabwa) Continue, please. (Official Hansard, June 21, 1990, 402)

The above interaction illustrates how gender is reproduced in the institutional setting of parliament. Turyahabwa was echoing the sentiments of the chauvinistic society that produced him. As we have already seen, culture and morality provide formidable tools for men's control of women in Ugandan society. The laughter and foot stomping of Turyahabwa's colleagues signified an untroubled attitude or an endorsement of his remarks. Indeed, culture as a tool for preserving the male power structure came up repeatedly during this particular debate. Several male members found it unacceptable that the age of defilement, or statutory rape, was raised from fourteen to eighteen years; custom, they argued, allowed for sex with any girl who had reached the age of puberty. The general mood that surrounded the debate of that particular bill was frivolous. The chairman's total dismissal of the desperate pleas for intercession from the female members showed his acquiescence to the frivolous manner in which the issue was being treated.

The chairman of the CA, James Wapakhabulo, was a lawyer, a veteran of parliamentary politics with national and international experience, and a former cabinet minister. Thanks to his impressive vitae, which includes work experience ranging from clerk to the East African Legislative Assembly to legal officer in the attorney-general's office of Australia to senior legislative draftsman in Papua New Guinea, Wapakhabulo knew the parliamentary procedures like the back of his hand. In addition, he had a knack for presiding over large meetings. His deputy, Victoria Mwaka, on the other hand, was a professor of geography whose seventeen years of work experience were exclusively in the academic field at Makerere University. Her rise to political power was indeed meteoric, as she had never participated in formal politics. Wapakhabulo described his background to me:

I had been in active politics right back from 1968. . . . When I became minister in 1986, I also became an ex officio member of the NRC. I stood for the 1989 parliamentary elections, which expanded the NRC, and came in on my own right. I was of course very determined to serve and because I had been working in a parliamentary body before, I was knowledgeable, I knew some rules. So I was able to fit in quite easily.

Contrast that with Mwaka, who informed me that

I had never thought of becoming a politician, but when I was appointed by the president to contest for the chair for the CA, by then I was on sabbatical in Dar es Salaam [Tanzania] and they just sent me an air ticket that you're wanted by the president. I came, never campaigned, and when we went through the elections for the chair, I was elected deputy chairperson with an overwhelming majority of 226 out of 284. I'm not a politician, I'd never been a parliamentarian, and I'd never thought of becoming a politician.

Their different backgrounds and personal skills had a significant bearing on the way each steered the House as alternate chairpersons. Gender had an even more significant impact on their performance. Wapakhabulo had firm control of the House right from the start, whereas Mwaka faltered, slipped, and was defensive, reinforcing gender stereotypes. Wapakhabulo's sessions moved swiftly, and he had the solid backing of male colleagues who constantly reminded him of his competence: "Mr. Chairman . . . I must say how happy I am at the excellent manner in which you have steered our deliberations. . . . and I am confident that the good humor, the wit, and the friendly atmosphere that you have set . . . will remain with us to the end" (Ogola, CS, *Proceedings of the National Assembly,* July 12, 1994, 795). "Mr. Chairman, I propose that . . . you endeavor as much as possible to attend this assembly so that your colleague and deputy learns from your experience and expertise." (Steven Ongaria, CS, *Proceedings of the National Assembly,* July 8, 1994, 703).

Mwaka's sessions, on the other hand, were continuously bogged down with procedural technicalities as one male delegate after another raised "points of order" challenging the manner in which Mwaka was conducting House business. Mwaka said, "Delegates tried to derail me, taking advantage of the fact that I'm not a lawyer; they tried to confuse me. Because I am a woman they thought that I would not manage." While it is true that her sex was under assault, Mwaka was personally ill prepared to deal with the disrespect and aggressiveness exhibited by male delegates. For example, an exasperated male delegate once stood up and interrupted the proceedings with a "point of order":

OKULLO-EPAK: I have been raising my hand and I am not given a chance to speak . . . Do you have difficulties seeing me from your position, Madam Chairman [sic!]?
MWAKA: I have no problems with my sight. . . . Okay, you can speak. What do you want to speak? (*Proceedings of the Constituent Assembly,* August 29, 1994, 1743)

The impertinence of the rhetorical question and the fact that it was a woman in the chair were not coincidental. In all the months that I observed parliamentary business during this study, no such tone was used in addressing a male chairperson.

Another male delegate actually shouted, "That's rubbish," in reference to a ruling that Mwaka had made as assembly chairperson (Adoko Nekyon, CS, *Proceedings of the Constituent Assembly,* July 25, 1994). When his colleagues demanded that the chair rule the delegate out of order for directing such utterances to the chair, she argued that the man was enti-tled to his opinion. "If he thinks I'm rubbish, let it be so. . . . but I know that I'm not rubbish. Let's continue." Reflecting on that incident during our interview, Mwaka told me that it was strategic for her to let him get away with it:

> If I had said, "Let him withdraw," it would not have gone on the record. Once you withdraw they don't mention it at all, . . . So today it's on record in the Hansard. . . . The House was so unhappy with my decision; Nekyon was frozen in his seat because he thought that I was going to explode, ask him to go out because he'd insulted the chair. But then he'd have marched out as a hero because I'd have jumped out of my skin. But I decided to keep my cool so tactfully with a smile and the man was frozen on his chair.

In fact, withdrawn statements are not struck from the record. Mwaka's stated reasons for not taking a stern position with the rude delegate and her interpretation that he "froze in his seat" were her way of legitimizing her action, her way of challenging patriarchy. In searching for a personal strategy to deal with a powerful institution, she inadvertently repro-duced dominant gender stereotypes. By adopting a nonassertive method of dealing with the aggressiveness and rudeness of the male delegates in both cases, Mwaka conformed to expectations that a woman should avoid confrontational behavior, especially in public. She yielded her power as chair to abusive men and in so doing accentuated the power re-lations arising from gender relations in the wider society. Had she "ex-ploded," she would not have been "motherly." Male delegates continued to take advantage of this, which sustained the perception of her incompe-tence and unsuitability as chair. One of the local newspapers passed the following verdict on Mwaka's performance in its editorial: "Her rulings are so off the wall, they are bizarre. . . . Madam chairperson, why don't you take a long leave out of town? And the CA? If the professor can't shape up, then let her ship out" (*Monitor*, September 23, 1994).[12]

Comparing Mwaka's record with that of the NRC vice chairman, Hajj Moses Kigongo (who was also NRM vice chairman), shows that her per-formance is attributable to gender.[13] Like Mwaka, Hajj Kigongo assumed the chairmanship of the NRC with very little legislative experience; he had been a successful businessman before joining NRM politics in the

1980s. Moreover, Kigongo's formal education was very limited and did not even include a high school diploma. Although Kigongo made several errors and blunders, it hardly caused a dent on his record and the media took little note of it. Kigongo's confidence and skillful control of the House impressed me as I did my fieldwork, not to mention the visible respect that parliamentarians exhibited toward his chairmanship. All this suggests that Mwaka's femaleness, Kigongo's maleness, and the gender dynamics at play in the House accounted for the difference in their performance.

It is also "doing gender" when gender-insensitive female politicians articulate antiwomen arguments in the House. It lends legitimation to women's subordination and sounds doubly valid coming from a woman legislator:

> While we advocate for equality, we should be aware that women and men have special different roles to play from time immemorial. We are definitely aware that a cock cannot lay eggs and a hen cannot crow. . . . We must therefore appreciate the efforts and contributions of men which have enabled us to be where we are today. (Beatrice Bakojja, AA, *Proceedings of the Constituent Assembly,* September 1, 1994).

By highlighting the "natural differences" between men and women, this female legislator provides a powerful reinforcer and legitimator of hierarchical arrangements. A woman NRC representative opposed the argument raised by another woman legislator that the Ministry of Women in Development should be represented on the proposed Uganda National Council of Science and Technology and said, "If we are not careful enough, Mr. Chairman, we may push the issue of women's representation too far and probably push it to a ridiculous extent" (Gertrude Njuba, (historical MP),[14] Official Hansard, July 5, 1989, 44–45). The male legislators were more than happy that a woman was voicing their sentiments, as evidenced by their loud "Hear, hear!" and foot stomping.

Yet nonconformity to gender expectations may hold potential for the women's movement in Uganda, as exhibited in the course of CA proceedings. In this case women were provoked, but they did not take it sitting down; they walked out in protest. It all started when a male delegate who had previously worked with the Ugandan diplomatic corps said:

> Mr. Chairman, I am speaking as a career diplomat, and when I was learning diplomacy, my professor told me two things. He said there is direct line up between a diplomat and a lady in the use of words except that they are in the opposite direction. In that what they say is always the opposite—what the diplomat says will be the opposite of what the lady will say. When a lady

says "no," she means "perhaps" [laughter], and once she says "perhaps" she means "yes," and when she says "yes" then she means "no" [laughter]. (Akisoferi Ogola, CS, *Proceedings of the Constituent Assembly,* July 12, 1994, 799).

Several women delegates requested the chair to call the ex-diplomat to order. He immediately defended himself by arguing that he was merely cracking a joke and added, "A country which has no sense of humour is no [sic!] worse that an atomic bomb." Female delegates were outraged:

Point of order. . . . Is the speaker holding the floor in order to impute that we ladies do not normally mean what we say? At least that is what I understand him to be saying and I wonder whether that is in order, Mr. Chairman. (Hope Kabirisi, *Proceedings of the Constituent Assembly,* July 12, 1994, 799)

Is he . . . in order to sit in this hall and rebuke women . . . by implying that they just do not know what they want, they do not know what to say, they do not mean what they do? Is he in order Mr. Chairman to use even sexist analogies in this hall? (Miria Matembe, *Proceedings of the Constituent Assembly,* July 12, 1994, 800)

I do know how to take a joke on a good day, but Mr. Chairman I find the comments . . . offensive. Is he in order to suggest that I do not mean what I say simply because I am a woman? (Anonymous, *Proceedings of the Constituent Assembly,* July 12, 1994, 800)

Chairman Wapakhabulo, however, did not share the women's outrage and he let the ex-diplomat get away with a mere slap on the wrist. Amid peals of laughter, foot stomping, and derision from the male delegates, the chairman ruled:

The honourable made a joke . . . the ladies in this House were disturbed and a point [of order] was raised. I asked honorable Ogola whether that was what he meant to say. "In other words, do you intend to crack a nasty joke at the expense of ladies?" I asked him and he said he did not intend that. Then he proceeded at one stage to say . . . and he was actually interrupted as he was finishing to say that which more or less could have been an apology. So could you say it so that we hear it?

Ogola, however, insisted that he had nothing to apologize for. Adding insult to injury, he appended, "If somebody has not got a wide scope in life, I am not going to apologize for her ignorance. . . . There is a Russian saying [laughter] that a frog in a pot can only see the size of the sky which is equal to the mouth of the pot. . . . some of us have lived in a pot with a larger mouth; therefore, we are able to see a large part of the sky." At that point, the women delegates walked out of the House in protest. The chairman interpreted their action lightly: "We take it that the ladies are going out for lunch, they are not walking out on you . . . " [laughter]. Another male colleague actually patted Ogola on the back, saying, "some of us really appreciate the analysis given by Honourable Ogola, and if the analysis can reach our understanding of the political situation in this country, surely some people who feel they cannot understand his analysis should leave us" [applause] (Jack Sabiiti CS, *Proceedings of the Constituent Assembly,* July 12, 1994, 801). The debate continued as if nothing had happened.

One male delegate dismissed the walkout strategy as defeatist, irrational, and immature. He pointed out that women had in the past cracked jokes at the expense of men in the House, but the men had not walked out. Applauding the four "iron ladies"[15] who had not marched out with their colleagues for their demonstration of "capacity of tolerance and zeal of leadership to bear some strong words . . . because as a leader you are supposed to be sometimes criticized, but if you cannot bear this type of joke . . . how are we sure, Mr. Chairman, that the future leaders who are likely to be the opposite sex will steer us properly?" [applause]. (Matayo Kyaligonza, CS, *Proceedings of the Constituent Assembly,* July 12, 1994, 804). Yet another male delegate sarcastically pleaded with the chairman to "coach our language in handling gender issues because it is becoming too much. . . . we cannot possibly now talk about a woman without having certain ladies raising up arms" (Ben Wacha, CS, *Proceedings of the Constituent Assembly,* July 12, 1994, 804). A male *New Vision* reader wrote a letter to the editor suggesting that instead of "acting in a cowardly manner," the female CADs should have been grateful to Ogola for identifying an inherent female weakness. Another correspondent rebuked the women for walking out and blamed them for "making themselves vulnerable by flying off the handle." In his view, the unprincipled women delegates "owe[d] their electorate an apology for running away from the front-line" (*New Vision,* July 19, 1994).[16]

In this rare show of overt resistance, female delegates defied their oppressors. By walking out in protest, they made a historic statement of extreme importance. The men who opposed the walkout were merely expressing their nervousness and agitation at seeing the ruffled feathers of the "crowing hens." They found it threatening to see women who were doing gender unconventionally and inappropriately. Indeed, West and Zimmerman (1987, 145) argue that insofar as sex category is used as a fundamental criterion for differentiating people's (men's and women's) actions, we are always doing gender. By staging a walkout, women violated the gender norms; they were being assertive and aggressive. Gender was evoked to interpret their action in terms of behavior that is supposedly natural to women: flying off the handle (read hysterical), being vulnerable, and being cowardly. Because women legislators had not done gender appropriately, they were being called to account: "They owe an apology to their electorate." Meanwhile, the real culprits—the gendered institutional arrangements—went unquestioned and were left intact. Had similar action been taken by men, it would most likely have been described as principled, valiant, and gallant.

Special committees represent a distinct space in which women are more likely to do gender unconventionally, underscoring the point that the masculine character of the main chamber operates to maintain the status quo. Typically, men dominate committees that deal with traditionally male issues, such as the national economy and business. Women, on the other hand, are overrepresented on less prestigious committees, such as the committee on government assurances and commissions. As one member put it, "When it comes to wheeling and dealing, we can't beat the men; they gang up against us and keep us out of all the good things . . . such as the prestigious committees" (Rosette Ikote, AA). Nevertheless, in my study, female MPs were much more active in the committees than they were in general chamber debates. They seemed to be more comfortable debating in the smaller, less formal settings, as indicated by higher levels of contribution. My analysis revealed that female legislators actually spoke or indicated a wish to speak on the committee floor at least two and a half times more often (in proportional terms) than they spoke on the main chamber floor.

Furthermore, women were more likely to face down their male aggressors in the committees than they were in the main chamber. For example, the sessional committee on natural resources and tourism, wildlife, and antiquities convened to discuss a sensitive and confidential issue that required an individual vote of committee members. One of the female members of that committee hesitated in giving her response to the chairman. A male colleague chastised the female member for "wasting the committee's time." The response of the female member was swift. "Don't harass me, I'm thinking," she told him. Affronted by the retort, the male MP stormed out of the committee room. Given the size, formality, and ambiance of the main chamber, such a reaction would have been less likely to occur. Indeed, in the months that I spent observing parliamentary business in the main chamber such confrontation was extremely rare.

The Dialectics of Sexual Politics in the House

The issue of women's sexuality as a means of keeping women in their subordinate positions deserves separate treatment. Feminists have argued that sexual practices are one of the most important modes of effecting and perpetuating women's oppression (Evans 1978; McCaghy 1985; Wise and Stanley 1987; Sawicki 1991). Such practices may take the form of unwelcome sexual advances, sexually motivated physical contact, or verbal communication of a sexual nature. At the other end of the spectrum they may take somewhat more subtle forms, such as depicting women as primarily good for sex through the media and in other public forums. Sexual harassment is best defined by the effect the behavior has on the recipient, that is, a sense of being harassed, regardless of the intentions of the harasser (Collier 1995).[17] As with other forms of gender violence, sexual harassment stems from the power and status accorded to men in patriarchal societies (MacKinnon 1979; Ucko 1994).

Sexual prowess in most African cultures symbolizes men's power and is intricately linked with the institution of polygyny and culturally endorsed male promiscuity. What makes sex an extremely insidious tool for oppressing women is that in its commonest form it is often interpreted as normal, complimentary, and even flattering to the victims. Sexual acts are associated with the personal, and rarely do the victims perceive them as political (Toubia 1994). In the parliamentary setting wherein all legislators are ostensibly equal, sexuality is one way that male MPs gain and exercise their power over female MPs. My interviews reveal that women in the House are not spared this hideous form of oppression. The behavior of male legislators reveals the systemic and pervasive control that patriarchy exerts over social life, making sexual harassment appear natural, normal, and right (Wood 1994, 24).

Not all women parliamentarians I interviewed were willing to openly discuss the issue of sexual harassment.[18] A few told me that they preferred not to talk about it; others denied ever having been victims of it. However, further probing and couching the question in a less direct fashion almost always revealed that sex was an issue that most women legislators had to deal with on a day-to-day basis. As the examples below illustrate, many did not regard the repetitive sexual remarks directed at them as problems, let alone sexual harassment.

> Sexual harassment, no; but sexual remarks go with the territory. But I know how to deal with those. When a male colleague says to me, "Oh, you look juicy!" I respond, "Well, give it a try" [laughter]. He calls me "sweetheart" and I call him "darling" . . . they realize that it will get them nowhere and we continue to be friends. (Esther Opoti, CS)

> You know, I don't like using the term "sexual harassment." This has become a cliché [laughter]. But yes, it happens. . . . It depends on who it is coming from, what kind of mood I am in, but most of the time I tend to brush it off.

Like the other day when I wore a short sleeveless safari suit and this man was making comments that were uncalled for, I mean . . . but he thought he was being funny. So I also looked at it from that point of view, that he actually doesn't mean it badly. It is the culture; he thinks he's flattering me. If I turned around and said, "You're insulting me," he'd be shocked. (Winnie Byanyima, CS)

Of course the sexual remarks will always be there, but the harassment depends on the character of the woman. If somebody harasses you and tells you, "I want to have a love affair with you" and you say no . . . even if he continues pestering me for a long time, I'll just stand my ground. (Juliet Bintu, AA)

When you stand up to make a contribution, you hear remarks from behind: "Look at her bum!" . . . Oh yeah, believe me . . . "Ah this one is too beautiful to be here, she should be home taking care of her man." But it depends on how you have been molded to deal with it. Somehow you have to ignore it, pretend that you haven't heard and get on with what you're doing. (Ruth Aliu, AA)

I believe that women who are harassed ask for it, the way we present ourselves . . . the man may think that you also have a bit of interest. Before you talk to a man ask yourself, What do I expect from this person? What am I advancing to him? How am I approaching him? What's the attitude I am presenting to him? (Betty Akech Okullu, AA)

"It only happens to women who ask for it" is a justification often heard in rape cases. It has been used in Ugandan courts both as a defense and a mitigating mechanism for rapists (Tamale 1992). Many women have internalized this justification, thus shifting the blame from the culprits to the victims. "Brushing it off" both literally and mentally was the method adopted by all victims of sexual harassment in my study. Even the most radical feminists among the female legislators I interviewed adopted passive methods of dealing with it and did not consider it serious enough to warrant retaliatory action. Even when a male colleague made physical contact of a sexual nature, the women legislators either blamed themselves for his action or simply ignored it.

> AKIIKI:[19] Oh gosh god. They do all kinds of funny things [laughter]. I don't even know where to begin [sighs]. . . . This guy, you know, he calls me into his office one day, he asks his secretary to bring some coffee, blah, blah, blah and we talk. The conversation is going nowhere so I say, "Okay thank you, bye-bye." So he gets

> up to open the door for me and . . . [illustrates by grabbing her
> left breast with both hands].
> SYLVIA: Oh my god, really?
> AKIIKI: Uh-huh. I couldn't believe it; you can't imagine such a
> thing. All of them are the same.
> SYLVIA: What did you do?
> AKIIKI: I just brushed off his arm and walked out [laughter].

The crux here lies in the member's contradictory statements; she cannot believe what her male colleague did to her, yet she concedes that his behavior is commonplace when she adds that "all of them are the same." In other words, this particular MP could not believe that a "respectable" fellow parliamentarian would treat her as basely as "other" men outside parliament. Forgetting that sexual harassment is simply a way that men objectify women as a means of maintaining their power and control over them, this female legislator thought that her personal attributes and status would protect her in this particular environment. The bottom line is that to these men, she was a woman first and a parliamentarian only in a secondary sense.

Women parliamentarians operate in a power sphere in which their "honorable" status is at best precarious, as is powerfully demonstrated in the following emotional experience shared by another member in my study:

> One time I went over to say hello to a male colleague. I don't know; maybe I caught him at a bad time. . . . maybe he had had other things on his mind [chuckles nervously] and then he sort of grabbed me here [points to her crotch]. I was shocked; I literally went down on my knees. I said, "Please, please, I have a lot of respect for you." . . . But I wasn't angry; I thought maybe it was my mistake, maybe I took him for granted. I just learnt a lesson that time—that sometimes you have to be careful with men. You don't take . . . by nature they can misbehave simply by the way you present yourself. (Akwasi,[20] AA)

Again, this case offers a glimpse into the contradictions confronting women caught between the domains of power. When Akwasi reasoned that it was men's "nature" to behave in such a manner, she played into the sex-gender-desire normative and thus reinforced and reinscribed the power structures propped up by the heterosexual matrix (Butler 1990; Disch and Kane 1996).[21]

The attitudes and reactions reported here are by no means unique. Many studies have found similar results from victims of sexual harassment elsewhere (McCaghy 1985; Clerk 1985). What better way to reinforce and protect a particular structure of oppression than to "enculturate" or engender in the victims a belief that such behavior is natural and hence largely invisible? Throughout history systems of oppression have always had within them mechanisms of ideological legitimization. Through socialization, society "molded" these women to understand that sexual attention certifies their worth and that the mature way to deal with unwanted sexual attention is to not embarrass the man. The same culture will be passed on to these women's children and their children's children. This form of oppression is fortified and buttressed by the victims, who actively promulgate its ideology.

Harassment is sometimes utilized as a mechanism to marginalize and bypass female legislators. Just as Hollywood starlets had to sleep with the movie director or the movie mogul to get the better parts, women MPs are expected to "put out" in order to access the privileges of the institution. Hence women parliamentarians miss out on many beneficial international conferences, tours, and consultations designed for parliamentarians that routinely arrive at the desks of top administrative officials. They are systematically bypassed or boldly informed that their names will not be included on the list of participants unless they extend sexual favors to the powers that be. After requesting me to turn off the tape recorder, a female MP in a voice thick with emotion said, "Imagine I am married . . . even if I wasn't married, but each time you go to them with a problem they tell you that you have to sleep with them first before they can help. . . . It's terrible, whenever they look at us it's our sexuality that they focus on" (Gibwa, AA).[22] None of the male MPs interviewed complained of such harassment. Because men occupy the majority of top administrative or executive posts, they are less likely to be harassed in this manner.

The National Assembly has adopted a modus operandi that functions as a means of keeping female MPs in their subordinate position. For example, no formal regulations exist that cater to women MPs who wish to take maternity leave. Thus a woman representative may be forced to leave a two-week-old baby at home and rush to parliament simply to get her signature in the attendance book for that badly needed sitting allowance. She may or may not sit through the day's business, and even if she does, her concentration level may not be very high. The numerous appeals from women legislators to parliament and to the business and welfare committee to address this serious problem have either fallen on deaf ears or been received as a joke.[23]

Sometimes women's arguments on the assembly floor are dismissed or trivialized on the basis of fanciful speculations about their sexuality, as one attractive and unmarried MP revealed to me:

> There's one time when I contributed to the day's debate . . . and as we were
> moving out of the House, this male colleague attacked my arguments on the
> grounds that the stand I took was because I was not married and starved
> sexually. Can you believe it, he said, "You young men should get this
> woman and give her a good whopping in bed." He used very nasty words
> and I was so embarrassed. You know, someone who pushes you to the level
> of wanting to slap him? (Najjita, AA)[24]

Thus women's sexuality becomes another convenient tool for men to impose silence and compliance on female politicians. Ultimately, the legislative work of female MPs is adversely affected. This may, in part, explain the apparent reticence and diffidence that generally characterize women parliamentarians on the chamber floor. In the course of their regular legislative work, women also have to deal with the psychological anguish, feelings of belittlement, and increased self-consciousness occasioned by sexual harassment.

During Constituent Assembly debates delegates often used sexual examples to demonstrate details of particular situations, often at the expense of women legislators. During the CA proceedings one male delegate sent the House into an uproar when he used a sexual allusion to illustrate a point. "If I was put in Luzira [prison] for raping the minister of Women in Development . . . while defending the constitution . . . [laughter]" (Elly Karuhanga, *Proceedings of the Constituent Assembly,* August 30, 1994, 1786). The minister of Women in Development only drew a louder uproar from the House when she raised a half-serious point of order, "Is it in order for the member to bring his fantasies of wishing to rape me [laughter]? Maybe he has been longing to do it and I have refused" (Specioza Kazibwe, *Proceedings of the Constituent Assembly,* August 30, 1994, 1786). The matter was swept under the carpet when the chairman ruled, in the same spirit of banter, that an open application by the male delegate had been openly rejected by the minister. In this case the minister tactfully used "counterhumor" to deal with a humiliating situation.

The power and privileges that accrue to parliamentarians offer many women MPs some degree of independence, financial and otherwise. For example, the daily sitting allowances and opportunities to purchase vehicles at subsidized rates have turned many female legislators into the primary breadwinners in their households. However, as the statement quoted below indicates, all this often comes with personal (and often sexually related) costs for the women legislators:

> My entry into politics has made me much more of an independent person.
> . . . Before I could never imagine really doing anything on my own. I always

had to go from work to home, home to work, and if I was lucky maybe my husband would take me out once in a while, once in a year [laughter]. But when I got into politics, it suddenly opened my eyes really. I used to commute fifty miles daily to and from Kampala because I had to be home with my husband and then one day I said, "What is all this madness?" . . . Now, without thinking twice about it, I tell him, "Look, I am tired, I am not going to make it tonight," not because I'm being stubborn . . . but you know as a human being, you've got to think about yourself too. My husband fretted about it for some time; he imagined all kinds of things but eventually he settled down. . . . Other times I have to be weeks on end in the village, in the constituency. But I think . . . you know the rumor mill—by the way Uganda is so small, it's like a small town, I think that the reason why some marriages have broken down for my colleagues is actually because some women take license to behave any or how. Anyway, it always gets back to the husband somehow and that's when you find people falling out and breaking up and doing all this and that. (Rosette Ikote, AA)

Thus their newly acquired independence leads many female MPs to run the risk of losing the trust of their spouses and partners, who interpret financial independence as being equivalent to promiscuity. One male legislator explicated this point:

When women become politicians, there is bound to be some friction at home because you see politics involves going and coming back late at night, it involves traveling in the constituency, staying overnight. . . . now some men can't take it. Some men just cannot stand a situation where a woman comes home after midnight; it's cultural. Culture dictates that men find women at home [laughter] and not vice versa, . . . Don't ask me whether it's right or wrong but I know some men can't stand that. . . . they think that their wives are up to other things, you know . . . extralegislative work [laughter]. (Manzi Tumubweine, CS)

New Vision (March 19, 1996) quoted a forty-three-year-old engineer, Francis Angasa, as having told a *New Vision* reporter in a random opinion survey conducted on the streets of Kampala that he would not mind his wife's joining formal politics, "on condition that she [makes] sure politics does not get in the way of her biological functions like giving birth. I would expect her to bring up the children normally and not leave it to the housemaid. She should also cook, wash for me and entertain the family." His major fear, reported the newspaper, was "of her sleeping with her superiors and leaving him for them" (*New Vision* March 19, 1996, 15). The same report quoted a trader from a local market, Daniel Kiwanuka, as having said, "I would rather die of poverty than send my dear wife into politics for a better income. When your life gets spoilt [sic!] from there, you don't blame her because you could have stopped her." The views of both Angasa and Kiwanuka, two men from diverse socioeconomic backgrounds, confirm what Tumubweine said in the above quote. The attitudes of male parliamentarians who regard their female colleagues as sex objects place the public and private lives of the latter in extremely awkward positions. Indeed, such complications have resulted in (or at least contributed to) several separations and divorces for women in the House (also see *New Vision*, August 20, 1996, 11).

Although Western feminism celebrates the exposure of sexual harassment as a success story, African feminists are yet to embark on that battle. Indeed, the concept of sexual harassment is often described as Western and alien whenever it is mentioned in the African context. Issues of sexual harassment appeared relatively late in the women's movement of Western countries, first receiving attention in the late 1970s. In Britain it was not until 1986 that the landmark case of *Porcelli v. Strathclyde Regional Council* recognized sexual harassment as illegal. It achieved visibility in the United States in the 1991 Senate confirmation hearings for Clarence Thomas (Collier 1995). Such issues are bound to appear even lower on the priority list of the African women's movements, which operate in the context of neocolonialism and underdevelopment. This is because sexual harassment pales in the face of battles involving basic human needs, which the African women's movement must address. For example, African women are still struggling to obtain education, clean water, medicines, and the right to own property. In the face of such monumental struggles, unwelcome sexual jibes, lewd taunts, and other sexual overtures may seem ridiculously inconsequential. Yet, as I have argued, these struggles are directly linked to what has been made to seem "inconsequential." It is all part of the efficient working of patriarchy.

As the preceding stories illustrate, Ugandan women do not welcome inappropriate sexual advances from men. They face a somewhat contradictory situation, acknowledging the adverse effects of unwelcome sexual attention from their male colleagues while trying to convince themselves that personal integrity and professionalism will protect them from any "real" harm. It is also part of the female legislators' strategic concessions (conscious or unconscious) in dealing with patriarchy as they continue to access positions of power.

Notes

1. Even then, the story was relegated to the "WomaNews" section of the *Chicago Tribune*. It is very common even in Uganda for reports on women politicians to be run on the inconspicuous women's page of local newspapers.

2. Also see article 12 on citizenship rights, article 21 on equality and freedom from discrimination, article 31 on the rights of the family, and article 32 on affir-

mative action for marginalized groups and the establishment of an equal opportunities commission. Furthermore, the entire document employs gender-neutral language in contrast to the 1967 constitution, which employed masculine nouns and pronouns, interpreted to encompass the feminine.

3. See article 20 of the 1967 constitution.

4. Article 4(1)(c) of the 1967 constitution laid down the criterion to be followed in determining the citizenship of persons born outside Uganda: "Every person born outside Uganda after the commencement of this Constitution one of whose parents or grandparents is or was a citizen of Uganda, *provided that his father was a citizen of Uganda . . . at the time of the person's birth or, in case of the father's death before that person's birth, at the time of the father's death* (emphasis added). Minors followed their father's citizenship (Articles 4[2–3]). Whereas a foreign woman married to a Ugandan man was eligible for registration as a Ugandan citizen, the reverse was not true for a foreign husband of a Ugandan woman (Article 4[4]).

5. See proposed article 131(1) of the draft constitution.

6. NAWOU is an NGO formed in 1992 with the following general objectives: to coordinate and facilitate efforts and initiatives of women's NGOs and community-based Organizations; to network, promote, and develop a common vision for women's empowerment; and to engage in capacity building for women's effective leadership at all levels.

7. Between August 30, 1994, and August 3, 1995, nine major dialogues were held on a range of themes and topics concerning women's constitutional issues, for example, dialogues to discuss amendments on gender and representation, women's and children's rights, and the rights of persons with disabilities. Female CADs met with women parliamentarians as well women's NGOs and CBOs and exchanged views on pertinent issues (NAWOU 1995).

8. Rhoda Kalema is the only woman who voted against the amendment. In her interview, she explained that her primary objection was against what she perceived as an attempt to tie marriage to property rather than the welfare of children. Kalema believed that some women adopted an "emotional" and "personal" stand on the issue, thus invalidating their arguments. Her view was that in the Ugandan context, in which polygyny is practiced "loosely," most customary marriages not being registered, a blanket constitutional provision such as that proposed by the amendment would not achieve justice.

9. Rosabeth Kanter (1977, 219–221) found that one of the ways token women in her study responded to performance pressures was to find ways of becoming socially invisible. For instance, some women deliberately kept a low profile, avoided controversial situations, and were happy to play background roles that kept men in the foreground.

10. The same was found to be true for many postapartheid women parliamentarians in South Africa who explained to researcher Hannah Britton that they experienced a form of identity crisis when entering parliament (Hannah Britton, "Women Have the Numbers but Not the Power," *Parliamentary Whip*, April 18, 1997).

11. In her classic book *Body Politics*, Nancy Henley conducted a psychoanalytic study of how nonverbal behavior bound to people's power relationships. She notes: "The 'trivia' of everyday life—touching others, moving closer or farther

away, dropping the eyes, smiling, interrupting—are commonly interpreted as fa-cilitating social intercourse, but not recognized in their position as micropolitical gestures, defenders of the status quo—of the state, of the wealthy, of authority, of all those whose power may be challenged" (1977, 3).

12. The newspapers were relentless in their persecution of Professor Mwaka, as the following headlines suggest: "CA collapses in Mwaka's lap," *Daily Topic,* September 21, 1994; "Mwaka stumbles again, . . . and again," *Monitor,* September 23, 1994; "Mwaka returns, fails to steer CA," *New Vision,* September 21, 1994; "'Am not a super computer'—Mwaka," *Monitor,* September 30, 1994. The diver-sity of the newspapers exhibiting such hostility toward Mwaka is evidence that the reasons behind it were not political as such. The persecution was so bad that the Constituent Assembly Commission wrote a letter to newspapers dated Sep-tember 26, 1994, in which it rebuked the press for its persistent attacks on Mwaka.

13. President Museveni, the chairman of NRM, was also the chairman of NRC. Thus, prior to the 1995 constitution, the executive and legislative arms of the NRM government were fused. In practice, Museveni only rarely chaired NRC sessions and Haji Kigongo practically assumed the role of chairman or speaker.

14. Historical members in the NRC were those who made up the original coun-cil while the NRA was still fighting the bush guerrilla war in Luwero.

15. I interviewed two of these four women; both told me that they did not walk out because they appreciated Ogola's words as a joke and were not offended by them. The women who walked out, on the other hand, told the *New Vision* out-side the assembly building that they had indeed walked out in protest over "Ogola's offensive and dirty sexist talk" (see "Matembe Leads Walk Out," *New Vision* July 13, 1994, 1).

16. In contrast to the views expressed by male citizens, a letter sent to the edi-tor of the same newspaper by a woman said, "That the majority of men regard women as inferior at best, and pieces of property at worst, is not news to most of us. Nor indeed, were Ogola's utterances. It is one of the common stereotypes about women held in our society." Supporting the walkout, she continued, "It is up to the rest of us to offer all the support we can muster in demanding for the full equality of women, and also to raise the consciousness of men in Uganda to the realization that sexism is critically dysfunctional to our common goal of over-coming backwardness and underdevelopment" (Audrey Busulwa, "Decision to Walk Out Was Appropriate," *New Vision,* July 28, 1994).

17. Rubenstein (1992, 2) defines sexual harassment as "unwanted conduct of a sexual nature or conduct based on sex which is offensive to the recipient."

18. Some were only willing to discuss the issue on condition that I turned off the tape recorder. All the male legislators I interviewed denied the existence of sexual harassment in the House.

19. In order to protect the informant's confidentiality, I use a pseudonym in this case.

20. A pseudonym is used here to protect the informant's confidentiality.

21. Another example of how women reinforce the heterosexual matrix can be seen in the following incident: During the CA debates a female delegate insisted on changing the general term "intending parties" (which was used in the draft constitution) to the specific words "men and women" regarding people's right to

marry and have a family. She argued that the former term was unacceptable because it accommodated "homosexuals and lesbians" (see *Proceedings of the Constituent Assembly,* September 8, 1994).

22. A pseudonym is used here to protect the informant's confidentiality.

23. Interview with MP Sarah Namusoke, January 23, 1998.

24. A pseudonym is used here to protect the informant's confidentiality.

6

Women's Legislative Activities Inside Parliament: Trends and Directions

The 1989 affirmative action policy created significant expectations among women politicians and legislators. Member of parliament Miria Matembe shared her expectations in regard to the increased number of women legislators after the implementation of the affirmative action:

> I was looking at women's entry into public life as a sort of light. I thought that in these countries of ours, where leadership is characterized by dictatorship, corruption, nepotism, dishonesty, hatred, envy, and all these things . . . I thought that when women come to the public scene, they would come in with humane qualities. You know, they say that women are emotional; we are supposed to have all this love or this sympathy, all the good qualities—which at times men use to abuse us—but which I think God gave us in order to counteract the other poor qualities of [laughter] men. I thought that our entry into public life would clean up the dirt that has been there. . . . I personally had wished to hear society say, "Hey, we had missed these women and we had done bad because if they had come to the public forum earlier we would have been spared so much suffering." . . . I had hoped that women would break through the ills of society and bring light into the otherwise dark rooms where men have been sitting for a long time making decisions that have not been good for society.

Matembe's rather idealistic belief is based on the underlying assumption that gender differences play a primary role in legislative activity; or, to put it differently, that an increase in the number of female legislators in the national assembly would bring their distinctive perspectives, concerns, and agenda into the arena of public policy and law. Such a notion can be extended to mean that women's traditional and/or feminist interests would increasingly be promoted in public policymaking, say, by bringing issues of the hitherto private sphere into the public realm. But do these assumptions necessarily hold true in the real world? Matembe's tone betrays some disillusionment and a tinge of frustration, suggesting that thus far her expectations have not been met. Has the incorporation of women brought only marginal differences to the goings-on in the House? Are men impervious to the concerns that women raise? Is the policy of affirmative action in politics a lost one?

In this chapter I seek to examine the trends and patterns of women's legislative activities in Uganda since the 1950s, when pioneer female legislators entered the legislative council (Legco) of the then Ugandan protectorate. Is legislative activity in Uganda gendered similarly to legislative activity in other parts of the world?[1] If so, what is the extent and the shape of the patterns of legislative activity? What explains these patterns? The principal focus of this examination is the legislative transcript (Official Hansards) of Uganda's parliaments, spanning the period from 1954 to the present.[2] The number of women parliamentarians increased by a factor of more than twenty-five during the four decades that are covered in this chapter. To find out if Uganda's legislative activity is gendered, I analyze intensively the successive Hansards, focusing on the types of (1) bills, (2) resolutions, and (3) arguments and questions introduced by female and male legislators in the assembly chamber. In the process, I try to frame the broad trends set by women legislators in the context of an institutionally male policymaking process. In examining women's engagement in the arena of policymaking, I look out for particular behaviors that display differences between women's and men's legislative activity.

The search for trends and directions in the way women legislate begins with an account of the general and particular legislative process adopted by the Ugandan National Assembly. This is extremely important for a comprehensive analysis and a correct understanding of how legislative activity is molded by the institutional character as it interacts with gender (Kathlene 1990, 242; Thomas 1994). During my interviews with them, several women legislators expressed a sense of frustration with the fact that their participation in mainstream politics was limited by existing norms and the infrastructure of legislative activity. In Chapter 5 I offered a detailed description of the physical environment of the main chamber of the national assembly and how it affected the operation of female MPs. This section outlines the specialized discourse of the legislative process and thus complements such a portrayal. In the second section of the chapter, I discuss general trends and directions. Finally, I explore some theoretical explanations for the gendered character of legislative activity.

The Parliamentary Procedure

As is the case with most commonwealth jurisdictions, in Uganda the procedure for enacting new laws or amending existing laws is a fairly detailed one. Almost all newcomers in parliament are barely acquainted with the technicalities of the legislative procedure; it takes months, even years, for anyone to grasp the fine elements of this conduct. Indeed, several men and women have left parliament at the end of their term of office without having made their maiden speech or without having gone beyond such speech. In the present parliament, this is clearly compounded by the numbers. There are 270 members of the House, for a population of only 18 million Ugandans. They sit for three days a week, very often to discuss arcane and boring matters about which very few members have either expertise or interest.

Article 91.1 of the 1995 constitution provides: "Subject to the provisions of this Constitution, the power of Parliament to make laws shall be exercised through Bills passed by Parliament and assented to by the President." The elaborate rules of procedure that regulate the legislative process from the moment a bill is conceived to the time it is given the presidential assent are laid down by the legislature itself at the commencement of its term. The procedure in place at the present time is provided in the 1995 constitution, the Uganda Government Standing Orders, and the *Rules of Procedure of the Parliament of Uganda, 1996*. I provide a summary of this procedure below.

1. Bills may be introduced into the House by government (through its cabinet ministers), by a standing committee of the House, or by any private member of parliament. All proposed bills begin in the form of a memorandum setting out its policy and principles.
2. The office of the first parliamentary counsel in the attorney-general's chambers then translates the memorandum into draft bill form. The draft bill must be submitted to the cabinet accompanied by a memorandum explaining the legal effect of its more important provisions.
3. After a cabinet draft bill has received cabinet approval, it is published in the official government gazette. The published draft bill is then distributed to all MPs and is slotted in the "order of business," which contains the schedule of all the bills to be debated at each parliamentary sitting.
4. Every bill progresses through a triple-tiered process consisting of three readings once it reaches the House floor. The first reading of a bill simply entails a reading of its short title as a way of introducing it to the House. The bill is then forwarded to the

relevant sessional committee of the House for scrutiny and comments. The committee submits a report on the bill at the time a motion is moved and seconded for its second reading.

5. Detailed debate on the merits and principles of the proposed legislation is carried out at the stage of the second reading. The House will either resolve itself into a committee of the whole House for purposes of debating the bill or the bill will be committed to a select committee that will report its findings to the House. At this stage there are set formal procedures for members of parliament to introduce new clauses and amendments or delete clauses from the draft bills.

6. At the conclusion of the full debate at the second reading stage, the bill is read a third time and is passed by parliament.

7. After a bill has been passed by parliament, assent copies are published by the government printer and are submitted for the presidential assent. The bill is finally published as law after presidential assent has been obtained.

The rules governing the language and manner of debate in the House are extremely formal; any departure from them may lead to a member's being called to order or even suspended from the House. For example, in parliament one says, "Mr. Speaker, sir, I beg to second the motion," not just "motion seconded." Members can only speak after they have risen to their feet and have "caught the speaker's eye." They are not permitted to read their speeches on the floor.[3] Members have to know when to stand up and sit down, when and how to bow before the Speaker, how to walk in and out of the House chamber, when and how to address the Speaker, cabinet ministers, and other colleagues in the House, when and how to interrupt another member, and the proper language used in the House. Rules are set out for the admissibility of members' petitions, questions, statements, personal explanations, motions, and amendments to motions. With a few exceptions, all questions proposed for decision of parliament are determined through a majority vote. Such vote is resolved not through a secret ballot or a show of hands but by shouts of aye and nay.[4] This archaic practice inherited from the English House of Commons gives the Speaker the discretion to declare which of the two collective voices constitute the majority.

The formality and lengthy procedure of the legislative process is often justified with the argument that the people represented by the legislature have a right to long deliberations on laws that are considered sacred to them. There is need, therefore, to strike a balance between the rights of the majority to expect reasonable dispatch in the public business and the right of the minority to enforce the most careful scrutiny of these bills

(Miers 1989). But to whose advantage, men's or women's, does the specialized discourse work? Is such formality likely to be friendlier to males or females? What is the probable effect of such discourse on the legislative activity of those who do not find it particularly appealing? Does the legislative process and method hinder some legislators from pursuing their legislative agendas? I argue that the formality associated with the conduct of business in the House is another tool that facilitates the gendered institutional character of parliament. My analysis of the Official Hansards suggests that it is women, more than men, who are constantly reminded to follow the "proper rules of procedure" or conform to the multifarious practices in the House. The two examples offered below were both addressed to female MPs.

> Honorable Byanyima, I see your hand . . . I think you have forgotten . . . you stand up and catch my eye—I give you the floor. (the Speaker of the House, Official Hansard, September 12, 1996, 419)

> There is really a procedure for a member of parliament wishing to put question to a minister, and I do appeal to the honorable member that if this question is put in the normal way a member of parliament puts a question to a minister, I will definitely respond to it. (local government minister Bidandi-Ssali, Official Hansard, September 25, 1996, 478)

My observations in both committee sessions and assembly debates suggested that the onerous and intimidating rules of procedure in plenary sessions act to prevent many parliamentarians from effectively contributing to the debates on the House floor. Several MPs who keep silent or hardly contribute in the plenary sessions are fairly active in the committees. Although this was also true for some male members of parliament, it was much more common for female members. Such differences can be explained in part by the informal and more relaxed atmosphere that prevails in the committee sessions. Women, who are more familiar with the unofficial, casual "private" sphere, are bound to identify more with the committee sessions and to be alienated or neutralized by the formality and the legalistic conduct in the plenary.

General Trends and Directions

With incremental numbers of female representatives appearing in successive Ugandan parliaments, the culture of "crowing hens" has become more and more consolidated. Normally, women parliamentarians contribute to almost any issue under deliberation on the assembly floor. The range of topics varies from health expenditures to the defense budget.

Nevertheless, there are general trends and broad patterns that point to a gendered structure to legislative activity. These gendered patterns are discussed under two thematic subgroups, namely, women's interventions in the House, and the tactics and strategies that women employ.

Women's Interventions in the House

Clear trends are discernible in the types of issues that women focus on when it comes to the substantive business of parliament, such as debating specific bills, budgetary proposals, and motions. The favorite topics of parliamentarians can be gleaned from the Hansard records of members' annual discussion of the motion thanking the president for his state of the nation address at the commencement of every parliamentary session. Customarily, the debate on the address is open for any member to generally consider any matter of her or his interest (albeit related to the presidential address). Many parliamentarians use the address as a post-election "ode to the nation," in which they continue to harp on their main electoral themes and speak to the gallery. Women's pet topics include education, agriculture, health, peace, corruption, and the economy.[5] These topics reflect areas that female members are most familiar with professionally or spheres that directly affect their lives as mothers, wives, and homemakers.

But whatever topic they contribute to, female (more than male) MPs tend to perceive issues through a gendered lens. An unmistakable pattern demonstrates that women largely intervene on behalf of marginalized groups such as children, the poor, the elderly, and people with disabilities. But most especially, they consistently articulate for the specific interests of women.[6] In other words, the contributions of women MPs attempt to *engender* assembly debates by compelling the House to seriously consider the policy implications on gender relations in Uganda. Illustrations abound in the Hansard records of female MPs taking up the cause of women. This feature is a constant throughout time. A good example of this can be drawn from the colonial legislative council—the precursor to the independence parliaments. Challenging the governor's state of the nation communication to parliament, Barbara Saben, who was one of two women legislators in the assembly stated:

> There is no mention in the address either of the urgent need to probe the problem of the status of African women in our society. . . . I think I can tell you why, I would like to say that I think it is a man's world for men only. . . . All over the country women are urging that they should be given rights to land, rights to work and rights in their children. . . . I have been told . . . that any changes to be accorded in the status of women here must come from the District Councils but I would like to ask how can this be done

when for the most part it is men only who sit on these councils? I would also like to ask where do the women begin to improve their status when you have the whole weight of man's "vested interest" in keeping us where we are? I would like to ask for a statement of Government policy on where I begin. I would like to ask this without a vestige of "vested interest" coming from Government! (Official Hansard, January 16, 1958, 133–134)

Yet women MPs do not consider only general gender concerns. When, for example, the House resolves itself into a committee of supply to consider and approve the annual budgetary proposals from the Ministry of Finance, they are on the alert to see how much money has been earmarked for projects that will benefit women. Female parliamentarians usually take the minister to task, for instance, to provide a breakdown of the lump sum vote for the Ministry of Health, demonstrating exactly how much is proposed to be spent on reproductive health care. Similarly, on the expenditure figures of the Ministry of Agriculture, they will demand to know what measures the ministry has put in place to ensure that agricultural extension workers reach the rural women subsistence farmers who form the mainstay of Uganda's agricultural output. In addition, female MPs have highlighted women's suffrage rights,[7] the plight of women prisoners,[8] the exclusion of women from the formal economic sector,[9] issues of domestic violence,[10] the unjust position of taxing housewives,[11] and women's disadvantaged position regarding project-run ministries.[12] The list goes on and on.

The trend of executing the gender brief in parliament is also carried by the few women who sit on the front bench—cabinet ministers. In their capacity as heads of government departments, ministers are usually required to appear before parliamentary committees and the plenary sessions of the House to answer questions and defend their budgetary proposals. Female cabinet ministers generally do an impressive job of responding to questions and defending their ministries. In responding to questions, these women (unlike their male counterparts) use every opportunity to highlight the gender implications of their policies. As deputy minister of rehabilitation in 1987, Gertrude Njuba, for example, metaphorically emphasized the important but unrecognized role of women in agriculture:

Wherever we go, and unfortunately people think that the Ministry of Rehabilitation—because of its name—is responsible for making sure that agriculture is rehabilitated . . . People are saying we want tractors. We have not got those tractors. . . . Our traditional "tractors" . . . have been the women of this country. . . . Incidentally, Mr. Chairman, I do not know whether you are aware that this traditional tractor whenever you look at [any] budget, the tractor has been getting the least amount of vote in all the budgets and . . . in

> this year's budget, this tractor has not been taken care of at all. . . . The Ministry of Finance should assist us, if only at least to rehabilitate the tractor that has been working for us all these years. (Official Hansard, August 27, 1987, 87–88)

The deputy minister went ahead to criticize the finance minister for consistently cutting budget proposals submitted by her ministry and others which, she argued, leads to frustrating their work.

Female parliamentarians and other women's activists have been criticized by some scholars for what they perceive to be the rather limited agenda in the struggle against subordination and oppression. Human rights lawyer Oloka-Onyango, for instance, argues that Ugandan women activists ignore the wider human rights struggle of which challenges to gender oppression are an integral part. He contends that broad human rights issues (such as the right to organize, freedom of association, and freedom of expression), which also affect women, are generally ignored by the women's movement. By focusing exclusively on a narrow definition of gender issues without simultaneously remaining aware of and confronting wider and equally important human rights concerns, he argues, women activists are engaging in a rather futile exercise which, in the final analysis, can only lead to the truncated liberation of women.[13]

This argument has serious limitations. The contemporary human rights movement in Africa existed for decades before the emergence of the parallel women's movement. Indeed, it was precisely because the advocates (almost all of whom were men) of the mainstream human rights movement consistently ignored and/or marginalized women's rights that the latter activism arose. No one denies the mutuality of the struggles of mainstream human rights and women's human rights. Although women activists are always mindful of wider human rights issues, I think that they are quite justified to focus on the gender aspects of human rights *for the moment*. This must be done until such a time when such issues are considered mainstream and are given the prominence they deserve. Women parliamentarians should not, therefore, feel guilty about being branded "women's representatives." By explicitly carrying the "gender brief," they are deliberately laying the necessary political seedbed for a more integrated and holistic human rights agenda.

Another trend discernible in the parliamentary activities of all parliamentarians, but most especially in those of female MPs, concerns the inclination to make a case for the "modernization" of their specific constituencies. Women parliamentarians have a way of presenting the pressing problems in their constituencies with a passion that is not common among their male counterparts. Unlike men, they do not seem to be inhibited from putting emotion into their submissions, often evoking laughter from their colleagues.[14] Although emotions are frequently considered a sign of weakness, especially in the public arena, this style of delivery has proved quite effective for women because it draws attention to whatever issue they are making. Modernization issues for members of parliament are of crucial importance given the fact that Uganda's human development index (HDI) falls below the average for the "least developed countries in the world."[15] Members of parliament are therefore competing for the meager national resources to develop and modernize their constituencies in the areas of constructing road networks, initiating modern farming techniques, introducing electric power, constructing and facilitating schools and health care centers, and sinking boreholes.

The fact that female MPs are drawn into legislative and constituency work concerning gender interest, in addition to sharing the modernization agenda with their male counterparts, means that they have a disproportionate workload, a double official burden. It becomes a triple burden when they add their "unofficial" duties of homemaking and child care.

Concerning the generational characteristics of women legislators, there are distinctions between the first generation of women legislators and their contemporary descendants. The Hansard records show clearly that almost all the women from the pioneer generation of MPs (up until the 1960s) stood out as remarkable debaters—people who could hold their own despite their small (almost miniscule) number. For example, in 1966, at the height of the constitutional crisis characterized by political intimidation and rampant defections from the opposition to the ruling Uganda People's Congress (UPC), Florence Lubega was one of the few MPs who stood up to the government:

> There is no harm at all, Mr. Speaker, in pointing out to Government what part of its duty, or what part of its obligations is not being properly fulfilled, or what is lacking in its plan for the welfare of our nation. . . . We are not here, Mr. Speaker, to joke, we're not here to please each other, not even to earn popularity amongst our fellow parliamentarians. We are here, Mr. Speaker, to perform certain duties, and perform them to the best of our ability [*Hear, hear!*]. Mr. Speaker, sometimes I sit here and I feel very sad when I see some of our best speakers in the House, after crossing the floor of the House, sitting so quiet as if nothing needs to be put right [*Hear, hear!*]. (Official Hansard, January 12, 1966, 432–433)

Reacting to Lubega's submission, the deputy speaker lauded her in words laced with paternalism: "Honourable members, I have not been in the House long enough; but I think we must congratulate ourselves for having a lady of this calibre in the House" (Official Hansard, January 12, 1966, 439). Pumla Kisosonkole, who was president of the Uganda African Women's League (UAWL) and vice president of the Uganda

Council of Women (UCW), also impressed the House with her contribution to the debate on whether or not Europeans and Asians should continue to enjoy reserved seats in the Legco of independent Uganda. Pointing to the fact that there was no special representation in the British parliament for non-Britons, she rejected the proposal (Official Hansard, October 3, 1957, 155).

In contrast, only a proportion of women who have served as legislators in more recent times debate with comparable articulation and vivacity. Almost to a woman, contemporary female legislators are wary of adopting radical positions in opposition to the prevailing status quo. There are several possible reasons to explain this distinction. First, because the number of pioneer female legislators was negligible, women MPs probably worked very hard to ensure that they did not let their lot down. Second, a plural political system was in existence in all pre-1970 legislatures. In other words, there was more than one political organization in contention for political power. Opposition politicians added a certain vibrancy to the debate as they locked horns with members of the government. Such oscillation is largely lacking in the monolithic movement-type legislatures in which consensus building supersedes bifurcated debates. The words of Prime Minister Kintu Musoke provide eloquent testimony of the situation that currently exists in the Ugandan legislature: "When members speak freely and at the end of the day they convince one another leading to emergence of a consensus. . . . That phenomenon of consensus building is the beauty of the Movement System."[16]

Third, and most important, almost all first-generation female MPs emerged from "political families," either as wives or daughters of male politicians.[17] In contrast, as noted in Chapter 4, only a quarter of the forty female MPs interviewed for this study laid claim to having come from "political families." Having a political husband or father, no doubt, leads a woman (consciously or unconsciously) to have interest in national politics or to emulate his deeds. As MP Florence Lubega declared, "I was a politician when I was nine years old . . . when I used to sit at the feet of my father who was a great politician and listen to what he said."[18] In other words, such women never felt like "fish out of water" when they decided to join politics. Many contemporary female legislators not only lacked previous connection to any political persons but entered the political arena for the first time when they were elected to office.

Tactics and Strategies That Women Employ

The need for women in politics to employ tactical strategies in order to work effectively in a male-dominated environment has been noted. A review of the Hansards from the 1950s to the present immediately reveals a striking trend: male chauvinism. Consider the following excerpts drawn from the Hansards of the 1960s:

> I would like to inform the hon. Member [Mrs. Lubega] that one of the causes of juvenile delinquency is the deprivation of parental love, and I would also urge her to see that in the Uganda Council of Women, they do not indulge in fighting for independence for women to an extent that instead of being in the home to look after children, they go out and leave the children roaming around, so much so that they come to the city and therefore they become juvenile delinquents [laughter]. (S. K. Okurut, Official Hansard, January 12, 1966, 437)

> Mr. Speaker, in Africa it looks rather funny for girls or women to put on these mini-skirts . . . and when [they] sit they cut [their] legs like men. This is very bad. (J. Ekaju, Official Hansard, July 26, 1967, 1170)

> Women are trying to provoke men and also are trying to be like Europeans whereas in fact we are Africans. . . . We have got our own culture, but the way they paint their lips is not welcome by men as a whole. And also wearing these mini-skirts is really tempting. (C. B. Katiti, Official Hansard, July 26, 1967, 1170)

True, these MPs may have been victims of a time when gender awareness in Uganda was still minimal. Moreover, the fact that there were only two women in the legislature meant that female parliamentarians were considered an aberration not to be taken seriously. But consider the following extracts drawn from more contemporary times:

> I want to inform my colleague who is holding the Floor that . . . as per Genesis, chapter 3 [laughter] . . . the first thief was a woman and she stole from the middle of the garden of Eden by eating the forbidden fruit. (Cosmas Adyebo, Official Hansard, February 25, 1997, 1379)

> It is the women who must be responsible for rejecting men because men's ability to refuse a woman is almost zero. [laughter] . . . The other source of rape is the dress. . . . Some women dress in such a way that men feel that these people are ready. . . . A woman who knows she is quite big puts on a pair of trousers which is [sic!] not fitting her. What is the purpose of such a dress? These are things which we have to try to remove if rape is be eliminated. . . . Then there is the question of women hanging in dark places alone and in places where the men are already drunk. . . . a woman leaving the house at about 8 o'clock up to 9 walking around. What do you expect? (Adoko Nekyon, Official Hansard, June 14, 1990, 359–360)

> I stand to support the bill [on rape] and also to emphasize that as we stand, there is need to protect the weaker sex by passing such a stringent legislation. . . . On the other hand, however, allow me to state that the erosion of our African culture has somehow contributed to immorality. . . . Mr. Chairman, we need to build a society with high standards of morality. Unless we do this, unless we awaken to these realities, to some of these challenges—and I am sorry I have to comment on our mothers, the women—and we allow our women to dress the way they like, you know [laughter]. . . . We have to scrutinize the problems that cause this phenomenon of rape. (Abu Mayanja, Official Hansard, June 13, 1990, 344–345)

The patronizing attitude of these legislators in a time of affirmative action, gender sensitivity, and political correctness, not to mention the presence of fifty-one female legislators in the House, is very telling indeed.

Although women parliamentarians first gained numbers in the fifth parliament (National Resistance Council) after the implementation of the affirmative action policy, it was not until 1996, when the sixth parliament was elected, that they organized themselves into a women's parliamentary caucus. The name of the caucus is something of a misnomer because it does not reflect the alliance of marginalized groups represented in parliament. In addition to women, the caucus encompasses MPs representing people with disabilities, workers, and youth. Female MPs have identified male MPs thought to be gender sensitive and have offered them permanent membership in the caucus. Being identified as a gender-sensitive male MP is based on an observed track record in voting for and speaking up for the interests of the caucus. Women parliamentarians realized the need to ally themselves with all these categories of MPs in order to build needed support.

The primary objective of the caucus is to lobby for bills and influence their direction to make them sensitive to the interests of the marginalized. Since its membership is varied, the caucus moves cautiously, taking on issues of specific interest to the allies. Avoiding divisive issues is vital to its success. It identifies key issues on the parliamentary agenda that it wants to address, since it cannot afford to place too much on its platter. For various reasons the caucus is not as active as women parliamentarians would like it to be, but it has nevertheless registered some positive results. Many MPs offer their support to the caucus in the hope of gaining a block caucus vote for their own interests when the need arises. One of the most effective strategies adopted by the caucus is identifying a sympathetic male MP to present their position on the assembly floor. If a woman stood up to defend gender issues, the majority of her male colleagues would simply "switch off." For example, in 1996 there was debate over the local governments bill, which sought to decentralize Uganda's system of administration. After lobbying the relevant parliamentary committee working on this particular bill, the women's caucus requested a male committee member to articulate their amendment on the issue of who was to elect the women's quota of one third at the different levels of the local councils. The draft bill had proposed that an electoral college be entrusted with this task, but the caucus thought otherwise. Thus Obiga Kania, the committee chairman, made a case for the caucus:

> Mr. Chairman . . . the caucus of women presented a position to the committee . . . I have the text of a brief amendment they have kindly asked me to move and the committee adopted this amendment as its position. It is on clause 114(2) to remove all the words after "shall be by" and replace them with "universal adult suffrage through secret ballot." The reasons which they gave, which convinced the committee are as follows . . . .[19] (Official Hansard, December 11, 1996, 1078)

Given the controversial nature of the amendment, it would probably not have succeeded had the caucus not lobbied the committee and taken deliberate steps to package it in palatable wrappings for the House. Several men opposed the amendment, arguing that an electoral college was "more convenient" for electing affirmative action women leaders.

In addition to winning the electorate issue in the local governments bill, the women's parliamentary caucus also registered two amendments. Section 2(c) reads, "The objectives of the Act are . . . to establish a democratic, political and gender-sensitive administrative set-up in local governments." The amendment introduced the words "democratic" and "gender-sensitive" to the original bill tabled. Section 48(3) was added to specifically provide that "at least one third of the executive committee members at the parish or village level shall be women." Furthermore, the women's caucus is currently working to influence the pending land bill to ensure that it caters to women's needs. The domestic relations bill, which is also due for tabling before their term of office has expired, is another landmark piece of legislation that the caucus is preparing for. This bill, the product of over ten years of research and pressure from women's interest groups, proposes to reform and consolidate all key legislation regulating gender relations in the domestic arena.

Members of parliament, especially men, are fond of quoting old proverbs and "traditional wise sayings" to back up a point that they are advancing on the assembly floor. Women employ a combination of proverbs and humor to augment important issues. Evoking traditional wisdom to make counterarguments is especially effective for female MPs. Miria Matembe, for example, quoted the Runyankore proverb *Ngu obusasi nibumanywa akakumu* "It is the hurt finger that knows best how much it pains" when defending the position that women are best placed to talk about "women's issues."[20] Florence Lubega emphasized a point by citing a Kiganda proverb, *Agali awamu, gegaluma enyama* "Teeth that are close together bite meat better than those that are spread out," meaning that there is strength in working together.[21] Women MPs also use proverbs as a rousing tool, a way of attracting the attention of the House to what they are saying. When, for example, Barbara Saben commenced her contribution by quoting the Spanish proverb "Women seldom say anything worthwhile but any man who does not listen to them is mad,"[22] she must have successfully jolted her colleagues to full attention.

Female politicians tend to drive their points home by evoking their "unique female qualities" as a rhetorical strategy to fall back on when everything else seems to have failed. For example, when appealing to government to put an end to the insurgency in northern Uganda through roundtable negotiations with the rebels, Betty Akech-Okullo reasoned:

> Mr. Speaker, I do not believe in the issue of saying we put out fire with fire. When you put out fire with fire, there is a lot of destruction that comes along the way as you try to put out that fire with fire. Therefore, as a woman and as a mother who knows how difficult it is to bring life into this world and knows how painful it is to lose this life senselessly, especially innocent young lives, I think that we should look at ways and means of reconciliation, of forgiveness. (Official Hansard, February 27, 1997, 1424)

Barbara Saben also used this tactic back in the 1950s. By turning a derogatory and sexist remark made to her into a positive act, she eloquently contributed to a controversial motion:

> Sir, on previous occasion in this House I was likened to a wife, and today with the permission of the honourable House, I would like to try and take up my duties once again as a housewife and tidy up what I consider the menfolk—my menfolk on this side of the House and others opposite—have done to make the disorderly work of this House. Men usually do disorder a House and what I would like to try and do now is try and tidy up and put things in order. . . . May I begin, like all good housewives, with tidying up what is least difficult. (Official Hansard, October 3, 1957, 146)

Saben's style worked. It gained her the full attention of the House (evidenced by an absence of the usual disruptive interruptions) and a loud applause at the end of her lengthy submission. A familial term had been used to refer to a female parliamentarian. Instead of rejecting it, she embraced it and manipulated it to accentuate her point. She took a sexist remark meant to make a woman MP appear less threatening in the context of parliament—a patriarchal political structure—and turned it on its head.

The parliamentarian women's caucus realizes that it is not enough for women to enjoy big numbers in leadership positions: Being "in power without power" is not what Ugandan women want. Thus women parliamentarians have found it imperative to empower themselves in order to have a real impact on parliamentary agenda and national policy. As women MPs, they have identified the need to master the legislative processes and to effectively balance their parliamentary duties with their other responsibilities. For example, the caucus has organized training workshops, mainly through the Forum for Women in Democracy (FOWODE), in which they learn practical skills in different areas, ranging from macroeconomic policy and management to gender budgeting.[23] Such workshops prepare caucus members for key debates in parliament.

When women's legislative work is conceptualized as a convergence between their own emancipation and modernization, it conjures up the schema of women in development (WID), that is, the struggle to provide, inter alia, improved access for women to health care, education, credit, markets, and land. Women legislators are aware of the limitations embedded in WID programs and, as part of their empowering program, are equipping themselves with the skills to overcome the underlying structural conditions that deny women such rights in the first place.[24]

However, despite the positive legislative and policy changes that reflect women's needs and concerns, the procedural and substantive legislative activity remain fundamentally untouched. This is partly because women's increased political participation with the inception of the affirmative action policy is a relatively recent phenomenon. Surely, a decade of policy change is too short a time to make an impact on structures and patterns that have been in place for centuries. Since the NRM government established a gender ministry and instituted affirmative action programs, the women's movement has been pushing for a clear policy framework for mainstreaming gender in all sectors of society. Such policy is meant to offer guidelines for all development practitioners, including parliamentarians. In December 1997 government adopted the National Gender Policy (NGP) as an integral part of the national development process. The significance of this policy for parliamentarians is that it supplements the constitution as a legal basis for challenging any bills or policies that are not gender responsive.

Regardless of the total percentage of women's representation in the national assembly, women have made their mark on the policymaking history of Uganda. The names of women such as Barbara Saben, Pumla Kisosonkole, Florence Lubega, Rhoda Kalema, Victoria Ssekitoleko, and Winnie Byanyima have their place on the prestigious list of great Ugandan statespeople. The general trends indicate that women's mere presence in parliament not only influences the way bills are debated but also readjusts the focus on public policy issues. In view of this, how are the gendered patterns of legislative activity in the different Ugandan legislatures to be rationalized?

Theoretical Explanations for the Trends

Various theories have been offered to explain gender differences in legislative activity. Some scholars attribute such differences to socialization (e.g., Jaros 1973; Weissberg 1974; Sapiro 1983). Thomas and Welch contend that

> the attitudes and behavior of women state legislators are expected to be a reflection of two separate socializing influences. Socialization as legislators teach "the rules of the game" and how to operate within them. Socialization as women in a society still engaged in gender specific public and private roles will . . . impel women legislators to give high priority to issues that address this dual status. (Thomas and Welch 1991)

Kathlene (1989) hypothesized that American female legislators have greater concern than their male counterparts for interpersonal relationships because of differences in the socialization and life experiences of men and women.

A related explanation claims that fundamental value differences between the sexes are responsible for the gender differences in political values and moral orientation (Shapiro and Mahajan 1986; Canover 1988). This explanation, which is not dissimilar to Matembe's reasoning in her introductory words to this chapter, stems from the "woman-centered" or "women culture" perspective that gained a lot of attention in the mid-1970s. Proponents of this view argue that women constitute a unique source of values for society, resulting from the different roles that men and women play in patriarchal society (see Chodorow 1974, 1978; Gilligan 1982; Eisenstein 1983; Massey 1985). Thus the political attitudes of men and women are allegedly molded by their differing world experiences. Woman-centered analysts further argue that women should capitalize on their feminist identity (as opposed to mere sexual identity) and consciousness in order to "revolutionize" the male-oriented values that dominate in political culture (Ruddick 1980; Rich 1976). This, they contend, is the only way women can resist the pressures toward assimilation and conformity with existing norms in any male-dominated institution (Freedman 1979; Carroll 1992). Dolan and Ford (1995) investigated the degree to which possessing a feminist identity influences the legislative behaviors and priorities of female state legislators in the United States. They found some significant diversity in the assignments and priorities of feminist and nonfeminist female legislators.

The main weakness with the woman-centered conception of women's culture, as Susan Carroll (1992, 26) points out, is that "it is generally rooted in an essentialist, often biologically based, notion of gender difference." Such perceptions in fact regress to the position that contemporary feminism has been criticizing, which discerns gender differences as fixed or static (Randall 1987, 28–35). Moreover, conceptions of a woman's culture are based on assumptions of a common, universal women's experience, overlooking the diversity among the experiences of women (hooks 1984; Lorde 1984; Anzaldua 1990). To the extent that it ignores differences based on race, ethnicity, class, and religion, the woman-centered perspective is problematic. Grimshaw (1986, 224) concedes that "the life experiences and activities of women, centered as they have tended to be, more than those of men, around the 'microcosm' of household, family and the physical and emotional care of others, may provide space more easily than those of men for questioning some dominant social priorities." However, she rejects conceptions of a "woman's culture" or "female ethic." Such conceptualization, she correctly argues, erroneously assumes a consensus among women, a different mode of reasoning (rather than different concerns) for women, and obscures ways in which notions of caring have been used oppressively (Grimshaw 1986, 187–226).

For Ugandan women parliamentarians, the dual concerns for "women's interests" and "modernization" programs clearly reflect their struggle against gender oppression within the wider struggle against underdevelopment. Their experiences and material existence within the sociopolitical setup of Ugandan society have a direct bearing on their legislative activity. The general trends and directions of women's legislative work accord increasing legitimacy to women's issues and perspectives at the highest policymaking institution in the nation. And by doing so, they begin poking holes, albeit tiny ones, in the patriarchal institutions of the state.

Notes

1. See, for example, Kirkpatrick (1974), Mezey (1978), Johnson and Carroll (1978), Thomas and Welch (1991).

2. Due to years of civil war, anarchy, and looting in Uganda, several copies of the Official Hansard were missing from the various libraries that I visited.

3. In some rare cases, with the permission of the Speaker, members may read their speeches to the House.

4. Some exceptions require a secret ballot, for example, a bill seeking to amend any provision of the constitution and the election or removal of a person holding office under the constitution.

5. The list of "pet" topics for male MPs is generally similar to that of female MPs, with the notable addition of national security.

6. Studies elsewhere also found women legislators to be more verbally supportive of women's issues than men. This was true in the United States (Johnson and Carroll 1978; Diamond 1977; Carroll 1984), Norway (Bystydzienski 1992), the United Kingdom (Norris and Lovenduski 1995), Australia (Considine and Deutchman 1994), and India (Prabhavathi 1991; Chopra 1993).

7. Pumla Kisosonkole, Official Hansard, August 8, 1957, 74.

8. Barbara Saben, Official Hansard, October 4, 1957, 232.

9. Florence Lubega, Official Hansard, March 10, 1965, 1331–1334.

10. Ida Bikorwenda, Official Hansard, January 30, 1997, 1, 235.

11. Victoria Mwaka, Official Hansard, August 13, 1996, 294.

12. Betty Akech Okullu, Official Hansard, August 14, 1996, 331.

13. "Gender and Politics in Africa: Reflections from Uganda," paper presented at a roundtable discussion held at Dartmouth College, January 27, 1997.

14. It is difficult to gauge emotions from reading the Hansards. However, I noted this pattern during my field observations of the proceedings both in the main chamber and in the committees.

15. See UNDP, *Uganda Human Development Report* (Kampala: UNDP, 1997), 6, where it is reported: "While the country continues to register modest improvement in human development, globally it remains among the countries with the poorest human development indices. In 1994 Uganda's HDI score fell below the average for sub-Saharan Africa (0.38) and most striking is the fact that it also fell below the average for the "least developed countries in the world."

16. Official Hansard, August 7, 1996, 244.

17. The fact that participation of most pioneer female legislators was legitimized by their affiliation to their political husbands or fathers was also found to be true in studies conducted in the United States (Kirkpatrick 1974; Gertzog 1979), New Zealand (Baysting et al. 1993), Australia (Sawer and Simms 1984), and Canada and the United Kingdom (Kohn 1980).

18. Official Hansard, January 27, 1966, 795.

19. The reasons advanced here were similar to the ones I outlined in Chapter 4 on this very issue.

20. Official Hansard, August 7, 1996, 219.

21. Official Hansard, July 2, 1969, 237.

22. Official Hansard, January 16, 1958, 132.

23. Gender budgeting refers to an examination of one of the most important policy instruments of government—the national budget—to analyze how it addresses the needs of different groups of women and men with the aim of making it gender sensitive. Australia and South Africa are the only two countries so far that have experimented with the gender-budgeting initiative.

24. WID policies that are supported by international financial agencies simply seek to pursue the modernization paradigm across the gender divide (see Oloka-Onyango and Tamale 1995). For this reason, many feminists in Third World countries are increasingly demanding more comprehensive gender and development (GAD) policies.

7

Into the Trenches: Women Legislators and Their Constituents

On a warm October morning in 1997 President Museveni's convoy was trapped in a heavy traffic jam on a Kampala road. Thousands of rally fans had thronged to a motor rally, bringing traffic to a standstill. For ten minutes, the *wanainchi* engaged in mild banter with the president, who sat back waving and smiling. *"Ssebo otufuze bulungi naye obwavu bututta,"* they yelled, "Sir, you have ruled us well but we are dying of abject poverty" (*Sunday Monitor*, October 12, 1997). Communications of this kind from *wanainchi* to the head of state reflected the overall sentiment of the majority of Ugandans at the time when this study was undertaken. The same sentiment was continuously repeated in the constituency in which I followed a female parliamentarian interacting with her constituents. Most constituents were demanding that the relative political stability be translated into economic prosperity at the micro level. This demand poses the primary challenge for most members of parliament as they interact with *wanainchi* in their local areas. The demand invariably transcends gender lines, but the manner of its articulation illustrates the different ways in which women legislators are approached by their constituents.

In this chapter I closely examine the personal experiences of one member of parliament in her local constituency. The case of Winnie Byanyima provides a glimpse of a Ugandan woman MP in action outside the National Assembly. The constituency visit took place a few days before the start of local governments election in early November 1997 and was conducted in the western town of Mbarara, a three-hour car journey from Kampala. For four days I observed Byanyima—the parliamentary representative of Mbarara municipality—interact with a wide range of her constituents. The experiences related here may not necessarily reflect those of the majority of female legislators for a number of reasons. For example, Byanyima's constituency is relatively small because she does not hold an affirmative action seat representing a whole district. Furthermore, the unique intricacies of local politics pertaining to each constituency, coupled with the personal political style and approach of individual representatives, invariably influence the "trench experiences" of every female representative. Therefore, this chapter is only intended to give readers some idea of how gender, politics, and other social dynamics interact in determining the decisions, trends, and politicking of female MPs when they are out in the field of their local constituencies. Finally I draw some general distinctions between the constituency activities of district affirmative action women representatives and those of county female MPs like Byanyima. In sum, I attempt in this chapter to clarify the operative "social nuts" and "political bolts" exercised by Ugandan women politicians on the ground. In order to put Byanyima's trench experiences into perspective, I begin with a brief description of her background and the constituency she represents.

Background

Honorable Winnie Byanyima can talk to anyone, anywhere, at any time about any topic with an amazing display of intelligence.

—Foreign diplomat accredited to Uganda

Winnie Karagwa Byanyima was born in 1959 in a place called Ruti, about three miles from Mbarara town. She is the second born in a family of four daughters and three sons. When Winnie was two years old, her father, Boniface Byanyima, was elected to the new Ugandan parliament and served as a Democratic Party representative for northeastern Ankole from 1961 to 1971. Byanyima thus grew up in a political family, a fact that greatly influenced her life.

When I was growing up, the job I respected most was that of an MP, seeing my father serving people. . . . I always used to pick up the *Uganda Argus*, following every little thing about either my father or his colleagues who were from the Democratic Party who would come to our home. Then I'd also read what [President] Obote had said because my father was always criticizing Obote. So I was always reading politics, and by the time I was in primary seven I was reading the Hansards and I knew the rules of the House—you know, someone rising on a point of order or information and the speaker's ruling. . . . When I went to senior one I went to a boarding school and I didn't like it because I was missing many things that I enjoyed with my father, like sharing his politics with him. In the second term I smuggled some Hansards in my suitcase and I was reading them at night and the nuns caught me and asked me never to bring them back.

Byanyima's mother is a teacher by profession who gave up her teaching when her husband joined politics to stay home with their children. She is a very enterprising and capable woman who hardly ever depended on her husband's income. Having grown up in a convent, she is also deeply religious. She encouraged her children to read about the lives of saints in books such as Thomas à Kempis's *The Imitation of Christ,* St. Augustine's *Confessions, Mary: Mother of Faith*, and *A Grain of Wheat: The Story of St. Bernadette of Lourdes.* Perhaps it is this side of Winnie Byanyima's life that explains her pro-life stance in the controversial abortion debate, her ardently feminist views notwithstanding. Winnie's childhood upbringing clearly influenced her present political career; from Tolstoy novels to Leslie Stemp's *Speeches and Toasts: How to Make and Propose Them,* Winnie culled and cultured an interest in politics from a tender age.

Byanyima's parents were part of the Ugandan educated elite, although the family home in Ruti did not enjoy typical urban amenities like running water and electric power until the 1980s. Byanyima used to walk approximately two miles to her primary school in Mbarara, fetch water from a nearby river, and do her homework under the light of a kerosene lamp. For her ordinary-level secondary education she left home for a reputable girls' Catholic boarding school and later transferred to a Protestant coeducational boarding school. In 1979 Byanyima obtained a scholarship to study aeronautical engineering at Manchester University in England. She also holds a master's degree in mechanical engineering from the Cranfield Institute of Technology. As a student at Manchester University, Byanyima was actively involved in student politics.

> I became a very, very left-wing young student. I joined the Socialist Workers' Party, read all the texts—the *Communist Manifesto,* Engels, Marx. I also got involved in the exile groups fighting Amin. Soon after Amin left power, many groups emerged vying for power in Uganda. There was the Kanyeihamba group which I joined. Then we opened a DP branch in London and I was on the executive as assistant publicity secretary. So by the time I was in university I was active in exile politics. When the 1980 elections came, I was an activist in the DP campaigning for many candidates across the country even up to Arua. Museveni and others had tried to get me to join UPM [Uganda Patriotic Movement] but I said, "No you don't have a chance of winning; all of you should join DP." They wouldn't of course but I promised them that if the votes were rigged and Semwogerere [the DP leader] didn't go to the bush and they go, I'd join them.

Museveni's guerrilla bush war was launched in February 1981. Three months later he contacted Byanyima in England, reminding her of her promise to join them in the struggle. She was recruited immediately but asked to work clandestinely within Uganda. Thus Byanyima returned to Uganda in 1981 and took up a job as a flight engineer for Uganda Airlines. She worked at the corporation until it became too risky in 1984.[1] She "defected" to the bush and joined the National Resistance Army (NRA) guerrilla forces. While in the bush, Byanyima did not engage in direct combat but served as an administrator and a courier for the NRA high command.[2] Her employment record also includes serving as the chief Ugandan diplomat to UNESCO in Paris from 1988 to 1993. She resigned from that job to return to Uganda and run for the Mbarara municipality Constituent Assembly (CA) seat in 1994. Two years later, she won the same seat in the parliamentary elections. In addition to her parliamentary work Byanyima has been the president of Forum for Women in Democracy (FOWODE) since its inception in 1995. She has no children and has never been married.[3]

Byanyima has a gentle but firm voice and she speaks very deliberately, as if to ensure that her listeners do not miss a word of what she has to say. Her demeanor is complemented by her six-foot frame. When she joined active national politics, she never felt a need to stand on the affirmative action ticket because, in her words,

> I had been involved in politics for much longer than all the males who wanted to stand in my constituency despite the fact that one of them was a cabinet minister. I had over the years acquired political skills, I had capacity to organize, and to convincingly speak in public. I had picked these up over the years being in politics and I could see that I was better than most men. So there was no need for me to go for this seat which is supposed to enable a woman who is beginning in politics. I was not a beginner so I went straight for the direct seat and I hoped that by taking it I would be adding to the number of women participating in the process.

Mbarara municipality consists of three divisions (equivalent to subcounties), which in turn have six subdivisions called wards (equivalent to parishes). Together the six wards carry a total of fifty-one cells (equivalent to villages). The municipality includes about 45,000 people, most of whom are petty traders and lower-class workers. About a third of her constituents own land in the municipality and engage in subsistence farming. The community of Mbarara municipality is extremely cosmopolitan and consists of people from all over Uganda. I heard many constituents speaking Luganda, Rutooro, Rukiga, and even Itesot, in addition to the native Runyankore language.

In addition to fighting for women's rights, Winnie battles corruption in the public sector. Her struggle for clean government has brought her into sharp conflict with many government officials, including municipal council officials. Byanyima waged a big struggle against the corruption of the mayor and his team; finally an independent commission of inquiry found them guilty of practicing graft.[4]

For God and Her Country

When Byanyima and I arrived at Byanyima's Mbarara residence cum office at around 9:30 P.M. on October 31, 1997, a coordinators' meeting was already under way. The rented house that serves as Byanyima's residence and office in Mbarara town is small and nondescript. With an orange-tiled roof and whitewashed walls, the dwelling contains a living-room/dining area, a study, two bedrooms, a kitchen, and a bathroom. It is furnished modestly with only the basics that Byanyima needs during her regular bimonthly weekend visits to the constituency. She employs two full-time staff members, a housekeeper, and an office manager.

Approximately twenty people sat in the sitting/dining area, strategizing on how to root out corrupt municipal council members and replace them with untainted people in the impending local government elections. These people form the pinnacle of Byanyima's campaign network, which goes under the name Unity. Byanyima took over the chair and the meeting proceeded until 1:00 A.M. The meeting introduced me to a strange new political language. For instance, Unity members were speaking of "going for a lineup," which I subsequently learned refers to lobbying for and preparing a list of candidates you support; "going for *kakuyege*," on the other hand, means door-to-door campaigning for your candidates;[5] "*Kankwite*" is the local lingo defining a secret political meeting of core or trusted supporters to discuss sensitive matters.

The organization of the Unity network, which has been in place since the 1994 CA elections, is very structured and elaborate. At the apex of the Unity team is member of parliament Byanyima. Six male coordinators from each of the wards constitute the next level in the hierarchy and work very closely with Byanyima. She explained that all six ward coordinators are male by design because of the practical fact that men find it easier to stay out of their homes late than women do. It would, for example, be more difficult for female coordinators to regularly leave their home responsibilities to attend late-night political meetings.

Under the ward coordinators are village coordinators, one from each of the fifty-one cells or villages. Each village coordinator has a team of about thirty grassroots mobilizers who comb the village canvassing support and acting as Unity's feelers for *wanainchi* concerns and grievances. Many village coordinators and mobilizers are women. The Unity network is most active during election time or when the MP has a program in the area. Some of the more diligent coordinators hold regular bimonthly meetings with their mobilizers throughout the year. Given the fact that Unity team members work exclusively on a voluntary basis, I wondered where they got all the inspiration; what is in it for them? Byanyima explained that she encourages all her coordinators and mobilizers to pursue their own political ambitions, the ultimate formula being "support me and if I win I will in turn support you." Indeed, the entire Unity team of coordinators and mobilizers were aspiring for local council seats at various levels; they hoped to utilize Byanyima's political capital as a platform to win their own seats. Byanyima attributes her organizational skills, exhibited by the efficiency of the Unity network, to her reading of texts on revolutions coupled with her practical experience in the NRA guerrilla war. Very few other members of parliament can boast of such an elaborate and active working group in their constituencies.

Day two of our stay was a Saturday with a full schedule for the MP. It started with a visit to a slum area of the town called Biafra. Byanyima was recognized by everyone as we drove through the dusty rows of semipermanent buildings. Half-naked children chanted, "Winnie, Winnie, our woman, Winnie!" She greeted and waved to *wanainchi* everywhere we went. Byanyima sought out a woman called Madrin who is very influential in this particular slum because she is the biggest landlady in the area. Madrin is a trained nurse in her sixties who inherited a lot of land from her father. She owns most of the semipermanent buildings and shops in Biafra. Like many of the slum residents, Madrin has succumbed to alcoholism. But because of the power she holds in the area, she commands a lot of veneration and fear from her tenants. It therefore made good sense for a politician such as Byanyima to deploy someone like Madrin to gain the support of the hundreds who occupied the slum valley.

Luckily for Byanyima, Madrin was sober when we found her at nine o'clock in the morning. She was busy mobilizing slum dwellers to clean up and dig a pit latrine. A few men and women were sweeping the dirt compound, some were cooking in soot-blackened pots, others were drinking a local brew in a nearby hut. One man clad in an army uniform with a gun slung over his shoulder emerged from the hut and staggered to the small bench where Byanyima was sitting, only to demand some money from his parliamentary representative. In a stern voice, Byanyima advised him never to drink with his gun, as it poses a risk to others. Several other people who appeared intoxicated requested Byanyima for money, but she told them that she had no money for alcohol. However, she peeled a few thousand-shilling notes (equivalent to US$1) from a wad of money and gave it to a disabled woman and some fly-covered children.[6] She informed the crippled woman about the newly constituted affirmative action seats for people with disabilities at all the local council levels and advised her to actively participate in electing a representative. Finally, Byanyima managed to engage Madrin in a private conversation and briefed her on the politics of the upcoming local government elections. The latter promised to work with the Unity group in amassing support for their candidates.

Our next stop was at the Mbarara municipal council hall, where a council meeting was scheduled for 11:00 A.M. The sole item on the agenda was a discussion of the launching of a road repair project to cover 3.8 kilometers of municipal roads. On the way to the council hall Byanyima's car was waved down by a group of rowdy construction workers working on a new building in town. Byanyima asked the driver to stop and we climbed up a steep, muddy embankment to get to where the sweat-drenched men were working. They did not have anything specific that they wanted to discuss with their MP but simply wanted Byanyima to pay them political homage by stopping for a chat. She took the opportunity to inform them about the road repair project that was going to begin. When we left them twenty minutes later, the construction workers seemed happy to have secured her audience.

The council meeting set off with all of us singing the national anthem followed by self-introductions by the fifty-three people in attendance. Seated at the high table were the mayor, the town clerk, Ministry of Local Government engineers, and Byanyima. It was attended by local councilors at the level of LC III and above. The central ministry of local government had put up 200 million in Uganda shillings and the municipal council, another 50 million toward this project. This money was only enough to reseal 3.8 kilometers of tarmac roads. The meeting had to decide, among other things, which priority the roads were. Mindful of the corrupt track record of the local councilors, Byanyima did not mince her words at this meeting:

> My eyes are wide open regarding this project. I'm hiring extra eyes, extra ears to make sure that no one diverts money from this project. We have a graft cancer in our municipality, but we in parliament are extremely serious on how each shilling we budget for is utilized; I want to see transparency in procurement and employment. And during this campaign period please don't make political capital out of the road project by borrowing the road equipment to work on small roads in your areas.

Byanyima was boldly lecturing to the mayor and his team as they shifted uncomfortably in their seats. She went on to condemn the council for not making arrangements to find alternative premises for women selling second-hand clothes along the roads that were going to be repaved. "It is a contradiction when we're elected to work in the interest of the people but harm them in the process." One of the council executives responded by remarking that it would be too expensive for the council to find temporary premises for second-hand clothes traders, a comment that played directly into Byanyima's hands.

The plight of second-hand clothes traders, 90 percent of whom are women, had a long history in Mbarara municipality. During the 1980s a piece of land had been demarcated in downtown Mbarara specifically for constructing market stalls for these women traders. However, when the market was completed, the corrupt council allocated the stalls to other traders and ordered the women to sell their merchandise from a dirty back-street space. The women defied the council order and, left with no choice, resolved to conduct their business from the downtown street pavements. It was a very uncertain and precarious way of conducting business, since they were vulnerable to the vagaries of the weather and the whims of the tax collectors. These women traders had sought the intervention of Byanyima as soon as she joined the municipality politics, and their plight has been one of the persisting issues on her constituency agenda.

Fired by the council's lackluster attitude, Byanyima decided to personally call on the second-hand clothes traders and forewarn them about the impending road project. She advised them to look for alternative premises for their business during the three-month period. As we walked along Mbaguta street by the old taxi park, Byanyima addressed about one hundred women who traded in second-hand clothes. We were led by a woman called Madina, who was one of the local Unity team mobilizers. Ever the politician, Byanyima took the opportunity to campaign against the incumbent council by stressing that council members did not care about the traders' welfare. She impressed upon the traders the need to sweep the council clean in the upcoming local council elections and put in place a council that would address the women's pressing problem. Byanyima explained that the mayor and his team had not obtained the money to repair roads in Mbarara town, as *wanainchi* had been told. Rather, the money had been obtained through her sweat in parliament; she had convinced the ministry to include Mbarara among the four towns selected nationwide for road repairs.

Byanyima was dressed in an elegant outfit of the style worn by West African women, headgear and all. Her eyes were protected from the harsh afternoon glare by a pair of expensive designer sunglasses. Clearly Byanyima took no pains to try to blend in with the majority of her constituents. This had both a positive and a negative effect on *wanainchi*. On the plus side it created the sense of a distinct and special figure, a true leader of the people. However, by the same token, those distinguishing factors served as constant reminders to *wanainchi* of the status gap between them and their leaders, as well as the hopeless economic position they occupy in society. This conflict was clearly reflected in the manner in which the traders received her. Although most of them were very attentive and greeted Byanyima respectfully, there were some disgruntled voices among the audience. One woman, for example, kept interrupting the meeting with angry comments such as, "Winnie, what do you want with us? I gave you my vote twice but what have you done for me personally? The only time we see you is when you're begging for votes." I noted that one woman standing near this audacious woman kept nudging her to stop. Several others also did their best to protect Byanyima from the barrage of contemptuous remarks that emanated from two male supporters of the incumbent mayor who tried to disrupt the meeting. Byanyima kept her cool and tried to reason with the disgruntled woman by enumerating the things she had done for the municipality and pointing out how difficult it was for her to attend to all her parliamentary duties in Kampala and pay personal calls to all her constituents at the same time.

Byanyima was scheduled to address a public rally at the Catholic social center at 5:00 P.M., so we proceeded to the center from Mbaguta Street. The large hall was filled to capacity by the time we got there, the majority in the audience consisting of young men and relatively few women (because of their home responsibilities, perhaps?). On such occasions Byanyima personally foots bills such as renting the room and hiring the public address system she used to address the gathering. All expenses incurred during MPs' visits to their constituencies are supposed to come out of a monthly allowance of approximately Ug.shs. 2.4 million. For forty-five minutes, Byanyima educated the crowd on how the upcoming elections were to be conducted, briefing them on the legal requirements thereof. She also told them about the road repair project. Thereafter she allowed for a question/answer session lasting until 7:00 P.M. Although initially puzzled, I finally understood why Byanyima left more time for the question/answer session. It is during such sessions that she expounds upon her favorite topics. Thus a question might be posed about the poor plantain harvests. In response, Byanyima addresses the question and then goes on to cover a wide range of topics close to her political agenda.

From the Catholic social center we proceeded to the final task of the day. At approximately 8:00 P.M., we drove to another slum area of Mbarara and walked about fifty meters through a banana plantation to the home of Hajj Kasumari and his wife, Janet. Close to 150 men and women waited patiently for Byanyima to address them, and more people kept trickling in. They gathered in a small compound that stood between two rows of mud and wattle houses, each row divided into five one-roomed rental homes. There were a couple of benches reserved for the guests, but most of the people present either sat on the grass or remained standing. Apart from the moonlight, the only other source of light in the compound were two dim bulbs hanging from either corner of the parallel dwellings. It was a chilly night and most people were wrapped in jackets and sweaters. The general ambience was homely and jovial.

Byanyima was warmly welcomed and she greeted everyone present, many by their first names. Janet led her into a room in which her husband lay indisposed with a fractured leg. Fifteen minutes later they emerged from the room and Byanyima started addressing the gathering. She introduced me to the people as a friend and researcher who had traveled all the way from Kampala to see "the great people of Mbarara." Byanyima talked about the road project, the upcoming local council elections, and the general welfare of the constituency. Again she allowed for more time to answer *wanainchi*'s questions. The variety of questions posed by *wanainchi* indicated that their primary concern was personal economic survival. For example, there was one primary teacher who wanted Byanyima to help him and others in his category to secure the equivalent of six months' worth of salary arrears from the district education office. Another asked her to bring *entandikwa* (small government loans) to the people of Mbarara. As we were leaving, one woman gave me a letter to deliver to Byanyima in which she requested a loan of Ug.shs. 300,000 to set up a small business.

Again there were a few bold people who openly accused Byanyima of neglecting her people and only returning to them at election time. With a lot of patience, she belabored to explain that her work in parliament does not permit her to visit even her own parents. She had opened an office in Mbarara so that *wanainchi* could take their grievances and concerns to the office manager. Through the same manager they could schedule appointments to see her when she came on her regular visits to the constituency. Byanyima challenged *wanainchi* to make use of the facility. She also reminded them of the credit scheme that she had introduced in Mbarara town, which was designed to assist in alleviating their poverty. In 1996 Byanyima persuaded a U.S.-registered credit organization known as Pride Africa to open a branch in Mbarara town wherein *wanainchi* could receive collateral-free loans with minimal interest.

A bottle of soda was supplied to everyone present at the meeting. Apparently this was routine practice at such meetings and the people expect it, so it is part of her regular budgeting during her constituency visits. It serves both as an incentive for *wanainchi* to turn up and as a gesture of gratitude to them on the politician's part. At the end of the meeting several women approached me for a chat. The conversation ranged over a number of topics. One woman told me how proud they were that their

MP had honorable friends such as I back in Kampala and how proud they were that women were beginning to shine in Ugandan society. By the time we left the Kasumari homestead at 10:00 P.M., I was exhausted from the long day's events. Byanyima, however, seemed to have an inexhaustible source of energy. She continued to consult with some Unity coordinators when we returned to her home-office. In addition, the telephone never stopped ringing. Even when I dozed off sometime after 1:00 A.M. she was talking politics to one of her coordinators.

Sunday morning greeted us with an incessant drizzle that had been pattering for the better part of the night. I woke up early to peruse the pile of work files that were stacked on a table in Byanyima's study room. There were eleven in all, each neatly marked: New Mail, Minutes, Projects Support File, Education-General, Education Sponsorships, Employment, Letters and Documents, Land Issues, Women's Councils, Expenses-General, and Invitations and Miscellaneous. The list reflects the range of constituency issues that Byanyima regularly deals with. For example, the thick education sponsorship file is filled with desperate letters written by young boys and girls whose parents either have died or can no longer afford to pay their school fees. As a last resort they turn to their MP for financial assistance. Similarly, the employment file is full of letters from unemployed constituents to Byanyima requesting her to use her good office to secure jobs for them. The bulk of letters in her letters and documents file also constitute *wanainchi*'s requests for financial assistance.

How does Byanyima deal with the thousands of cases that reach her desk seeking different kinds of assistance?

> I identify desperate cases; I keep a list and categorize them. If it is a request for a loan, I direct them to this group which I brought—Pride Africa—which gives them loans. So with such people I don't have to do much. I try to help people seeking employment by writing letters of recommendation and things like that. . . . Regarding school fees, I do what I can. Right now I am paying fees for seven orphans, but I just can't afford to meet all those requests. Thank God for the universal primary education program which government introduced recently, but you'll find secondary school, even university students requesting for assistance. I have to turn most of them away; it's a big problem.

This underscores the point earlier observed that *wanainchi* do not care much for wider political issues apart from those that directly concern bread-and-butter issues and their day-to-day survival.

Land is another problem that dominates much of Byanyima's time in the constituency. Even as I studied the work files that wet Sunday morning, *wanainchi* started streaming in to see their MP. Three elderly women in their sixties and seventies arrived before nine o'clock and sat waiting to see Byanyima. One of them clutched a tattered file folder that held evidential correspondence and documents proving her title to a piece of land under dispute. She was a victim of a 1960s government policy that had declared most of the land around the municipality the property of Mbarara municipality. This policy automatically reverted *wanainchi's* freeholds (*bibanja*) into urban leaseholds owned by the council. In many cases the municipal council leased people's land to so-called developers, forcing *bibinja* holders, such as this old woman, off the land for a minimum compensation. As Byanyima explained,

> What happened was that all these people, mostly old people who can't read English or write who had their *bibanjas* . . . their land was being targeted by a corrupt council. They were not going according to the plan as long as you wanted to build a house or even to speculate on land they would give you the land and give you a lease that you must develop it in two years. And then people who were there would suddenly find themselves being fenced in and being told that council has given the land to me. The person may not even develop it but sell it for a couple of million to another person, having got it for free from the council. This is what is happening and these poor people find themselves homeless.

The old woman could not afford to hire an attorney, and Byanyima was her only hope. The council had leased her piece of land to a businesswoman who had constructed a school on it without paying her any form of compensation. She wanted Byanyima to intervene and protect her rights. The MP acted by writing to the council and requesting it to furnish her with copies of the record documents that transferred ownership to the school owner. She also arranged for a meeting with the businesswoman with whom she hoped to reach an amicable solution.

We had to leave for the cathedral in time for the eleven o'clock service. By that time Byanyima had not seen even half of the constituents who waited to see her. She promised to deal with them after church. Byanyima had invited another male MP from a nearby constituency in the district to be her guest at the church service, and we set off with him following closely behind. The cathedral sits magnificently on top of a small hill, and when we arrived it was packed with worshipers. I expected to see ushers scurrying around the MP to lead her and her guests to some special seats, as is often done in Protestant churches I have visited. But no one seemed to take particular notice of Byanyima. She simply asked us to follow her to the front platform, and we settled ourselves on an extra bench near the pulpit. Byanyima later commented on this:

I find it quite disturbing when I go to church and no one pays any attention. I think that I've got a lot more ego than I had before joining politics. Before I joined politics if there was no seat, I didn't make a big deal out of it; I would stand through the service. But now if within five minutes I haven't been offered a seat I feel quite offended [laughs]. I think when you join politics you tend to become more egoistic, you want to be heard more than you want to listen. You literally have to hurt yourself to listen to people!

Apparently the Catholic church in Mbarara takes separation of the state from the church literally. Byanyima's whispered request into the ear of the church catechist to allow her say a few words and introduce her visitors after the sermon was brazenly ignored.

After the service, Byanyima spent almost thirty minutes greeting and talking to constituents. *Wanainchi* took advantage and approached her here in the church yard; one by one they consulted and aired their grievances. She listened patiently and counseled cheerfully. To her utter surprise, one woman asked Byanyima, "How's your baby?" It is public knowledge that Byanyima has never borne a child, so she politely told the woman that she has no baby. In an embarrassed voice, the woman uttered some apology and added that someone had told her that she (Byanyima) had delivered a baby. This was not the first time the issue of children had come up since we got to Mbarara. In the thrift market the day before, a dealer in second-hand clothes had asked Byanyima when she hoped "to start a family." Somehow, a childless woman is not perceived as whole in most Ugandan cultures. It was as if Byanyima's female supporters were asking her to round off all her achievements by conceiving a child.

Sunday afternoon, a victory party was organized for Byanyima in Ruti ward. It was the last of the six wards to formally congratulate her on winning the municipality parliamentary seat in July 1996. The celebrations were held at Ruti rehabilitation center for the disabled, whose director was a female councilor in the municipality—one of the few councilors who supported Byanyima. We arrived at the center at 4:30 P.M. and found a big crowd of about 1,000 supporters waiting for Byanyima. A large papyrus shed adorned with colorful mats and balloons had been constructed for the occasion. In front of the high table, on a carton draped in Byanyima's campaign posters, sat a big cake. Crates of soda and a variety of eats were served, and women's groups sang and danced in praise of Byanyima. At one point Byanyima herself stood up and joined in the traditional dancing. *Wanainchi* cheered and clapped. The highlight of the entertainment, however, was the *kyevugo*—a special poem composed for important occasions. Traditionally, among the Banyankore, *okwevuga* (recital of the special poem) is reserved for talented men who repeatedly recite lengthy verses in a single breath, at the end of which the audience responds "ehh" in agreement. In more recent times, with women's increased empowerment and their greater visibility in positions of power, a few women have started conducting *okwevuga*. The woman who recited the *kyevugo* on this occasion worked the audience into a frenzy as she excitedly wiggled around in praise of Byanyima and her mother. "*Yamweta Karagwa ati, 'nakuraga Mbarara.'*" "She named her daughter Karagwa [the inheritor] and said, 'you will inherit Mbarara.'" The audience all responded in loud unison, "Ehh."

The carousing was punctuated with several speeches by local council officials, Unity team coordinators, and other local dignitaries present. The Unity candidate for mayor was one of those who addressed the crowd.[7] Although women were more intimately involved in the overall organization of the party, men stole the show by dominating the limelight at the microphone, delivering speeches and taking most of the credit. Byanyima later confirmed my suspicion, remarking that women generally had a greater spirit of voluntarism than men but always tended to remain in the shadows on occasions such as this one. Such behavior doubtlessly stems from a deeply engrained social upbringing that encourages women to work and remain in the "private" sphere and men to embrace the "public" domain.

In her speech, Byanyima summarized the political achievements she had attained so far for her constituency. She talked about the credit organization, a branch of Pride Africa; her role in moving a constitutional amendment to end urban leases; and her role in securing Ug.shs. 250 million for repairing the municipality roads. Furthermore she addressed *wanainchi* on the issue of women's representation on the local councils:

> We gave you women an opportunity to have one third of the local council seats. We fought for it in the CA and now it is in the constitution. It's not for nothing . . . not for you to become powerful and be bosses. But it's so that you can defend the interests of women. You see before this, when a woman was battered and left outside, she'd go to an LC I or an LC II court and face eight men and one woman. She'd put her case and her judgment would be made from a male perspective, by men who are probably themselves batterers and believe in it. And the one woman would be overpowered and overruled. So we've given you numbers so that you can use them to defend such a right for women. This is a good thing for the men too because when a woman joins the council she becomes a leader and she learns many new things, broadens her horizons and she can solve many problems in the home. So you'll have a real partner rather than a dependent.

In order not to antagonize her male constituents unnecessarily, Byanyima always rationalized women's rights in terms of benefiting both men and women. By turning gender issues inside out to show the advantages men can reap from respecting women's rights, she makes them more palatable to her sexist male constituency.

On the final day of our stay in Mbarara, Byanyima rose early to pay a visit to her elderly parents in Ruti before the usual stream of constituents started arriving at her office for consultations. Her parents' home is a huge old mansion standing in the middle of a banana plantation. Only her father was home when we arrived. The old Byanyima had a touch of malaria but nevertheless welcomed us very warmly. He graced me with a tour of his rich but dusty library as Winnie reminisced about the books she enjoyed reading as a child. The old man, who is the current national chairman of the Democratic Party, would give anything to have his daughter join the party. It was obvious how close father and daughter were, and he spoke about her with a spark in his wan eyes: "I'm very proud of my daughter because she's extending what I did in parliament thirty-five years ago; in parliament I fought government corruption and that's what she's doing, only that she's operating under a different name [NRM: National Resistance Movement]." Indeed, Byanyima's trench stories would not be complete without an exploration of her crusade against corruption.

Byanyima: Anticorruption Crusader

In addition to work as a gender advocate, Byanyima fights government corruption. Her struggle reaches from her local municipality trenches into the national arena as she attacks and challenges cabinet ministers and senior civil servants. It is no accident that Byanyima is the vice chairperson of the parliamentary public accounts committee (PAC). As expected, Byanyima's struggles come with a heavy political and personal cost. To take on and threaten political heavyweights who have a lot of ill-gotten wealth at their disposal is not only bold but also very risky business. For example, they can easily buy and manipulate media space for countercampaign purposes. Counterattacks, innuendo, and malicious aspersions have been leveled not only against Byanyima but also against her family members and close friends in order to question Byanyima's credibility as an anticorruption crusader. Interestingly, as the example below illustrates, many of the counterattacks are clothed in gender terms.

In October 1997 accusations that connected the minister of state in charge of primary education, Brigadier Jim Muhwezi, to a dubious real estate contract were exposed in the national parliament. The contract involved a rental deal between the Ministry of Finance and a company called Meera Investments. The Ministry of Finance took out a twenty-year lease on a building owned by Meera at an exorbitant monthly rate of

Ug.shs. 50 million, payable two years in advance. Apparently, it would have made much more economic sense for the ministry to construct its own building instead of taking on such an expensive lease. A statement was read in parliament by MP Nobert Mao showing how Brigadier Muhwezi held indirect business interests in Meera Investments, whose registered proprietors were a Ugandan Asian businessman, Sudhir Ruparelia, and his wife. Although not a direct shareholder of Meera, Muhwezi was a major shareholder in another banking business, Crane Bank, the major partners in which were Ruparelia and Meera Investments. Interestingly, in 1990, as head of the main government intelligence agency, the Internal Security Organization (ISO), Muhwezi had arrested and prosecuted Ruparelia on charges of smuggling foreign currency out of the country. Muhwezi was therefore accused of having used his public office to influence the rental contract.

Although a parliamentary committee subsequently exonerated Muhwezi from the accusation that he was party to the multimillion rental deal, his credibility in the public eye has remained questionable for a number of reasons. For instance, it was also disclosed that the plush official residence of the commissioner-general of Uganda Revenue Authority was being rented from Muhwezi at a monthly cost of Ug.shs. 3.5 million. He was paid a year's rent in advance when Uganda Revenue Authority was aware that the job contract of the expatriate commissioner-general was expiring in three months and therefore the house would fall vacant within three months. Furthermore, the parliamentary committee that exonerated him exposed the fact that Muhwezi had used his office as chief of intelligence to influence the Central Bank to register Crane Bank in 1991.[8]

Over a third of parliamentarians signed a petition seeking to move a resolution to pass a vote of censure against Muhwezi. It read in part, "Your petitioners are dissatisfied with the conduct of the Hon. Brig. Jim Muhwezi Katugugu, Minister of State for Primary Education, and intend to move a motion for a resolution of censure in accordance with Article 118 of the constitution." The grounds for censuring the brigadier were based on alleged influence peddling, abuse of office, failure to account for his massive wealth (estimated at Ug.shs. 6 billion), and blackmailing parliament. Byanyima took on the brigadier and raised broader issues concerning his enormous wealth and breaches of the leadership code. On *Capital Gang*, a Saturday talk show[9] (airing on November 15, 1997), she challenged Muhwezi, who had telephoned in earlier:

> People want to know for example where you got 200 million cash to buy shares in Crane Bank, where you got millions and millions to build a mansion which people compare with the Gbadolite one of Mobutu [Seseseko], to

own shares in various companies, to buy lavish mansions in Kololo, in Bugolobi, in Old Kampala . . . How did you acquire your wealth while in a position of power, how did you make it so fast? (*Sunday Vision*, November 16, 1997)

She challenged Muhwezi to publicly declare his assets and how he came by them so as to "put the public to rest." An incensed but constrained Muhwezi responded:

> Honorable Winnie, first of all, what you're saying is your concoction but let us not go for that; we cannot be reduced to so many levels. . . . Can I ask you, what do you have to say about the following? That you claimed over 70 million for a small dilapidated vehicle you purportedly used in clandestine activities for NRM; that you supplied to the army a one shoe size which was a disaster to the army; that you lied to parliament that the chairs you bought for the embassy house when you were in Paris were for the embassy when you have them in your own house; that your sister was in financial problems and you used your influence to convince [the ministry of] defense to buy her old house in Entebbe; where did you get a car you drive as a gift from somewhere?; and is it true that you have been collecting allowances from parliament for attendance even when you have been outside the country?

Byanyima dismissed all the allegations as untrue and promised to publicly declare her assets, since questions had been raised about her propriety. Indeed, four days later, Byanyima made a personal statement before parliament, declaring her personal wealth and armed with official letters, receipts, and other documentary evidence to disprove all the accusations raised by Muhwezi. From her declaration, Byanyima had relatively few worldly assets and concluded her statement with sober words:

> Mr. Speaker, I am not an angel. I too have my faults like anybody else. Parliament's role in controlling corruption is not so much from a moral standpoint. Our main concerns should be the political and economic consequences of corruption. The pastors and mullahs can take care of the moral questions, although all are linked. (Official Hansard, November 20, 1997)

She challenged other leaders to follow her example and promised to table a private member's bill amending the leadership code to make it mandatory for government leaders to declare their wealth publicly together with that of their spouses and children.

Byanyima received many congratulatory calls from colleagues, and several members of the public wrote laudatory letters about her in the press (e.g., *New Vision*, December 3, 1997, 5; *The Monitor*, December 7,

1997, 5). Others, however, interpreted Byanyima's anticorruption crusade in a different light. One perceived her hour-long personal statement as an act of "over-indulgence" and "vanity" (*New Vision*, November 29, 1997, 4). In an exclusive club an agitated cabinet minister asked his colleagues, "What the hell does she think she is? How many testicles does she think she has?"[10] The November 28 editorial of a weekly newsletter, *Uganda Confidential*, portrayed Byanyima as a self-styled anticorruption crusader who was desperate and frustrated because "she is barren, which makes her a despised woman under traditional values." Sexualizing and trivializing Byanyima's politics and principles, the editorial advised Byanyima to quit the populist game and "to settle down, get herself a new man without strings,[11] and lead a normal married life. It is only then that Winnie will be at peace with herself."

Arguments linking a politician's private life and politics are never made in relation to male politicians in Uganda. It seems that (hetero)sexuality validates women's intellect, whereas it does not for men. This takes us back to sexuality and gender difference, which was discussed in Chapter 5. In patriarchal sexual politics, gender (i.e., femininity or masculinity) defines sexuality in such a way that it meshes with women's private and public lives, although it is absolutely irrelevant to men's public lives. Such double standards serve to rationalize gender inequality and domination.

Other critics described Byanyima as a disgruntled "movementist" and a disguised "multipartyist."[12] The movementist versus multipartyist label is invoked whenever a controversial issue is debated on the parliamentary floor. In this case it was absurd to brand the actors because the NRM government itself had pledged to fight government corruption when it was still in the bush.[13] Moreover, both Muhwezi and Byanyima actively participated in the NRA/M guerrilla war and are well-known movementists. Thus to imply that anticorruption campaigners were the same as multipartyists was preposterous. As Byanyima put it, "If the multiparty scarecrow is used successfully to divide and weaken the resolve of parliament to fight corruption, then we can all sit back and wait for the Movement to crumble under its own weight of graft" (*Sunday Monitor*, November 16, 1997, 21). Muhwezi's fate was finally sealed on March 3, 1998. In a hotly debated session, 148 members of parliament voted in favor of censure, with 91 against. The Ugandan parliament made history by becoming the first Commonwealth legislature to pass a motion of censure against a minister (*The East African*, March 9–15, 1998). True to the principle of separation of powers, parliament had held the executive to account.

Byanyima would never be able to win the battle against government graft single-handedly, and the significance of the support she receives from her colleagues in the form of information gathering, lobbying, and petition signatures cannot be underestimated. Indeed, the censure motion against Brigadier Muhwezi was moved by a male MP and seconded by a female county representative, Salaamu Musumba. However, it is Byanyima who constantly assumes the risk of standing on the front lines of the battle to openly challenge government corruption as the rest of her female colleagues render backdoor support. Vice President Specioza Kazibwe, who heads the anticorruption unit in the president's office, occasionally comes out with general public statements on the issue but has not seriously taken on any of her colleagues in cabinet, nor has her office actually done much to bring culprits to book. Indeed, she has diverted attention from the issue by declaring that nobody (including the MPs behind the crusade) is clean.

The limitations of a top-down affirmative action policy have already been discussed in Chapter 4. The majority of affirmative action women parliamentarians feel reluctant to openly take on issues that make government uncomfortable, since they feel that they owe their seats to government. The feeling of patronage toward government is even worse for female cabinet ministers. This is because of the system of patronage that permeates the mechanisms of the affirmative action policy and make women feel beholden for their positions. Female cabinet ministers constitute a minority and are also bound by the principle of collective responsibility. The latter operates in such a way that even individual censures of cabinet members are perceived to be affronts on the cabinet body as a whole. Breaking ranks in such a context would therefore be perceived as a betrayal of the movement that brought them into the fold.

Stepping Out of the Trenches: A Summation

The "trench area" for affirmative action female MPs is much wider than that of ordinary county representatives. This fact is crucial in determining the kind and method of work for the majority of female parliamentarians in their constituencies. First, the phenomenon of double representation (discussed in Chapter 4) means that these women leaders are inclined to organize most of their trench activities in conjunction with the parliamentarian representing the county in which the activity is to take place. Although the reverse is not necessarily true (i.e., county MPs always working in conjunction with women district representatives), it is important for affirmative action MPs to do this in order to avoid alienating their county colleagues by appearing to be more active than they are. In other words, affirmative action MPs have to be careful not to "step on the toes" of county MPs, as the veteran woman MP warned them in the FOWODE induction seminar.[14] This fact, together with the fact that they operate in a much wider area of operation with limited allowance or "facilitation" from government, creates real limitations on the kind of work affirmative action MPs can do.

Under the circumstances, the working programs of most of these MPs tend to focus on the "safer" and "nonthreatening" agenda of dealing with women's community-based organizations and groups and/or children's issues. They tend to deal more with local council women leaders in organizing seminars and workshops for purposes ranging from sensitizing women about primary health care and their legal rights to advising them on how to run a successful pig raising, beekeeping, or rabbit raising project.[15] This in a sense is paradoxical because it is these same women who emphasize that they are merely women representatives of districts and not "women's representatives." The contradictions associated with the affirmative action seat are exemplified in the words of MP Namusoke:

> I think MPs have two levels of operation. We have our legislative role in parliament; in parliament I represent the people of Rakai—men, women, and children. And although my springboard in the assembly is Rakai, the issues we normally tackle there are national issues. Then there is the level of the district itself; there my main concentration is women's issues—development for women and how their projects are progressing. How can we get the district administration to effectively serve women? Of course women are my major priority, but I also take an interest in all the other issues concerning district activities. (Sarah Namusoke, AA)

Other projects that are considered "developmental," such as fund-raising for a new school or constructing new roads in their district, are normally initiated and undertaken by the county MP concerned. In such cases, district women representatives are normally invited to attend the function without necessarily participating actively in the process that leads to it. Member of parliament Joyce Mpanga explained this point quite clearly:

> As soon as you become the district MP, you realize that you have an MP in every county of your district; yours is a kind of water lily, an umbrella of sorts above everybody else. If you don't pick what to do carefully, you may be treading on other MPs' toes. You have to liaise with them sometimes for activities; otherwise you may collide. I chose education because that's my specialty anyway. I chose women, I chose youth and other projects, which I am asked to do. The projects I have done in Mubende are largely educational. I have done fund-raising for primary and secondary schools. Together with ActionAid, we worked out a program and we have trained nine hundred teachers for both Mubende and Kiboga. Then I have also worked

in the area of Safe Motherhood. . . . I look at women in particular and try to
make them come into groups and get them taught because I am a woman,
anyway, I can understand their concerns better.

Furthermore, local constituents relate to women parliamentarians differently than they do to male MPs. By the same token, local constituents
generally perceive affirmative action district women representatives in a
different light than the county representatives, thus lending credence to
the maxim "Separate can never be equal." Affirmative action MP Winnie
Babihuga observed, for example, that whenever she attends any community function in her district at which a male county MP is present, it is the
latter who is officially recognized and called upon to "say a few words to
wanainchi." The county MP will then normally introduce her to the audience as part of his speech. This is despite the fact that all MPs theoretically enjoy equal status and that the male MP presides over the county
that falls within the jurisdiction of the wider district. Here not only are
gender relations at play but also the hierarchical fashion in which
wanainchi perceive the two types of representatives.

As is the case with most other fields, a woman politician has to work
twice as hard and shout twice as loud as her male counterparts in order
to gain credibility and the respect of the public. Winnie Byanyima is a
good case in point here; through her hard work and principled stand in
parliament, she has been honored as Parliamentarian of the Year (*New Vision*, December 27, 1997, 4) and as Woman of the Year (*New Vision*, December 31, 1997, 16). When Byanyima was addressing the construction
workers who waved her vehicle down that November morning, I
watched the men's attentive focus mixed with a touch of fascination as
they listened to their MP. It gave me the feeling that Byanyima had in
many ways surpassed the gender barriers that often result in female
politicians, not being taken seriously.

All parliamentarians understand that they ultimately owe their positions to the *wanainchi.* It was interesting to note that Byanyima's political
schedule did not include a meeting with the more privileged members of
her constituency. She made no effort to consult with or even meet those
people who form the middle class of Mbarara municipality. This fact sig-
nifies the importance of *wanainchi,* who constitute the masses in any constituency. No leader can afford to ignore these people, especially when
their numbers translate into vital votes, as they did at the time of the impending local government elections. Byanyima understood that important as her middle-class constituents were, their numbers were too small
in comparison to the grassroots *wanainchi.* Moreover, middle-class citizens hardly ever turn out for elections, especially local government elections. The strength that *wanainchi* (especially women who constitute the

majority) hold from their sheer numbers is a source of potential power to influence national politics in ways that they cannot imagine. The question then is, What stops them from utilizing this potential? The main problem lies in the political manipulation of a largely uneducated and impoverished electorate. Many of them perceive politicians cynically as a group of distanced elite who use *wanainchi* as stepping stones to attain their own selfish goals. As one senior citizen put it, "I have listened to hundreds of politicians in my lifetime and they all sound the same. . . . At the end of the day really our votes will go to the highest bidder—the one who lines our pockets best."

Notes

1. As the guerrilla war gained momentum, government suspicion of people like Byanyima increased on account of her ethnic origins and previous political activities.

2. Winnie has written about some of her experiences in the bush war; see "Women in Political struggle in Uganda," in Jill Bystydzienski, ed., *Women Transforming Politics: Worldwide Strategies for Empowerment* (Bloomington: Indiana University Press, 1992).

3. All these facts were used against Winnie as decampaigning tactics during both the CA and the parliamentary elections. See Chapter 4.

4. In 1994, thanks to Constituent Assembly delegate Winnie Byanyima, together with Mbarara municipality *wanainchi*, government set up a commission of inquiry to investigate alleged mismanagement in the municipality. The commission's report, published a year later, revealed a lot of corruption on the part of local councilors and recommended, among other things, that the council be dissolved and the town clerk dismissed and prosecuted. However, for some unknown reason, most of the commission's recommendations to date have not been followed by the ministry of local government.

5. The word *kakuyege* is derived from the Luganda word for white ants *(enkuyege)*, which typically array themselves in a line as they travel about hunting for food.

6. Byanyima told me that whenever she comes down to her constituency she makes sure that she carries money in small denominations to facilitate the numerous cash requests she receives from *wanainchi*.

7. In the March 4, 1998, LC IV elections, the Unity candidate for mayor lost to the incumbent. The *Monitor* newspaper reported the mayor-elect as having said, "I can't say I have defeated only those who stood against me, but also Winnie Byanyima because she camped in town for over a week to make sure I'm defeated" *(Monitor,* March 16, 1998, 32).

8. Given Sudhir Ruparelia's questionable history, the central bank had reservations about issuing him a banking license.

9. Winnie Byanyima regularly participates in a weekly morning radio talk show, *Capital Gang,* aired live every Saturday on one of the Ugandan FM stations. A wide range of current political, economic, and social issues are discussed on the show.

10. The story was related to Winnie Byanyima by a third party present at the club when the minister made the remarks. See commentary by W. Byanyima in the *Monitor*, February 5, 1997, 10.

11. Byanyima's present companion had previously cohabited with another woman and had a child with her.

12. A "movementist" is someone who supports NRM politics. This position does not allow for various political parties to actively participate in national politics but espouses an all-embracing umbrella type of politics, with every citizen being a member of the movement. A "multipartyist," on the other hand, is someone who supports multiparty politics.

13. Point 7 of the NRM ten-point political program speaks of the "elimination of corruption and misuse of power."

14. See Chapter 4.

15. I reached this conclusion from my interviews and conversations with affirmative action district representatives as well as my one-day trench experience with MP Margaret Zziwa (Kampala district representative). On October 25, 1997, Zziwa held a program that she had organized to meet constituents in four different meetings to brief them on the upcoming local council elections. All the gatherings that she addressed consisted of local women leaders.

8

Media-ted Portrayals of Women Politicians

The Media in Uganda

Research indicates that print and broadcast media have considerable power to frame and influence people's understanding of public life and the political process (Keane 1991; Imam 1992). The Ugandan media have a checkered history, having been censored and gagged by successive autocratic governments, but have enjoyed relative freedom during the National Resistance Movement (NRM) era. However, it may be argued that generally the media in underdeveloped countries such as Uganda have limited influence because the majority of the population has only limited access to them. For example, in Uganda today there are only two daily newspapers; the total circulation of the bigger daily is about 30,000 (2 per 1,000 people) (UNESCO, 1993, 2–116). Furthermore, according to 1991 statistics the estimated number of radio broadcasting receivers in use was 1,975,000 (109 radios per 1,000 people), and there were only 187,000 television receivers in use (10 television sets per 1,000 people) (UNESCO, 1993, 9.4).[1] Such per capita statistics are deceptive, however, because they understate the number of Ugandans who have access to media information. Therefore a number of limitations must be pointed out in regard to these official statistics.

First, the statistics refer only to the number of newspapers, radios, and television sets that are actually purchased. They fail to capture the number of people who actually read the paper or those who may congregate around an electronic transmitter to listen to or view the news. Thousands of Ugandans who do not spend a penny to buy a paper actually read one. A common sight in urban centers every morning is the huddle of nonpaying readers mulling around the newspaper vendors reading the one copy made available for the general public to read for free. In more rural parts of the country, once the paper arrives (usually a day or two late) the designated town "reader" will recount the stories that are most interest-

183

ing. Consequently, a single newspaper can circulate through six to ten hands, particularly in the rural and peri-urban sectors of the country. Even if the actual news copy is read by only a few, the stories are spread by word of mouth.

Moreover, the statistics omit a new phenomenon that has recently emerged in Ugandan society—the FM radio stations that have been in existence since 1994 and an upsurge in popular, leisure, tabloid magazines. The upsurge in FM broadcasting, which deals mainly with entertainment, has led to an increase in the importation of cheap, affordable radio transmitters. Even if the number of those buying FM radios has not increased phenomenally, the number of listeners certainly has, on account of the novelty of the phenomenon. The change from the dreary state-sanctioned programs of the official radio, as well as the numerous competitions, gimmickry, and prizes that are on, effectively promote listenership in what has quickly become a highly competitive market. But the most important aspect of these new forms of media transmission is the kind of short, "sound-byted" news items they carry, which are designed to appeal to those whose primary interest is in entertainment.[2] The tendency, then, is to purvey the sensational and the prurient, both of which affect the portrayal of women in the media in general and the portrayal of women politicians in particular.

There are various other indirect ways that news circulates among *wanainchi* in Uganda, the two most influential perhaps being radio Katwe and popular theater. Radio Katwe refers to an elaborate communication system transmitted by word of mouth among *wanainchi*. It derives its name from a trading township called Katwe, which lies just outside the capital city. During the colonial period Katwe developed into an outlet for African petty traders who could not compete with the big Asian-run businesses in Kampala. It accommodated large numbers of beer sellers, bakers, small printers, and local metal workers in crowded slum conditions. Katwe became an important center of communication during the years of fervent anticolonial struggle (Apter 1967).[3] Today, radio Katwe "transmitters" can be found dotting the countryside in almost all trading centers, with local bus and commuter taxi parks being the major sites of dissemination.[4] Rural women also get most of their news ("gossip" in common parlance) at common meeting places such as local markets and water-collecting areas.

Popular theater is another indirect source that the wider population can access for media messages and influence.[5] Whether the scripts reflect public opinions or help formulate them, there is little doubt that the mass media play a role in shaping the themes of the plays that reach the village stages in the form of popular theater. A Ugandan political play, *Maswanku,* dramatizes the intricacies of managing a palace among the Baganda aristocracy. A princess is depicted as a treacherous, manipulative plotter (characteristics stereotypically linked with women of power and influence in the media). The play was very well received by *wanainchi*, but it drew criticism from feminists for its negative sexist undertones (*Monitor*, January 17, 1997, 19). According to Guarav Desai (1990) popular theater in Africa has a functional discourse that can legitimate (or subvert) existing power structures.[6] With regard to the position of women, it is fairly clear that popular theater can engage in satire, farce, and comedy of a kind that targets women politicians. The net result is to perpetuate certain images and perceptions of such women.

Against this backdrop I devote the next few pages to an analysis of newspaper articles in order to show how women MPs are covered in Uganda's media. The heightened presence of women on the Ugandan political scene has proved to be profitable fodder for the male-dominated media. Examples of news coverage of women politicians have been provided in preceding chapters. In this chapter I demonstrate further how the Ugandan press perpetuates women's subordination by constantly feeding readers with demeaning, patronizing, stereotypical, and overtly hostile reports about women politicians. Through its biased, sexist reporting on women politicians, the media reinforce the gender hierarchy in patriarchal Uganda. They employ a wide range of methods in achieving this. First, they trivialize female politicians and the issues they represent. Second, they depict women in national decisionmaking in negative ways that influence the public to view women politicians as an anomaly. The analytical separation of the issues is a matter of convenience in presenting them and should not blind us to the fact that the trivial and prejudiced portrayals associated with media coverage of female politicians often overlap with the common goal of reinforcing the gender hierarchy.

Maintaining the Status Quo Through Trivialization

Detailed press coverage of women politicians typically does not appear in the Report from Parliament section of the papers, which summarizes serious details of House proceedings. These reports usually include condensed versions of what male legislators contributed to House debates; women's contributions are reduced to single dry sentences that read something like, "Among others who contributed to the debate were . . ." More detailed news about women parliamentarians, if it is reported, is usually buried in the inside pages of the women/gender section of the newspapers nestled among articles on beauty, fashion, and advice. The letters to the editor page of most newspapers is another forum in which the prejudiced public contribute unflattering comments about women politicians. The end result of all this is that female politicians are not taken as seriously as male politicians; their issues are perceived as trivial; and their achievements are belittled.

Six weeks before the May 1996 presidential elections, and only five weeks prior to the dissolution of the Fifth Parliament, President Museveni appointed Rebecca Kadaga as assistant deputy chairperson to the National Resistance Council (NRC).[7] Despite the fact that *New Vision* described the event as historic and reported quite positively on Kadaga's first day in the chair, the article did not make headlines but was printed in the Women's Vision section on page 19. Among other items, the same section carried an illustrative article on elaborate head ties worn by African women, advice correspondence called the Agony Column, the Exercise Corner for fitness tips, and a fictional column, Secret Diary of Christina. Given the gender-specific character of the issues covered in Women's Vision, it is quite likely that men (and women who consider its contents unimportant) just skim its pages. Finding Kadaga's story in the Women's Vision column gives readers the impression that it is a leisurely, secondary story, like the rest of the issues reported under that title. Its political character and significance are thus lost.

Another example of how press reports adversely affect issues raised by female politicians comes from a journalist's report on his coverage of the Ministry of Gender and Community Development two-day seminar that I personally attended. The seminar was organized in August 1996 by the MGCD for women parliamentarians and other representatives of marginalized groups, such as people with disabilities and workers. The objective of the seminar was to equip participants with information, sharing experiences, and identifying tasks ahead. The minister of gender, Janat Mukwaya, set the tone of the meeting in the opening session by requesting participants to temporarily drop all their titles and refer to each other by their first names. The purpose was to create a relaxed informal atmosphere in which pertinent issues concerning women politicians could be openly discussed.

During the first session a number of important issues were raised, including the various strategies that women in parliament could adopt in contributing to the process of empowering women in Uganda. Miria Matembe's only contribution to this session was in form of a quick comment, after which she excused herself and left to attend another meeting. She had stressed the need for women MPs to meet regularly and sensitize themselves on short-term and long-term implications that bills introduced in parliament may have for Ugandan women. Matembe cited the statutes on privatization and value added tax (VAT) as two examples of laws adversely affecting women that women had helped enact in the recent past.

The next morning newsstands all over the country carried a *New Vision* front-page headline, "'Women MPs are Ignorant'-Matembe" with a story that proclaimed:

> Mbarara Woman MP Miria Matembe has said ignorance of women parliamentarians has contributed to the suffering of their colleagues by unknowingly participating in making oppressive laws. Matembe told a seminar for women parliamentarians and representatives of special interest groups yesterday at Hotel Equatoria that women legislators do not know what to do in parliament. (*Sunday Vision*, August 25, 1996, 1)

The *Sunday Vision* reporter ignored all the important issues raised in the MGCD seminar and wrote a sensational story in which he not only quoted Matembe out of context but also misrepresented her four-minute contribution to the entire debate. An important seminar thus came to be depicted as a frivolous insult-hurling contest and its issues receded into virtual nonexistence. Male politicians are also misrepresented in the press but never in such a demeaning, patronizing style. In most cases an "apology" will follow in a subsequent issue of the newspaper. The apparent double standard that characterizes the media treatment of male and female politicians makes it extremely difficult for women MPs to overcome the barriers they face in national politics.

Depictions of Women Legislators

Apart from trivializing issues raised by women politicians, the media perpetuate stereotypes about women by presenting female legislators as people who are basically apolitical and ignorant of the complexities of public life. If two female MPs stand on different sides of the fence on any subject being debated on the floor, it will be interpreted as a female feud (women at their best); for men it is construed simply as "differing." For example, *The Crusader* of August 8–13, 1996, reported that Byanyima and Matembe "locked horns" on an issue concerning what the paper described as Matembe's "pet theme of women's emancipation." Notably, the same report recorded a male MP as having "challenged" Matembe's views.[8] Hence the man was portrayed as having taken exception to Matembe's view by way of a mature challenge; the women, on the other hand, were portrayed as having engaged in an immature fray. In fact, the report prompted an enraged reader, Gorretti Kyomuhendo, to write:

> When Matembe and Byanyima begin "locking horns," I feel sorry for the
> people of Mbarara who entrusted them with their mandate. . . . We cannot
> afford to have you going for each other's throats because then, our cause
> will be lost. You should not wash your dirty linen in the House, what will
> the men think of us? (*Crusader*, August 15–20, 1996, 4).

Evidently the message that such reporting sends to the reading public is
that women are not playing their role in serious politics. It also distracts
women politicians by rechanneling a lot of their political energy into
counterbalancing the negative and trivial reports.[9]

Newspapers talk approvingly of male legislators while depicting female MPs as incompetent misfits in the House. *The Monitor* of March 1–4,
1996, ran the following headline: "Of the Best, Idle and Disorderly in the
NRC." The article credited Kizza Besigye for his "serious, original, and
articulate" contributions; described the "brilliant" arguments of profes-
sors George Kanyeihamba, Tarsis Kabwegyere, and Mondo Kagonyera;
praised Abu Mayanja for his "tactful" debates and Israel Mayengo for his
"short and precise" points. In contrast, the women mentioned in the
same report were portrayed negatively: Beatrice Lagada was dubbed
"the fiery woman"; Victoria Sebagereka and Loi Kiryapawo were reported as contributing only "when they thought men were disfavoring
women and stifling their rights." About Beatrice Bakojja the paper said,
"Except for her bright appearance nothing else showed she was in the
House." Wafana Masaba's "bizarre fashions" were said to have "over-
shadowed her presence and sealed her mouth." Similarly, in the wake of
the 1996 general elections, the editorial of the *Monitor* newspaper (June
24–26, 1996) ran the following commentary:

> The performance of most of [the women NRC members] was very disap-
> pointing. For many, there is almost nothing to show as their six-year
> achievements. . . . Apart from Miria Matembe (who unfortunately assumed
> that use of militant and embarrassing language would yield positive re-
> sults), many of the women have passed more as bench-warmers and sleep-
> ing beauties in the NRC than legislators.

The media have portrayed deputy speaker Betty Okwir as incompetent, blaming parliament for compromising merit in favor of affirmative
action. One reporter put it boldly:

> There were about 270 people to choose from but the honourables, after pick-
> ing a capable speaker (Wapakhabulo), chose to downplay the importance of
> his deputy. . . . Ability as a yardstick was relegated to the back seat while
> parochial considerations like gender, region, religion, political inclination
> entered the fray. (*Monitor*, February 25, 1998, 3).

Several MPs (both male and female) condemned the above report in defense of Okwir. Reacting to the snide remarks directed to the deputy speaker, MP Aggrey Awori stood up in parliament and said, "I am disappointed in the media. When the press maliciously attacks you [Okwir], me as a member of this House I stand up to protest" (*Monitor*, February 27, 1998, 2). Such negative reporting on women politicians serves to undermine their power base. Sreberny-Mohammadi and Ross (1996) argue correctly that a gendered news agenda has the total effect of undermining the status and career aspirations of women politicians.

Women politicians are further painted as incompetent through reports which suggest that women cannot succeed in the public sphere because their "natural" place lies in the private sphere. Thus sweeping statements such as the following appear often in the local newspapers: "Nearly all our women politicians have failed marriages or are merely hanging on to long-cold marriages either for the sake of the children or as a public relations ploy."[10] The message advanced by the argument is clear: If you're a woman, you have to choose between your marriage and politics; you can't have them both. It does not matter that the same standard is not applied to male politicians or that the ratio of failed marriages outside parliament is much higher than that inside parliament.

At a Forum for Women in Democracy (FOWODE) seminar female legislators confronted a representative of the press media with the following blunt question: "Why does the press portray women politicians in such a negative manner?" He defended the media by arguing that it simply reflected the values and interests of wider society and reminded female MPs of the fact that theirs was a business; "We only report what we think will sell." The only problem is that the type of news coverage of women politicians that sells for the media largely portrays them in negative, stereotypic images. Indeed, Ugandan female legislators are discovering what women leaders in other parts of the world already know about the sexist culture prevalent in mass media (e.g., Phillips 1980; Braden 1996; Norris 1997).

References to women politicians often include irrelevant descriptions that draw attention either to their physical characteristics or to their femininity and derogate their stature as unserious and incapable politicians. As one member noted:

During the CA, I was very disappointed with the press. We were portrayed very, very negatively; they wouldn't talk about our positive contribution in the House but would report on our physical looks. The *Monitor* went as far as giving us nicknames. I was the "Yellow Pumpkin," Rhoda Kalema was the "Grandmother." Hope Mwesigye was called the "Most Beautiful," yet she made some of the most brilliant contributions in the CA. Janet Bagarukayo was described as always dressing like a member of the

"Mother's Union" and Beatrice Byenkya was the "Sleeping Beauty" [laughter]. (Tezira Jamwa, CS)

When the female MP laughed in this context, it was not because she found the sexist classifications funny. It was a sad kind of snicker that did not reach her eyes, a laugh used as a mechanism to cope with a depressing and hopeless situation.

Using diminutive variants of women's names, such as "Aunt Cissy" instead of "Honorable/Ms. Cecilia Ogwal" (as is often done with male politicians) in reference to a very powerful Uganda People's Congress (UPC) leader and MP is demeaning (see *Daily Topic*, October 4, 1994). Ogwal has also been described as having "an unsexy, masculine voice" (*Crusader*, July 25–30, 1996, 7). When *The Crusader* interviewed Mary Mutagamba, the campaign leader of presidential candidate Paul Ssemwogerere during the 1996 elections, the introductory words of its report (carried in the Variety section) were "wearing an affectionate smile across her little face," thus depicting her not as a serious, effective person but a fragile, ineffective leader (February 2–9, 1996, 7). The vice president has been painted as a juvenile, unimportant person by descriptions referring to her as "baby-faced" (*Monitor,* November 21–23, 1994), "chubby-faced" (*Sunday Monitor,* August 10, 1997), and "good Catholic DP girl" (*Monitor,* November 21–23, 1994; August 10, 1997). Elsewhere, *New Vision* characterized Kazibwe as a *Nnalongo* (mother of twins), "the mother of four" (November 21, 1994), bringing her domesticity and sexuality into bold relief while pushing her political role to the background (cf. Kiguli and Kiguli 1997). Significantly, male politicians are never referred to as "father of . . ." or "uncle." If they are belittled, it is often in satirical cartoon images. The derogatory, patronizing words used to describe female politicians, on the other hand, occur in serious news articles.

Sexual innuendo about female politicians is daily fodder in the Ugandan press. In November 1994, when Specioza Kazibwe was appointed vice president of Uganda, for example, *The People* carried a cartoon of her swearing in with a caption that read, "Thigh Power!" The *Crusader* (June 14, 1997, 7) was more direct: "Specioza Kazibwe . . . is endowed with a bounteous bosom, a feature that is highly regarded in the beauty world as an attribute of sex appeal." Sexualizing a woman who had ascended to a position of power in this fashion was the media's way of downsizing her to make her appear less threatening. Another report in the *Monitor* insinuated that it was easier to recall how women CADs dressed than to remember what they contributed to the debates. Picking on one particular female delegate, the reporter wrote that Hope Kabirisi wore dresses with "long revealing slits" and "had the habit of moving in and out . . . in any sitting," supposedly to attract the attention of her male colleagues (*Moni-*

tor, August 5–9, 1994, 11). The enraged Kabirisi refuted the story in a strongly worded personal statement in the CA, to which the same reporter replied: "I must confess I felt sorry hearing you reading out in a trembling voice, this statement to the CA . . . I have received more congratulations for that piece than any other article I have [ever] written. And not least some of your fellow delegates even advised that we write more of such stuff" (*Monitor*, August 26, 1994). I sought out this particular reporter during my research in the hope of gaining a better understanding of the objective behind that particular report. In a rather elucidating explanation, he told me that the story was meant to give the public the "human, nonpolitical side of legislating." Although he insisted that he would have given the same detail had the "culprit" been male, one cannot miss the parallels in using *women* to demonstrate the *sexual, nonpolitical* side of politics.

Paradoxically, many of the female reporters who have started to make inroads into the male media world seem to have bought into the masculinist culture of biased sexist reporting. The aforementioned stories, "Locked Horns" and "The Best, Idle, and Disorderly," were authored by Charlotte Kawesa and Nabusayi Wamboka, respectively. Another woman reporter, Loy Nabeta, covered a regional conference on African women in decisionmaking for *The Monitor* and wrote a special report entitled "When Intelligent, Beautiful, Smart Women Met in Entebbe":

> All said, the conference was a rare collection of very beautiful smart and intelligent women from various parts of the world with mostly the Kenyan and Tanzania parliamentarians breathing fire. Uganda's firebrand, Miria Matembe, was there flying the flag. (*Monitor*, February 28–March 1 1996, 3)

One wonders if Nabeta would have described male parliamentarians as "very handsome, smart, and intelligent." By calling attention to the parliamentarians' physical appearance, Nabeta focuses her readers' eyes away from the important issues that these women politicians discussed. Juxtaposing "beauty" and "intelligence" in the report suggests incongruence and abnormality, as if the two were not supposed to go together.

Negative portrayals of women politicians by women journalists can be attributed to the resentment that rises out of the normative operations of patriarchy discussed in Chapters 1 and 4. It also results partly from the traditional training that female reporters receive. And it comes as no big surprise in view of the fact that almost all the leaders in public and private media charged with the power of selecting what, at the end of the day, deserves column or air space are men. Women in the media, therefore, count for very little in regard to enhancing the image of female politicians.[11]

Most women politicians try to keep a low profile in the hope that it will render them invisible to the assaulting pens and cameras of journalists. This is in stark contrast to male politicians who, as several women MPs told me, go as far as paying journalists a retainer just to keep the press spotlight on them. "It took me up to my last year in parliament to realize that these men who always appeared in the press pay reporters who sit in the gallery; so you can see that even politics has gone commercial" (Ruth Aliu, AA). The journalist I interviewed for this study corroborated this observation, adding that although this was more commonly practiced by men, female MPs were not exempt from the practice either.

Of the women interviewed for this study, 94 percent were dissatisfied with press coverage of their activities. Deputy speaker Betty Okwir shared a few practical suggestions:

> *New Vision* described me as "a humble former headmistress of St. Catherine Girls' School" and predicted all kinds of negative things about my performance. . . . The media should do something as we approach the twenty-first century as far as the changing image of women is concerned. I expect the press to try to participate actively in promoting women in government. I've had this idea for some time now, of initiating a program for the press to come to terms with women in politics. I thought someday in future we should raise money and organize workshops under the theme of the media and the changing image of women. Women should be interested in the press and the press should be interested in what women are doing not only in politics but also the important role they play in the development of our nation.

Officials from women's NGOs with whom I talked were also of the view that even though media coverage of female politicians is not always blatantly sexist, it leaves a lot to be desired. As the assistant general manager of the Uganda Women's Finance and Credit Trust (UWFCT) put it, "If you *really* want to know about women's contribution to the House debates, go to the gallery because you certainly won't get it from the papers."[12]

Notes

1. Compare these statistics to 1990 estimates for the United States, where there are 1,611 dailies with a total circulation of 62,328,000 (249 per 1,000 people) (UNESCO 1993, 2–116). Also compare the broadcasting estimates for the United States, where 534,800,000 radio broadcasting receivers (1,000 radios per 1,000 people) and 205,500,000 television receivers (814 sets per 1,000 people) are in use (UNESCO 1993, 9–12).

2. Much of the news reported on FM radio stations in Uganda is lifted directly from newspapers; public radio also carries several programs on *Today in the Press* in various local languages.

3. Apter provides a background to the growth of Katwe: "The small traders were just those whose knowledge of rudimentary bookkeeping and organization was necessary for the political organization. . . . Traders from Katwe used their establishments as their offices. Local beer halls served as meeting places. Trading was not a full-time occupation and each trader also had his small farm or plot of land. . . . The line between rural and urban never became strict because the trader was almost invariably a farmer as well (Apter 1967, 241).

4. Needless to say, as with all words transmitted from mouth to mouth, radio Katwe is not the best source of accurate reporting. As the "newsweb" widens, facts usually get distorted with embellishments, exaggerations, and misquotes; still, the gist of it will get around.

5. African theatrical activity, which has mass appeal, predates colonialism. Ngugi wa Thiong'o describes precolonial African drama thus: "It was part and parcel of the rhythm of daily and seasonal life of the community. It was an activity among other activities, often drawing its energy from those other activities. It was also entertainment in the sense of involved enjoyment; it was moral instruction; and it was also a strict matter of life and death and communal survival" (1986, 37).

6. From the late 1980s many African feminist organizations turned to popular theater as an alternative way of increasing accessibility to positive information about women to *wanainchi* and as a tool for empowering women. "The important aspect of Popular Theatre is that it is one of the few communication media where the woman is an active participant both as communicator and audience. It gives the women, especially the ones at the grassroots level, a voice denied to her by radio, television, film or print" (Lihamba and Mlama 1992, 108).

7. Many suspected that this move was calculated to lure women's votes in the impending presidential elections (see *New Vision*, April 23, 1996, 19).

8. Also see "Matembe, Byanyima clash," *New Vision*, August 16, 1994.

9. See, for example, Winnie Byanyima, "I Didn't Go for Matembe's Throat," *Crusader*, August 29–September 3, 1996.

10. See Odoobo Bichachi, "Museveni's Government a bad Example to the Youth, *Monitor*, July 15, 1997.

11. The chairperson of the Uganda Media Women's Association told me that despite the potential in a two-way linkage between the association and women politicians, it was hardly utilized. She also pointed out that the association was not as active as it should be.

12. Interview with Rose Kiggundu, December 29, 1995.

9

Conclusion

This book set out to investigate the role of women in formal politics within the larger context of patriarchy and underdevelopment in Ugandan culture. Important stages on the road to political emancipation and equality for women include (1) the establishment of seats reserved for women from the grassroots level to the national legislature, (2) the establishment of a ministry of women's affairs, and (3) greater access to high decisionmaking positions. Because the voices of more than half of Uganda's population had been excluded from formal politics for decades, the 1989 sex-quota experiment formed an important landmark in the political history of the country. It heralded a new era for women.

Female membership in the national legislature grew from 5 percent in 1989 to 17 percent by 1996. Only seven years into the affirmative action experiment, not only had the numbers of women representatives risen to 18.8 percent but tangible results had been achieved, as evidenced by the strong prowomen provisions in the 1995 constitution. These provisions were born out of the strength of the women's caucus in the Constituent Assembly. Yet these advances have made only a marginal dent on the overarching dominance of patriarchal forms of doing politics; women are still considered intruders in a preserve that was previously almost exclusively male. The door has certainly been opened, but there is a force pushing it closed from the inside that women have to get past.

Although African and Western countries have different socioeconomic and political histories, this examination revealed several parallels with regard to women in politics.[1] These findings point to the common denominator of patriarchy; the bold contours that delineate gender hierarchies are indeed cross-cultural. But the challenges posed by patriarchy for the women politicians in my study are inextricably tied to cultural and historical factors that are specific to the African and Ugandan contexts. Most significantly, Ugandan women, unlike women in the West, always participate within a matrix of imperial domination and underdevelopment. Some of these factors express themselves subtly or anachronistically. Others are more direct and debilitating.

Although not all female MPs consider "representing women" to be their primary role in the House, my analysis and observations revealed a clear trend in that direction, as the majority of them expend a good deal of energy and time both in the House chamber and in their local constituencies making a case for women. This was true regardless of how they entered parliament, through either the affirmative action channel or the traditional door. There is, therefore, an unarticulated unity of purpose between the issues that most female MPs pursue and the goals of women's emancipation in Uganda. Indeed, the greatest challenge currently facing women legislators and Uganda's feminists is how to change gender equality from a constitutional mandate to a social and cultural reality.

Women politicians face similar problems and challenges irrespective of their mode of entry into the legislature. This study has demonstrated that gender affects the social interactions of male and female legislators and is also intricately built into the parliamentary institutional framework. Applying to the analysis a conceptual framework that took into account both the gendered microstructure and the macrostructure of gendered sociopolitical organization was extremely useful. Such a framework clearly exposed how the social reproduction of gender in female (and male) parliamentarians reproduces the gendered political structures. The political domain, as patriarchally constituted, makes it extremely difficult for women to create the requisite space for political autonomy. In this sense affirmative action is reminiscent of what Stacey and Price (1981) refer to as "trappings without substance," a hollow-shelled victory that has little potential to shatter the institutional aspects of sexism in Uganda.

At the same time, the study has not painted a roundly pessimistic scenario for women in politics. It has revealed that patriarchy in Uganda is not entirely constraining but has some elements that women can exploit to improve their standing, as attested by the debate and organization around the promulgation of the 1995 constitution. Affirmative action as a policy allowed individuals previously restricted to the private sphere to enter the public realm. Indeed, the unprecedented presence of women in Uganda's parliament has had (and continues to have) a significant influence on the political landscape of the country. In particular, it has resulted in a shifting of political sites and a relocation of power (albeit slight), spurring a new kind of political self-organization for Ugandan women.

Nevertheless, the study has also revealed that the right of women to participate in politics as autonomous actors is still greatly curtailed in both overt and covert ways. I have demonstrated how prevailing gender relations together with the underdeveloped economy (rooted in neocolonialism and imperialist domination) operate to limit or otherwise shape the performance of women legislators. Cultural socialization, which molds "public (political) men" and "private (domestic) women," and the gendered order of state institutions and ideologies jointly operate to ensure the perpetuation of the status quo.

Culture and morality are useful tools for men to use in dominating women. Men in Uganda tend to have a very selective idea of culture. When it suits them to do so, they will invoke custom and traditional values. Thus when women step out of the "private" sphere to claim their rightful space in the "public" arena, traditional values can be invoked to remind them of their "proper" place. But the same men will hasten to strike down custom as outmoded and archaic if it stands in their way to power and privilege. Ugandan women have internalized traditional concepts and stereotypical images about women, which sometimes leads them to resent "deviant" women who take the path to national politics. This explains the woman-on-woman verbal violence and denigration that was demonstrated in many of the elections in which women were contesting against each other. It also explains why so many of the women parliamentarians are wary of being labeled feminists or of adopting radical postures.

The male-dominated media in Uganda represents one of the patriarchal pillars that serve as a conduit for perpetuating gender subordination and oppression. Operation of the old-boy network within the male political elite is extended to include the fraternity of reporters, journalists, and editors who serve as gatekeepers to what makes news. By portraying women politicians as an aberration or as intruders in the serious male game of politics, they perpetuate the gendered public/private divide. The people, *wanainchi,* internalize these ideologies, which create and/or fuel feelings of resentment toward the women who participate in formal politics. Eliminating the hostility that exists toward women and among women in high politics will be a painstakingly slow process. It will take sensitization, achieving greater gender balance in national politics, as well as the radical transformation of existing political structures.

This analysis has further illustrated that the benefits of the affirmative action experiment are limited by its being a top-down policy imposed by the state. Without advancing women's strategic gender interests at all, the National Resistance Movement (NRM) government gained the support of women legislators by offering them access to the political world of male power. It is quite clear that women very strongly support the NRM government because it "gave" them access into the political arena. At the same time, such mediation has the demobilizing and depoliticizing effect of nipping in the bud any popular opposition to the fundamental structures of gender inequality within Uganda's political economy. In other words, the state is not a guaranteed ally in the struggle for gender equity. Thus it is extremely important for the women's movement in Uganda to maintain a critical distance from the state. Such distance must be marked both conceptually and pragmatically. In the first instance, activists need to stop "thanking" the NRM for having "delivered" them from the bondage of oppression. The NRM position is a minimalist one that addresses only the most blatant aspects of sexual discrimination in the political arena; it is not hard to imagine less sympathetic governments simply scrapping many of the reforms achieved so far. Hence activists should view the affirmative action experiment merely as a structure of political opportunity within which to advance the emancipation of women in all spheres of life.

Female parliamentarians need to recognize that the achievements they have registered thus far are the result of efforts on their own part—individually and collectively. As the bastion and main perpetuator of patriarchy, the state will not make amends to women as a marginalized or oppressed group unless it is politically expedient to do so or there is considerable pressure compelling it in such a direction. In sum, the pressure must be maintained (albeit within certain necessary constraints, e.g., political pragmatism) and the women's movement must be ever vigilant against measures that substantively undermine gains made thus far. Failure to do so puts women in a precarious, nay dangerous, position whereby the state may co-opt their achievements or, worse still, conveniently remove the "favor" when it loses interest in preserving it.

The problem is exacerbated by the politics of patronage whereby resource-poor women (and men) in the context of an underdeveloped economy have little choice but to depend on the resource-controlling state as a vital backup for advancing their political careers. Complacent in their positions of power, many affirmative action beneficiaries hardly engage in serious self-analysis of their role in parliament, nor do they seriously or systematically question the gender implications of state-sponsored bills.

Moreover, the affirmative action policy has proved to be "class-centric," largely benefiting a minority of an educated, elite group of Ugandan women. In this sense the policy has perpetuated mainstream postcolonial politics, which excluded the voices of the largest section of the peasant population (men and women). In other words, the political situation of the majority of women, the ones who face the brunt of oppression and marginalization, at whom affirmative action was purportedly targeted, largely remains constant. Thus this study reinforces a point that has been made before: Affirmative action policies are essentially limited in that they neglect class-based interests (Sikhosana 1996). Indeed, the

1989 experiment is a reformist strategy that leaves the oppressive system intact. It does not look beyond the sex-gender redistributive aspect of its politics to deal with the underlying structural problems of the system. Thus it can be of only limited value to the women's movement in Uganda. Affirmative action needs to be recognized as a necessary first step toward the difficult road to transformative action that allows for a democracy with a wider base.

Ugandan women legislators are not totally unaware of the contradictions that constantly confront them in the process of their political work. Daily, women MPs have to negotiate a way around dilemmas related to issues of representation, power imbalances vis-à-vis the male politicians, as well as their sexuality, which is made an issue by their male colleagues, the media, and the prejudiced public. The work of female politicians in Uganda is in many ways a reflection of the constraints and contradictions arising out of a patriarchal sociopolitical setting existing in a peripheral area of the global economy. On the one hand, traditional gender roles and basic issues related to daily survival give shape to their political work. On the other hand, their contradictory status as marginalized women in positions of power sets them apart from the masses of Ugandan women. It is these very contradictions that are likely to foster further action for social change by female legislators; the sense of incongruity for these women is bound to precipitate into a particular form of political consciousness.

A strong women's movement is needed to back up women public officeholders and to raise their awareness in order to reconceptualize and recontruct political structures according to feminist principles (Bystydzienski 1992). Maxine Molyneux (1985) makes a compelling argument. Depending on the nature of the demands and claims, it is possible to distinguish between (1) organizations that aim to achieve women's emancipation or gender equality through strategic objectives to overcome women's subordination and (2) organizations whose demands arise from practical interests that do not necessarily challenge the prevailing forms of gender subordination, even though they arise directly out of them. Linking women's strategic needs to the practical ones will permit an increased level of consciousness among female politicians of the wider emancipatory agenda.

One of the questions that I hoped to answer as I began this study was whether increasing participation by women in formal politics would change women or whether women would change the politics of this country. At the conclusion of the study I have come to the view that both have taken place to a degree. Women have been changed as a result of participating in national politics and at the same time their entry into politics has certainly changed, albeit mildly, the politics of Uganda. The women who have tasted the fruits of national politics have gained from this exposure in many different ways. Most of them have become more assertive, self-confident, financially independent, and more acutely aware of women's rights generally, whether or not they directly espouse these issues in any conscious fashion. Ugandan women generally have benefited from this phenomenon: Seeing increasing numbers of women on the national political platform gives them confidence to join at the local government level and to stand up against abusive and controlling husbands. Because more women have infiltrated Uganda's high governing positions, the politics of this country will never be the same. Gender issues are not as easily ignored in government decisions as they were previously and there is a lot more gender sensitivity in the laws and policies of the country.

As a new millennium dawns, Ugandan women are likely to make even bigger strides in the political arena. Reconstructing existing male-dominated political structures is by no means an easy task, and in concluding this book, I offer female politicians in Uganda some suggestions on how to accomplish the enormous feat of reconstruction.

First, women legislators need to build upon the strength that they have already exhibited in the Constituent Assembly by forging a nucleus around which female MPs can build a common ground. The natural way to do this would be (1) to revitalize and reconstitute the Uganda Women Parliamentarians Association (UWOPA) with a new vision and a fresh agenda and (2) to collaborate with women's NGOs as well as government agencies such as the Ministry of Gender in realizing their redefined goals. The National Association of Women's Organizations in Uganda (NAWOU) and the Uganda Women's Network (UWONET) are two umbrella organizations that play a networking role for women's organizations in Uganda and have great potential to link women parliamentarians with grassroots women. The Forum for Women in Democracy (FOWODE) is an extremely useful resource not only for equipping female MPs with empowering skills but also for providing linkages to vital regional and international networks. UWOPA should open its membership to all female legislators, past and present, as a permanent caucus to be at the forefront of the struggle for women's political emancipation. In addition, UWOPA has great potential as a support group for women politicians to compare notes, discuss their problems, and take collective action to alleviate them.

Because of the diversity in women's interests and concerns, however, their unity and cohesion on gender issues cannot be assumed (Molyneux 1985). Therefore, at a minimum, women legislators must make a conscious effort to construct a common program as a basis of unity solidified by their shared gender inequality. This will entail a reconfiguration of their consciousness as well as their demands and claims. It will also require a good deal of commitment, sacrifice, and compromise. Instead of romanticizing unity, women parliamentarians should work hard to ward off outside pressures and detractors that constantly threaten it.

Second, with the favorable juridical context put in place by the 1995 constitution, women legislators have the enormous task of spearheading legal reform that will inhere with its spirit. Systematically and painstakingly, the constitutional rights won in 1995 will have to be brought in line with the day-to-day lives of Ugandan women. Priority should be given to eliminating laws that hurt women, such as the ones that endorse the patriarchal control of land and other forms of property. Since experience has shown that law-in-legislation is quite different from law-in-practice, the achievements of women parliamentarians in the legal arena should only be viewed as an initial but necessary step toward women's total emancipation. Involving feminist NGOs in their work as well as regularly touching base with the rural peasant constituents should be an integral part of the political agenda of women legislators. My study indicates that the relationship between female MPs and women outside parliament was at best tenuous. This trend of affairs will have to be reversed if formal legal equality is to translate into substantive equality. Women MPs should especially work with women activists in their efforts to equalize outcomes for women and men in all spheres of life.

Third, the Ugandan feminist movement in general and female politicians in particular can explore religion as a liberating ideological force for women in Uganda. For example, women leaders can embark on a vigilant campaign of working within existing religious welfare-oriented organizations such as the Mother's Union and the YWCA as a way of appealing to grassroots women. Women's councils provide an alternative structure that carries a great deal of underutilized potential for mobilizing and involving grassroots women. Such forums may be used to reconstruct the interpretations of rural women's life experiences and expectations as well as integrate their self-articulated needs into the wider struggle spearheaded by educated, elite women.

Fourth, reform in the electoral law would enhance the work of female legislators in Uganda. Having women who occupy the parliamentary affirmative action seats elected by universal suffrage instead of an electoral college would remove the hurdles that come with dealing with a relatively small, manipulative male-dominated electoral college and would also allow Ugandan women, as electors, to have a say in choosing the best possible female representative—one who would "act for" their concerns and interests. Furthermore, a limit of two five-year terms should be set for women standing on the affirmative action ticket, allowing for many more women to become involved in national decisionmaking. The ultimate goal, however, should be to attract more *wanainchi*, and this can only be achieved by whittling back the formalism and credentialism associated with Uganda's parliamentary system today.

Finally, as a long-term goal, Ugandan women, inside and outside parliament, must engage a two-pronged political struggle against underdevelopment and patriarchy. The agenda for achieving this is multilayered and complex and involves an altering of gender relations. It will take a total transformation in prevailing ideologies as well as social and political structures to confer substance and power to women's participation in politics: a redefinition of power and equality. This can be accomplished through the state's acknowledging and gainfully rewarding the productive and reproductive labor of Ugandan women; promoting gender awareness for men and women through education (formal and informal), the media, popular theater, and so forth; legal reform that scraps all forms of male oppression and dominance; and, most importantly, by establishing and consolidating links among women in policymaking, feminist (male and female) activists, women in academe, and grassroots women.

Although this study focused on women legislators in Uganda, its findings and implications will no doubt resonate for other African countries. It is my hope that it (1) will help women politicians around the continent become more sensitive to the barriers inhibiting their primary goal of improving the status of African women and (2) will act as a resource for them in dealing with the problems they encounter. Undoubtedly, the chant of crowing hens will one day reverberate around the four corners of Africa.

Notes

1. Although my study was not meant to be a comparative one, it is interesting to note these parallels. For example, as in most Western countries, the first few Ugandan women to enter Legco and the earlier assemblies were mostly from political families, just as female officeholders in both contexts have a general tendency to voice "women's issues," as compared to their male counterparts in the legislatures.

Appendix 1: Glossary of African Terms

Term	Language	English Equivalent
Busuti	Luganda	Women's traditional dress
Kabaka	Luganda	King
Kabaka Yekka	Luganda	The king alone
Kabila	Swahili	Tribe or community
Katikiro	Luganda	Prime minister
Lubuga	Luganda	King's sister
Lukiiko	Luganda	Parliament (of the Buganda kingdom)
Maama Kelele	Swahili	A loud, clattery woman
Mailo	Luganda	Freehold land tenure
Makabila	Swahili	Tribes or communities
Malaya	Swahili	Prostitute
Maswanku	Luganda	A small, sacred drum
Mugole wa Muchwa	Runyoro	King's sister
Nnalongo	Luganda	Mother of twins
Namasole	Luganda	Queen-mother
Nyina Mukama	Runyoro	Queen-Mother
Nyina Omugabe	Runyankole	Queen-Mother
Omunyana Omugabe	Runyankole	King's sister
Omwenkanonkano	Luganda	Equality
Ssaza	Luganda	County
Sekibobo	Luganda	King's father-in-law
Shuuka	Runyankole	Women's traditional dress
Ujamaa	Swahili	Familyhood
Wanainchi	Swahili	Common people

Appendix 2: Reflections on Methodological Issues

Methods

Three distinct categories of women politicians formed the subject matter of this book. First, members of the fifth interim legislature, known as the National Resistance Council (NRC), were the pioneer beneficiaries of the 1989 affirmative action policy; their term of office ended in June 1996. Second, delegates to the Constituent Assembly (CA)—a specially elected body that for sixteen months (May 1994 to August 1995) debated and passed a new constitution for Uganda.[1] Third, MPs elected to the sixth parliament—the National Assembly—in June 1996. As a result of the affirmative action policy, the number of elected women parliamentarians increased significantly. The numbers increased twenty-five-fold with the introduction of affirmative action; the total number of women in both the NRC and the CA was fifty; there are fifty-one women in the present assembly, who constitute between 17 and 18 percent of the total membership.[2] Needless to say, several women had overlapping memberships in two or three of the legislative bodies mentioned (see Appendix 3 and Figure 4.1).

The data presented here were collected in two phases. The initial stage covered a period of one year, from September 1995 to August 1996. This period witnessed presidential elections in May 1996 and general parliamentary elections in June 1996. The analysis in the doctoral dissertation ("When Hens Begin to Crow: Gender and Formal Politics in Contemporary Uganda," University of Minnesota, 1997) was based on data collected at this stage. The second phase lasted from August 1997 to January 1998; the data collected from this period was used to expand my analysis for this book. The methodology adopted was primarily qualitative; it took the form of field observation and in-depth interviews. Qualitative methods were best suited for my study because they allowed for contextuality, continuity, and personal experience, all of which were crucial to the research questions raised (Fonow and Cook 1991). The study is a social analysis of gender that sought to advance the experiences, perceptions, and interests of women in formal politics and to analyze how they affect their interactions. Thus it was important to pay close attention to the meanings women give to their experiences. Rather than maintain a subject-object relationship with the respondents, I adopted a strategy that allowed for feelings, emotions, and nonverbal information (Reinharz 1992, 18–45).

Paying attention to the interpretations of respondents illuminated sociohistorical processes and the structural contradictions that shape gender dynamics in

Ugandan politics. Intensive interviews that allow female respondents to reconstruct their past have the advantage of consciousness-raising—an important component of emancipatory "transformational praxis" (Freire 1972; Westcott 1990; Seitz 1995). The women politicians studied here are not only active agents of social change but are themselves a text for revealing and analyzing transformations in the sociopolitical map of Uganda.

I sat in on parliamentary debates for a total of sixty-seven days. For fifty-one days I observed business in the main chamber of the National Assembly. I spent sixteen days observing the deliberations of smaller specialized committees of parliament.³ Such observation occurred between the months of October 1995 and February 1996 as well as in August 1996. Detailed field notes were recorded throughout the observation period. Direct observation of the legislators in session helped me understand the context within which women legislators operate. Furthermore, direct observation provided me the opportunity to see things that may have routinely escaped the conscious awareness and perception of the interviewees. It also allowed me to note qualities that cannot be read from the Hansard record (e.g., feelings and body language). Finally, observations permitted me to move beyond the selective perceptions of others. This is critical, considering that all the interviewees with whom I talked reported their own perceptions of the situation. Combining their perceptions with my own (which were, of course, also selective) enabled me to present a more comprehensive view of the conditions and circumstances shaping the political participation of women legislators (Patton 1987).

Some of the issues I focused on during my observation included the following: Are male or female legislators called on more often? How frequently do women contribute to the debates? Which gender is more likely to interrupt the other in the debates? What kinds of topics do men and women tend to address? What persons and what issues invoke jeers, jokes, scoffing, and applause from the floor? Is the nonverbal communication among the legislators of any significance? Focusing on these specific aspects of gender interaction provided useful cues for sensitizing me to relevant information for the book.

I also sat in on two different in-house workshops that were specially organized for women parliamentarians; each was intensive and lasted for two days. The first was an induction seminar for the new cohort of women parliamentarians elected in June 1996. It was organized by Forum for Women in Democracy (FOWODE), a nongovernmental women's political organization. The second workshop was organized by the Ministry of Gender and Community Development (MGCD). These forums gave me a rare opportunity to observe women parliamentarians operating as a group in their own space and to hear them talking about their peculiar problems, priorities, and strategies.

In-depth, semistructured interviews were conducted with forty female legislators and fifteen male legislators.⁴ Male parliamentarians were included in the sample for comparative purposes in making a relative, insightful gender analysis. All interviewees were carefully selected through theoretical sampling (Glaser and Strauss 1967).⁵ Based on my observations of House debates, discussion with National Assembly staff, and reading of the Hansards (equivalent to the Congressional Record), I consciously sought out informants who represented a range of factors, including geographical region, political inclination, socioeconomic background, age, religion, and political experience.

A rough biographical sketch of the forty women legislators interviewed revealed that thirty hold university degrees and ten have a high school diploma (or its equivalent); twenty are married, eleven single, five widowed, and four divorced; ages range from 24 to 67, with a mean of 40.8; the number of children born to the MPs ranged from 0 to 7 with a mean of 3.1; religious affiliation fell under three categories: twenty-five Protestants, fourteen Catholics, and one Muslim.[6] Occupationally, the women interviewed included nine teachers, seven administrators, five agricultural officers, four lawyers, three businesswomen, three economists, two social workers, two journalists, one midwife, one engineer, and one doctor; two were fresh college graduates.[7] The lifestyles of the different female MPs radically differ (as with that of male MPs), ranging from chauffeur-driven MPs who live in the affluent suburbs of Kampala to MPs who easily blend into the crowd of *wanainchi* at the public taxi park. Generally speaking, however, women parliamentarians, by virtue of their education and income bracket, fall within the middle class. This means that their objective social class position distances them from the larger population of women in Uganda, who belong to the class of the peasantry.

In addition, I interviewed leaders of eight prominent women's nongovernmental organizations in Kampala (see Appendix 5 for a list of these organizations).[8] Sampling of the organizations was a process that was part of my eight-year involvement in the Ugandan women's movement. I was interested in professional organizations that work closely with grassroots women. All eight interviews were conducted before those with the parliamentarians. The purpose of these interviews was to explore links between the female political elite and the women's activist networks outside parliament. Finally, I conducted individual interviews with twenty grassroots women in the rural village of Nkozi, fifty miles from the capital city, to further examine whether there was a link between top women politicians and the rural women who constitute the overwhelming majority of the Ugandan populace.

The principal advantage of employing this methodological approach lay in its potential to elicit from the interviewees rich, detailed materials on a range of topics that could be used in qualitative analysis (Lofland and Lofland 1984). The interviews with male and female legislators provided insights into their subjective experiences, which simple observations at the field site could not. Talking to women outside parliament, on the other hand, provided me with a lens through which to analyze any impact that women politicians may be causing in the wider Ugandan society. All interviews with parliamentarians and NGO women leaders, which ranged in length from forty-five minutes to two and a half hours, were tape-recorded and transcribed verbatim. The bulk of interviews with legislators were conducted at the parliamentary building in Kampala; sixteen were conducted in their private offices; and five took place in the homes of the interviewees. All eight interviews with NGO women leaders were conducted in the offices of the various organizations. Interviews with the grassroots women were all conducted in their homes and were much shorter, lasting approximately thirty minutes. They were not tape-recorded; translated notes were recorded in a notebook.

Supplementary data was drawn from analysis of documentary research. Such documents included parliamentary Hansards, reports of the Constituent Assembly proceedings, newspaper reports, and other texts documenting the historical development of the lawmaking process in Uganda. Field notes were also kept on relevant television and radio programs by and about women politicians, relevant informal conversations with peers and journalists about women politicians, and observations at the National Assembly canteen, where MPs spend time between sessions.

The process of analyzing data was a continuous one throughout the fieldwork. Field notes were taken at the field site and following each interview session. Each set of data was analyzed after it had been put together. A more comprehensive analysis of the interview transcripts and field notes was done through both induction and deduction of the coded themes within the data (Lofland and Lofland 1984).

Reflections on My "Self" in the Field

I conclude the methodological section with a brief discussion of how my personal identity and various roles affected the research process, as well as some ethical questions that emerged from that experience. I engage in an exercise of self-analysis and self-reflexivity as a way of acknowledging the fact that my research, like all research, was by no means free of biases. Nor did I approach it from that value-free stance that the orthodox positivist approach advocates. Christman (1988, 73) reminds us that "researcher bias is present in all research . . . the problem selection, methodological stance, and theoretical orientation all reflect the researcher's position in society, world view, and personal experience." Instead of obscuring my study in a shroud of distancing objectivity and downplaying my personal role in the process of research and interacting with informants, I bring to the surface my "self" (see also Tamale 1996b). In this way I seek to do justice to the women politicians who were the subject of this study and the process of data collection and research (Krieger 1985, 1991). Feminist scholars and those from other subjugated social groups have moved away from the illusory positivistic approach and have made efforts to expose the role played by the subjective in the construction of knowledge (Smith 1974; Reinharz 1979; Roberts 1981; Collins 1986; Pierce 1995).

My self-positioning and my understanding of how the multifaceted roles I occupy affected the course of the research requires a brief biographical note about myself. Born in 1962 as the first-born in a family of six, my formative years were largely an African middle-class experience. I attended top-notch schools in Uganda, finally earning a bachelor of laws degree from Makerere University in 1985. Two years later, I entered Harvard Law School in the United States and pursued a master's degree in law. In 1988 I returned to Uganda and lectured in law for five years before returning to the United States to pursue a Ph.D. in sociology and feminist studies (the partial result of which is this book). As a member of the Association of Women Lawyers (FIDA), the Uganda Association of University women (UAUW), and several other organizations, I am very actively involved in the Ugandan women's movement and often speak out on women's rights issues in the local print and electronic media.

My personal history, as well as the connections I had within the women's networks, greatly facilitated this study. As a native Ugandan woman, I was close to the culture, language, local politics, and historical experience of the women and men I studied. This, I believe, brought a richness to the study that would be lacking had it been conducted by an outsider. For example, active involvement in the Ugandan women's movement since 1988 facilitated easy access to informants and often elicited their full cooperation. However, my outsider status as a nonlegislator and a nonpolitician in parliament also had an impact on the research process, particularly at the initial stages of the interviews. Some respondents (especially the men) perceived me with suspicion given my research topic; others were impatient with an academic exercise that encroached on their busy schedules. Several respondents (male and female) politely "endured" the mundane exercise by providing curt, laconic responses to my questions. At the end of the session they would say something like, "Good luck with your paper," obviously relieved to be through with me.

During the observation phase, despite my outsider status, I had minimal intrusive significance because my presence in the diplomats' gallery attracted little attention. That section of the National Assembly is normally occupied by officials from any government ministry that has a direct interest in the bill being debated on the assembly floor. Thus faces in the gallery change from time to time and draw little attention from the parliamentarians on the main floor. During the interview phase of my study, a few informants who had noticed my presence around the parliamentary buildings (e.g., in the main lobby or the canteen) told me that they had assumed that I was a journalist. Interestingly, many were relieved to learn that I was not and were more open to me than they would have been to a journalist.

My womanhood and feminist background proved to be useful assets to this inquiry concerning women in politics in Uganda. Several female legislators informed me how happy they were that a Ugandan female researcher was conducting a study of their experiences and problems. With the exception of a few cases, I struck an instant rapport with all female informants, many of whom requested me to avail them with both the transcripts of their interview and the final report of my study. During the interviews, conversation flowed freely and our shared gender status erased the inequalities arising out of both the nonlegislator/legislator status and the researcher/informant relationship. However, the same attributes did not work in entirely the same fashion with male informants. I noticed that most male MPs were not as enthusiastic about the study (because of the research topic, perhaps?). A few even related to me in a paternalistic fashion, largely disregarding the questions I put to them and instead engaging in self-absorbed monologues. Below is an excerpt from a transcript of an interview that took place in the office of a male MP.

> I think that affirmative action shortchanges women. It brings in too many women who are neither qualified nor ready for parliament. . . . I believe that I am more prowomen than the women MPs themselves, but because I engage in banter and jokes people think that I am a chauvinist. Women are not a threat to me and I can hold my own against any number of women in an intellectual argument. . . . [Son enters and

> briefly interrupts interview, touching my hand from across the desk and addressing
> son] Here's an intelligent young lady; I wouldn't mind having her for a daughter-in-
> law! . . . [Turning back to me] Where were we? (Wamala," CS)

I doubt that this honorable parliamentarian would have responded to a male researcher in a similar manner (not even in jest). The power that he possessed, first
as a parliamentarian and second as a man, accentuated the power dynamics at
play in this context.

This study was conducted against a backdrop of stresses and torn loyalties that
I constantly experienced in the field. Ethical issues always confronted me during
the course of the research. Most troubling was my experience with the rural peasant women whom I interviewed to shed light on the links between women parliamentarians and the grassroots society outside parliament. When I arrived in
the homes of most of these village women, they welcomed me very warmly. One
went out of her way to cut down a bunch of bananas while another rushed to
milk her only cow and offered me a quart, saying, "I know you city people only
get milk full of chemicals; here, have some of this; it's fresh from my small farm."
I was touched beyond words at these kind gestures extended to a total stranger
whom they would probably never meet again. I felt exploitative, knowing that
my purpose was to "extract" data from these women without offering any direct
reciprocal benefits. However, many of the female constituents I talked to both in
Nkozi and Mbarara expressed gratitude for having someone visit them and take
an interest in their problems and concerns.

With the women parliamentarians I always faced the dilemma of how much I
should disclose of the several "personal" stories that they related to me in the
course of the interviews, especially since in most cases such anecdotes illuminated
perfectly the gist of my analysis of the gender dynamics in Ugandan politics. Part
of this problem was dealt with by the decision to maintain their anonymity in
analyses that I deemed to be "sensitive." Redemption for me also came when I realized that my work was already having an impact on women parliamentarians.
For example, toward the end of my study I ran into an MP I had interviewed several months before and she said, "I didn't see you in parliament yesterday when I
made my maiden speech. I was thinking about you when I made the point about
Museveni ignoring women in his state of the nation address on modernizing agriculture, yet women constitute 80 percent of Uganda's agricultural production." In
July 1997, FOWODE invited me to act as a resource person at an evaluation retreat
for women parliamentarians, where I shared some of my study findings with the
female MPs. The discourse was so wonderful and mutually instructive that it
made the whole exercise worth every step of the way for me.

All in all, therefore, the personal attributes, experiences, and worldview I
brought to the research were extremely important and are in various ways la-
tently or manifestly reflected in the study.

Notes

1. The 1989 affirmative action policy favoring women in the political arena was
carried over to the Constituent Assembly.

2. The breakdown for the different bodies was as follows: In the NRC, 39 represented districts under the affirmative action program, 2 were directly elected on the open ticket, 3 were presidential nominees, 4 represented youth, and 2 were historical members from the original NRC; in the Constituent Assembly, 39 were specially elected for the women's seats, 2 were special presidential nominees, 1 represented workers' unions, and 8 entered in their own right after successfully competing with men; Presently, in the National Assembly, in addition to the 39 district representatives, 3 other women entered parliament on an affirmative action ticket favoring other interest groups, namely, people with disabilities (2) and the army (1), eight entered on their own merit after successfully competing with men, and one is an ex-officio member by virtue of her ministerial appointment (see appendix 3).

3. I observed parliamentary proceedings from the Diplomats' Gallery on the main chamber floor of the National Assembly. The two specialized committees that I observed were (i) committee on Gender and Community Development and (ii) committee on Natural Resources, Tourism, Wildlife and Antiquities.

4. Appendix 3 indicates the names of all the women parliamentarians I interviewed for this study (marked with an asterisk *). Thirty-one of these women held district affirmative action seats, six occupied regular county seats, and three were affirmative action incumbents who had unsuccessfully run for county seats in the 1996 race.

5. This means that I sought out those legislators who were likely to provide a broad range of backgrounds, ethnicity, experiences, and opinions based on my observations at the field site as well as consultations with National Assembly staff.

6. The Muslim woman I interviewed had actually converted from Protestantism at 22 years of age when she got married to a Muslim man. The general breakdown of religious affiliation in Uganda presently is 33% Catholic, 33% Protestants, 16% Muslims, and 18% indigenous beliefs (Reddy 1996: 959).

7. In comparison, the occupational breakdown of the 15 male legislators in my study was as follows: 5 accountants, 4 lawyers, 2 doctors, 1 pilot, 1 businessman, 1 engineer, and 1 teacher.

8. The Ministry of Gender and Community Development was the only governmental agency included in the eight.

9. I use a pseudonym to protect the identity of the interviewee.

Appendix 3: Women Legislators, 1950–1998

Legislative Council (Colonial Period)

1. Alice Boase, 1954–1956 (total number of MPs = 60)
2. Barbara Saben, 1954–1958
3. Pumla Kisosonkole, 1957–1958
4. Joyce Mpanga, 1959–1960*
5. Sarah Ntiro, 1959–1961
6. Frances Akello, 1959–1961
7. Eseza Makumbi, 1960–1961

National Assemblies, 1962–1986

1. Florence Lubega, 1962–1971 (total number of MPs = 92)
2. Sugra Visram, 1962–1966
3. Rhoda Kalema, 1979–1980 (NCC, total number of MPs = 156)*
4. Geraldine Bitamazire, 1979–1980 (NCC)
5. Theresa Odongo-Oduka, 1980–1985 (total number of MPs = 126)

National Resistance Council, 1989–1996
(total number of MPs = 280)

1. Abu Dominica — Woman Representative, Moyo district
2. Adima Betty — Woman Representative, Arua district
3. Aliu Ruth — Woman Representative, Soroti district*
4. Apio Irene — Woman Representative, Kitgum district*
5. Aryatugumya Kamugisha — Woman Representative, Rukungiri district*
6. Bahemuka Alice — Woman Representative, Hoima district
7. Bakojja Beatrice — Woman Representative, Mpigi district
8. Bigombe Betty — Nominated*
9. Bikorwenda Ida — Woman Representative, Bundibugyo district*

---

*An asterisk indicates women legislators interviewed for this study. Note that names are marked only once for those legislators whose names appear multiple times in the different legislatures.

10. Bintu Juliet   Youth Representative, Western region*
11. Birabwa Kiwanuka   Woman Representative, Luwero district
12. Bwambale Loyce   Woman Representative, Kasese
13. Byekwaso Gertrude   Woman Representative, Masaka
14. Ikote Rosette   Woman Representative, Pallisa district*
15. Kabasharira Naome   Woman Representative, Ntungamo district*
16. Kadaga Rebecca   Woman Representative, Kamuli district*
17. Kalema Rhoda   Kiboga county, Kiboga district
18. Kasule Kyambade   Youth Representative, Central Region*
19. Kazibwe Specioza   Woman Representative, Kampala district
20. Kazungu Justine   Woman Representative, Iganga district
21. Kiryampawo Loi   Woman Representative, Tororo district
22. Kulany Gertrude   Woman Representative, Kapchorwa district
23. Lagada Beatrice   Nominated
24. Lochoro Eunice   Woman Representative, Kotido district
25. Lorika Rose   Woman Representative, Moroto district
26. Masaba Wafaana   Woman Representative, Mbale district
27. Matembe Miria   Woman Representative, Mbarara district*
28. Mpanga Joyce   Woman Representative, Mubende district
29. Mugarura Ester   Woman Representative, Bushenyi district
30. Mukiibi Benigna   Woman Representative, Kibale district*
31. Mutagamba Mary   Woman Representative, Rakai district*
32. Mukwaya Janat   Nominated*
33. Mwonda Faith   Butembe county, Jinja district[1]
34. Namugenyi Noelina   Woman Representative, Kalangala district
35. Nampeera C.   Youth Representative, Buganda region
36. Namuyangu Jennifer   Youth Representative, Eastern*
37. Njuba Gertrude   Historical Member
38. Nkurukenda Florence   Woman Representative, Masindi district
39. Nkwasibwe Loy   Woman Representative, Kabale district*
40. Ntabgoba Jeninah   Woman Representative, Kisoro district*
41. Ogweng Molly   Woman Representative, Apac district
42. Oker Mary   Woman Representative, Gulu district
43. Okwir Betty   Woman Representative, Lira district*
44. Opio Albina   Woman Representative, Kumi district
45. Opoti Esther   Woman Representative, Nebbi district*
46. Rwabyomere Joan   Woman Representative, Kabarole district*
47. Sebagereka Victoria   Woman Representative, Mukono district*
48. Sekiziyivu Margaret   Woman Representative, Kiboga district
49. Wekiya Florence   Woman Representative, Jinja district
50. Zizinga Oliva   Historical Member

Constituent Assembly, 1994
(total number of CADs = 286)

1. Abu Dominica   Woman Representative, Moyo district
2. Adima Betty   Woman Representative, Arua district

3. Adio Winifred — Woman Representative, Soroti district
4. Akech Betty — Woman Representative, Gulu district
5. Akello Grace — Nominated
6. Bagarukayo Janet — Woman Representative, Ntungamo district
7. Bakojja Beatrice — Woman Representative, Mpigi district
8. Bikorwenda Ida — Woman Representative, Bundibugyo district
9. Bwambale Loyce — Woman Representative, Kasese district
10. Byanyima Winnie — Mbarara Municipality, Mbarara district
11. Byenkya Beatrice — Woman Representative, Hoima district
12. Egunyu Fiona — Woman Representative, Kumi district
13. Jamwa Tezira — Woman Representative, Tororo district
14. Kabirisi Hope — Woman Representative, Bushenyi district
15. Kakembo Mary — Woman Representative, Kalangala district
16. Kalema Rhoda — Kiboga county East, Kiboga district
17. Kalikwani Irene — Woman Representative, Kamuli district
18. Karaahwa Monica — Woman Representative, Masindi district
19. Kawoya Anifa — Woman Representative, Masaka district
20. Kazibwe Specioza — Kigulu South county, Iganga district
21. Kulany Gertrude — Woman Representative, Kapchorwa district
22. Lagada Beatrice — Woman Representative, Apac district
23. Lorika Rose — Woman Representative, Moroto district
24. Masiko Winifred — Woman Representative, Rukungiri district
25. Matembe Miria — Woman Representative, Mbarara district
26. Mavenjina Catherine — Woman Representative, Nebbi district
27. Mukiibi Benigna — Woman Representative, Kibaale district
28. Mukisa Solome — Woman Representative, Iganga district
29. Mukwaya Janat — Mukono South county, Mukono district
30. Mutagamba Mary — Woman Representative, Rakai district
31. Mwesigye Hope — Woman Representative, Kabale district
32. Mwondha Faith — Woman Representative, Jinja district
33. Nabafu Jennifer — Woman Representative, Mbale district
34. Nakyanzi Veronica — Ntenjeru South county, Mukono district
35. Nankabirwa Ruth — Woman Representative, Kiboga district
36. Ntabgoba Jeninah — Woman Representative, Kisoro district
37. Ogwal Cecilia — Lira Municipality, Lira district
38. Okorimoe Janet — Woman Representative, Kotido district
39. Okwir Betty — Woman Representative, Lira district
40. Oryem Alice — Woman Representative, Kitgum district
41. Opoti Esther — Okoro county, Nebbi district
42. Rainer Julliet — Woman Representative, Pallisa district
43. Rwabyomere Joan — Nominated
44. Sebagereka Victoria — Woman Representative, Mukono district
45. Sekitoleko Victoria — Butembe county, Jinja
46. Sempa Esther — Woman Representative, Luwero district
47. Ssemakula Hawa — Woman Representative, Mubende district
48. Ssentongo Theopista — National Organization of Trade Unions (NOTU)

49.	Turyahika Alice	Woman Representative, Kabarole district
50.	Zziwa Margaret	Woman Representative, Kampala district

National Assembly, 1996
(total number of MPs = 270)[2]

1.	Abu Dominica	Woman Representative, Moyo district
2.	Akech Betty	Woman Representative, Gulu district*
3.	Akello Grace	Woman Representative, Soroti district*
4.	Akumu Mavenjina	Woman Representative, Nebbi district
5.	Akwero Jane	Woman Representative, Kitgum district
6.	Alinyikira Ruth	Woman Representative, Jinja district
7.	Amongin Hellen	Woman Representative, Kumi district
8.	Baba Diri Margaret	Disabled Representative, Northern region*
9.	Babihuga Winnie	Woman Representative, Rukungiri district
10.	Bakoko Zoe	Woman Representative, Arua district
11.	Balemezi Lydia	Woman Representative, Mukono district
12.	Bigirwa Bernadette	Woman Representative, Bushenyi district*
13.	Bikorwenda Ida	Woman Representative, Bundibugyo district
14.	Bitamazire Geraldine	Woman Representative, Mpigi district
15.	Bumba Saida	Ex-Officio (minister)
16.	Bwambale Loyce	Woman Representative, Kasese district
17.	Byanyima Winnie	Mbarara municipality, Mbarara district*
18.	Byekwaso Gertrude	Woman Representative, Masaka district
19.	Byenkya Beatrice	Woman Representative, Hoima district*
20.	Egunyu Fiona	Ngora county, Soroti district
21.	Hyuha Dorothy	Woman Representative, Tororo district
22.	Ikote Rossette	Woman Representative, Pallisa district
23.	Jamwa Tezira	West Budama North county*
24.	Kabakumba Abwooli	Woman Representative, Masindi district
25.	Kabasharira Naome	Woman Representative, Ntungamo district
26.	Kadaga Rebecca	Woman Representative, Kamuli district
27.	Kafire Juliet	Kibuku county, Pallisa district
28.	Kakembo Mary	Woman Representative, Kalangala district*
29.	Kazibwe Specioza	Kigulu South county, Iganga district
30.	Kerwegi Rosemary	Woman Representative, Apac district
31.	Kuka Frances	Woman Representative, Kapchorwa district
32.	Lorika Rose	Woman Representative, Moroto district
33.	Matembe Miria	Woman Representative, Mbarara district
34.	Mpanga Joyce	Woman Representative, Mubende district
35.	Mukiibi Benigna	Woman Representative, Kibaale district
36.	Mukwaya Janat	Mukono South county, Mukono district
37.	Musumba Salaamu	Bugabula South county, Kamuli district*
38.	Mwaka Victoria	Woman Representative, Luwero district*
39.	Mwebesa Christine	Woman Representative, Kabale district
40.	Namumbya Sarah	Woman Representative, Iganga district*
41.	Namusoke Sarah	Woman Representative, Rakai district*

42. Nankabirwa Ruth   Woman Representative, Kiboga district*
43. Nayiga Florence   Representative for Disabled Women*
44. Nkalubo Annette   Army Representative*
45. Ntabgoba Jeninah   Woman Representative, Kisoro district
46. Ogwal Cecilia   Lira municipality, Lira district*
47. Okorimoe Grace   Woman Representative, Kotido district
48. Okwir Betty   Woman Representative, Lira district
49. Rwabyomere Joan   Woman Representative, Kabarole district
50. Wabudeya Beatrice   Woman Representative, Mbale district
51. Zziwa Margaret   Woman Representative, Kampala district*

Notes

1. Faith Mwondha replaced Victoria Ssekitoleko in 1994 when the latter was appointed regional representative (southern Africa) of the Food and Agricultural Organization (FAO).

2. Representatives for the Youth had not yet been elected at the time of publishing this book.

Appendix 4: Women's "Firsts" in National Politics

First black woman MP (nominated)	Pumla Kisosonkole[1] (1957)
First woman parliamentary secretary (Ministry of Planning and Community Development)	Florence Lubega (1963)
First woman to win an elective parliamentary seat in her own right (NCC, Kampala district)	Rhoda Kalema (1979)
First woman minister (Ministry of Foreign Affairs)	Elizabeth Bagaya (1973)
First woman vice president	Specioza Kazibwe (1994)
First woman deputy speaker of parliament	Rebecca Kadaga (1996)[2]
First woman deputy chairperson of a Constituent Assembly	Victoria Mwaka (1994)
First woman campaign manager for a presidential candidate (Paul K. Ssemwogerere)	Mary Mutagamba (1996)
First woman ambassador	Elizabeth Bagaya (1972)
First black woman city councilor (Kampala City Council and Mengo Municipality)	Rebecca Mulira (1962)*
First woman mayor (Mbale town)	Janet Wesonga (1967)

Notes

1. Mrs. Kisosonkole was (she died in late 1997) a native of South Africa and was married to the late Saza chief, *Sekibobo* (Mutesa's father-in-law). At the time she was also the president of the Uganda African Women's League and vice-President of the Uganda Council of Women. A meeting was arranged for me to interview Mrs. Kisosonkole but it aborted due to her deteriorating health.

2. Although Kadaga held office for only five weeks, technically she was the first woman to preside over the House. Honorable Betty Okwir was elected (by fellow parliamentarians) as deputy Speaker on the sixth parliament in August 1996.

Appendix 5: Women Cabinet Ministers, 1962–1998

Akumu Mavenjina	Minister of State for Public Service, 1996
Bagaya Elizabeth	Minister of Foreign Affairs, 1973
Byekwaso L. Gertrude	Minister of State, President's Office (Women in Development), 1989
Bbumba Syda	Minister of State, President's Office (Economic Monitoring), 1996
Bigombe Betty	Minister of State, Prime Minister's Office, 1986 In charge of Pacification of the North, 1988
Kadaga Rebecca	Minister of State for Foreign Affairs (Regional Cooperation), 1996
Kalema Rhoda	Deputy Minister of Culture, Community Development and Rehabilitation, 1979 Deputy Minister for Public Service and Cabinet Affairs, 1989
Kazibwe W. Specioza	Vice President and Minister for Agriculture, Animal Husbandry. and Fisheries, 1996 Minister of Women in Development, Youth, and Culture, 1992 Deputy Minister for Industry and Technology, 1989
Kuka Jane Frances	Minister of State for Gender and Community Development, 1996
Lubega Florence	Parliamentary Secretary (Equivalent to Deputy Minister) of Planning and Community Development, 1963
Mukwaya Janat	Minister for Gender and Community Development, 1996
Mpanga Joyce	Minister of State, President's Office (Women in Development), 1988 Minister of State for Education (Primary Education), 1989
Nkurukenda Flora	Deputy Minister for Local Government, 1989
Njuba Gertrude	Deputy Minister of Rehabilitation, 1986 Deputy Minister for Industry and Technology, 1988 Deputy Minister, Office of the Prime Minister, 1989
Odongo-Oduka Theresa	Deputy Minister of Health, 1981

Okwir Betty   Deputy Minister for Youth, Culture, and Sports,
                                   1989
Rwabyomere Joan   Minister of State for Agriculture, 1996
Senkatuka-Astles Mary   Minister of Culture and Community Development,
                                   1974
Ssekitoleko Victoria   Deputy Minister of Agriculture and Forestry, 1986
                               Minister for Agriculture, 1988

Appendix 6: Women's Organizations/Institutions That Participated in the Study

(Reporting Status of Officers Interviewed)

1. Association of Women Lawyers (FIDA-Uganda)—Chairperson
2. Uganda Media Women's Association—Chairperson
3. Action for Development (ACFODE)—Legal Officer
4. Uganda Association of University Women (UAUW)—Chairperson
5. National Association of Women's Organizations in Uganda (NAWOU)—Training Officer
6. Uganda Women's Finance and Credit Trust (UWFCT)—Assistant General Manager
7. Ministry of Gender and Community Development—Minister and Legal Officer
8. Forum for Women and Democracy (FOWODE)—Chairperson and Research Officer

Appendix 7: Male Parliamentarians Interviewed in the Study

1. Akida Alli Gabe — Jonam county, Nebbi district
2. Babu Francis — Kampala central division, Kampala district
3. Bambalira Jackson — Bwamba county, Bundibugyo district
4. Besigye Kizza — Historical member
5. Kagonyera Mondo — Rubabo county, Rukungiri district
6. Mayanja Abu-Baker — Busujju county, Mubende district
7. Mayengo Israel — Kyamuswa county, Kalangala district
8. Mwandha James — People with disabilities, eastern region
9. Ndawula Kaweesi — Kiboga west county, Kiboga district
10. Omara Atubo Daniel — Otuke county, Lira district
11. Rwakakooko Elly — Ruhama county, Ntungamo district
12. Tumubweinee Manzi — Rukiga county, Kabale district
13. Wanendeya William — Budadiri east county, Mbale district
14. Wapakhabulo James — Mbale municipality, Mbale district
15. Wasswa Lule — Rubaga north division, Kampala district

References

AAWORD. 1982. "The Experience of the Association of African Women for Research and Development (AAWORD)." *Development Dialogue* 1, no. 2: 101–113.

Adams, John. 1852–1865. *Works.* Boston: Little, Brown.

Adedeji, Adebayo, ed. 1981. *Indigenization of African Economies.* London: Hutchinson University Library for Africa.

Aidoo, Ama. 1992. "The African Woman Today." *Dissent* 39: 319–325.

Allen, Chris. 1991. "Gender, Participation and Radicalism in African Nationalism: Its Contemporary Significance." In Robin Cohen and Harry Goulbourne, eds., *Democracy and Socialism in Africa.* Boulder: Westview.

Amy, Douglas. 1993. *Real Choices: New Voices.* New York: Columbia University Press.

Andersen, Kristi, and Stuart Thorson. 1984. "Congressional Turnover and the Election of Women." *Western Political Quarterly* 37, no. 1: 143–156.

Anzaldua, Gloria, ed. 1990. *Making Face, Making Soul.* San Francisco: Aunt Lute Foundation Books.

Apter, David. 1967. *The Political Kingdom in Uganda.* Princeton: Princeton University Press.

Arblaster, Norberto. 1987. *Democracy.* Minneapolis: University of Minnesota Press.

Ardener, Shirley. 1975. "Sexual Insult and Female Militancy." In Shirley Ardener, ed., *Perceiving Women.* London: Malaby.

Ashe, Robert. 1894. *Chronicles of Uganda.* London: Hodder & Stoughton.

Asowa-Okwe, C. 1992. "Women Wage Workers in Plantation Estates in Uganda." Paper presented at a conference on historical trends in gender and work at the Center for Basic Research, Kampala, September 7–10.

Bacchi, Carol. 1990. *Same Difference: Feminism and Sexual Difference.* Sidney: Allen & Unwin.

Bashevkin, Sylvia. 1994. "Building a Political Voice: Women's Participation and Policy Influence in Canada." In Barbara Nelson and Najma Chowdhury, eds., *Women and Politics Worldwide.* New Haven: Yale University Press.

Baysting, Arthur, Dyan Campbell, and Margaret Degg. 1993. *Making Policy Not Tea: Women in Parliament.* Auckland: Oxford University Press.

Beckwith, Karen. 1989. "Sneaking Women into Office: Alternative Access to Parliament in France and Italy." *Women and Politics* 9, no. 3: 1–15.

Bledsoe, Timothy, and Mary Herring. 1990. "Victims of Circumstances: Women in Pursuit of Political Office." *American Political Science Review* 84, no. 1: 213–223.

Bobbio, Noberto. 1987. *The Future of Democracy: A Defense of the Rules of the Game.* Minneapolis: University of Minnesota Press.

Bogdamor, Vernon. 1984. *What Is Proportional Representation?* Oxford: Basil Blackwell.

Bolanle, Awe, ed. 1992. *Nigerian Women in Historical Perspective.* Lagos: Sankore Publishers.

Bookman, Ann, and Sandra Morgen, eds. 1988. *Women and the Politics of Empowerment.* Philadelphia: Temple University Press.

Boserup, Ester. 1970. *Women's Role in Economic Development.* London: George Allen & Unwin.

Braden, Maria. 1996. *Women Politicians and the Media.* Lexington: University Press of Kentucky.

Breitenberg, Mark. 1993. "Anxious Masculinity: Sexual Jealousy in Early Modern England." *Feminist Studies* 14, no. 2: 377–398.

Brenner, Johanna, and Barbara Laslett. 1991. "Gender, Social Reproduction, and Women's Self-Organization: Considering the U.S. Welfare State." *Gender and Society* 5, no. 3: 311–333.

Brown, Winifred. 1988. *Marriage, Divorce and Inheritance: The Uganda Council of Women's Movement for Legislative Reform.* Cambridge: Cambridge African Monographs.

Brydon, Lynne, and Sylvia Chant. 1989. *Women in the Third World: Gender Issues in Rural and Urban Areas.* New Brunswick, N.J.: Rutgers University Press.

Bujra, Janet. 1986. "Urging Women to Redouble Their Efforts: Class, Gender, and Capitalist Transformation in Africa." In Claire Robertson and Iris Berger, eds., *Women and Class in Africa.* New York: Africana Publishing.

Burman, Sandra. 1990. "Fighting a Two-Pronged Attack: The Changing Legal Status of Women in Cape-Ruled Basutoland, 1872–1884." In Cherryl Walker, ed., *Women and Gender in Southern Africa to 1945.* London: James Currey.

Burris, Beverly. 1989. "Technocracy and Gender in the Work Place." *Social Problems* 36: 165–180.

Burton, Clare. 1985. *Subordination: Feminism and Social Theory.* Sydney: Allen & Unwin.

Butler, Judith. 1990. *Gender Trouble: Feminism and the Subversion of Identity.* New York: Routledge.

Byanyima, W. Karagwa. 1992. "Women in Political Struggle in Uganda." In Jill Bystydzienski, ed., *Women Transforming Politics: Worldwide Strategies for Empowerment.* Bloomington: Indiana University Press.

Bystydzienski, Jill. 1992. "Influence of Women's Culture on Public Politics in Norway." In Jill Bystydzienski, ed., *Women Transforming Politics: Worldwide Strategies for Empowerment.* Bloomington: Indiana University Press.

______. 1995. *Women in Electoral Politics: Lessons from Norway.* Westport, Conn.: Praeger.

Canover, Pamela. 1988. "Feminists and the Gender Gap." *Journal of Politics* 50, no. 4: 985–1010.

Caplan, Paula. 1983. "Between Women: Lowering the Barriers." *Women and Therapy* 2, no. 2–3: 51–66.

Carroll, Berenice. 1972. "Peace Research: The Cult of Power." *Journal of Conflict Resolution* 6, no. 4: 585–616.

Carroll, Susan. 1984. "Women Candidates and Support for Feminist Concerns: The Closet Feminist Syndrome." *Western Political Quarterly* 37, no. 2: 307–323.

______. 1992. "Women State Legislators, Women's Organizations, and the Representation of Women's Culture in the United States." In Jill Bystydzienski, ed., *Women Transforming Politics: Worldwide Strategies for Empowerment*. Bloomington: Indiana University Press.

Carter, Stephen. 1991. *Reflections of an Affirmative Action Baby*. New York: Basic Books.

Castles, Francis. 1981. "Female Legislative Representation and the Electoral System." *Politics* 1, no. 2: 21–26.

Chabal, Patrick. 1992. *Power in Africa: An Essay in Political Interpretation*. New York: St. Martin's.

Chodorow, Nancy. 1974. "Family Structure and Feminine Personality." In Michelle Rosaldo and Louise Lamphere, eds., *Woman, Culture, and Society*. Stanford, Calif.: Stanford University Press.

______. 1978. *The Reproduction of Mothering: Psychoanalysis and the Sociology of Gender*. Berkeley: University of California Press.

Chopra, J. K. 1993. *Women in the Indian Parliament: A Critical Study of Their Role*. New Delhi: Mittal Publications.

Christman, Jolley. 1988. "Working in the Field as the Female Friend." *Anthropology and Education* 19, no. 2: 70–85.

Clerk, Dominique. 1985. "Zimbabwe Women: Finding Time to Act." *Kinesis* 9 (June): 29.

Collier, Rohan. 1995. *Combating Sexual Harassment in the Workplace*. Buckingham, U.K.: Open University Press.

Collins, Patricia Hill. 1986. "Learning from the Outsider Within: The Sociological Significance of Black Feminist Thought." *Social Problems* 33, no. 6: 14–32.

______. 1990. *Black Feminist Thought: Knowledge, Consciousness, and the Politics of Empowerment*. Boston: Unwin Hyman.

Connell, R. W. 1987. *Gender and Power in Society, the Person and Sexual Politics*. Stanford, Calif.: Stanford University Press.

Considine, Mark, and Iva Deutchman. 1994. "The Gendering of Political Institutions: A Comparison of American and Australian State Legislators." *Social Science Quarterly* 75, no. 4: 854–866.

Crawford, Neta. 1996. "Imag(in)ing Africa." *Press/Politics* 1, no. 2: 30–44.

Crompton, Rosemary. 1986. "Credentials and Careers: Some Implications of the Increase in Professional Qualifications Amongst Women." *Sociology* 20, no. 1: 25-42.

Curley, Richard. 1973. *Elders, Shades, and Women: Ceremonial Change in Lango, Uganda*. Berkeley: University of California Press.

Currell, Melville. 1974. *Political Women*. London: George Allen & Unwin.

Dahlerup, D. 1988. "From a Small to a Large Minority." *Scandinavian Political Studies* 11: 275–299.

Ddungu, Expedit. 1989. "Popular Forms and the Question of Democracy: The Case of Resistance Councils in Uganda." Working Paper no. 4, Center for Basic Research, Kampala.

Denzer, La Ray. 1976. "Towards a Study of the History of West African Women's Participation in Nationalist Politics: The Early Phase, 1935–1950." *Africana Research Bulletin* 6: 65–85.

Desai, Gaurav. 1990. "Theater as Praxis: Discursive Strategies in African Popular Theater." *African Studies Review* 33, no. 1: 65–92.

Diamond, Irene. 1977. *Sex Roles in the State House.* New Haven: Yale University Press.

Diamond, Larry, Juan Linz, and Seymour Lipset, eds. 1988. *Democracy in Developing Countries.* 4 vols. Boulder: Lynn Rienner.

Disch, Lisa, and May Jo Kane. 1996. "When a Looker is Really a Bitch: Lisa Olson, Sport, and the Heterosexual Matrix." *Signs: Journal of Women in Culture and Society* 21, no. 2: 278–308.

Dolan, Kathleen, and Lynne Ford. 1995. "Women in the State Legislatures: Feminist Identity and Legislative Behaviors." *American Politics Quarterly* 23, no. 1: 96–108.

Driberg, J. H. 1932. "The Status of Women Among the Nilotics and Nilo-Hamitics." *Africa (London)* 5, no. 4: 404–421.

Dunbar, A. R. 1965. *A History of Bunyoro-Kitara.* Nairobi: Oxford University Press.

Economic Commission for Africa. 1975. *The Role of Women in African Development.* New York: United Nations.

Eisenstein, Hester. 1983. *Contemporary Feminist Thought.* Boston: G. K. Hall.

Epstein, Cynthia. 1988. *Deceptive Distinctions: Sex, Gender, and the Social Order.* New Haven: Yale University Press.

Etim, Ekei. 1992. "Debt and Structural Adjustment Programmes: The Effects on Women in Africa." *Echo* 17–18: 18–22.

Evans, Laura. 1978. "Sexual Harassment: Women's Hidden Occupational Hazard." In Jane Chapman and Margaret Gates, eds., *The Victimization of Women.* Beverly Hills, Calif.: Sage.

Fairhurst, Gail, and Kay Snavely. 1983. "A Test of the Social Isolation of Male Tokens." *Academy of Management Journal* 26: 353–361.

Flammang, Janet. 1985. "Female Officials in the Feminist Capital: The Case of Santa Clara County." *Western Political Quarterly* 38, no. 1: 94–118.

Floge, Liliane, and Deborah Merrill. 1985. "Tokenism Reconsidered: Male Nurses and Female Physicians in a Hospital Setting." *Social Forces* 64, no. 4: 925–947.

Fonow, Mary, and Judith Cook, eds. 1991. *Beyond Methodology: Feminist Scholarship as Lived Research.* Bloomington: Indiana University Press.

Førde, Britt, and Helga Hernes. 1988. "Gender Equality in Norway." *Canadian Women Studies* 9, no. 2: 27–30.

Forney, Matthias. 1900. *Proportional Representation.* New York: E. W. Johnson.

Freedman, Estelle. 1979. "Separatism as a Strategy: Female Institutional Building and American Feminism, 1870–1930." *Feminist Studies* 5, no. 3: 512–529.

Freeman, Jo. 1975. *The Politics of Women's Liberation.* New York: McKay.

Freire, Paolo. 1972. *Pedagogy of the Oppressed.* New York: Herder & Herder.

Furley, Oliver. 1987. *Ugandan's Retreat from Turmoil?* London: Center for Security and Conflict Studies.

Geiger, Susan. 1982. "Umoja Wa Wanawake wa Tanzania and the Needs of the Rural Poor." *African Studies Review* 25, no. 2–3: 45–65.

______. 1987. "Women in Nationalist Struggle: TANU Activists in Dar es Salaam." *International Journal of African Historical Studies* 20, no. 1: 1–26.

______. 1990. "Women and African Nationalism." *Journal of Women's History* 2, no. 1: 227–244.

Gertzog, Irwin. 1979. "Changing Patterns of Female Recruitment to the U.S. House of Representatives." *Legislative Studies Quarterly* 4, no. 3: 429–445.

______. 1984. *Congressional Women*. New York: Praeger.

Gilligan, Carol. 1982. *In a Different Voice: Psychological Theories and Women's Development*. Cambridge: Harvard University Press.

Gladwin, Christina, ed. 1991. *Structural Adjustment and African Women Farmers*. Gainesville: University of Florida Press.

Glaser, Barney, and Anselm Strauss. 1967. *The Discovery of Grounded Theory: Strategies for Qualitative Research*. Chicago: Aldine.

Glickman, Harvey, ed. 1992. *Political Leaders of Contemporary Africa South of the Sahara: A Biographical Dictionary*. New York: Greenwood.

Goffman, Erving. 1967. "The Nature of Deference and Demeanor." In Erving Goffman, ed., *Interaction Ritual*. New York: Anchor Doubleday.

Goldschmidt, Walter. 1976. *Culture and Behavior of the Sebei: A Study in Continuity and Adaptation*. Berkeley: University of California Press.

Graham, C. K. 1971. *The History of Education in Ghana from the Earliest Times to the Declaration of Independence*. London: F. Cass.

Griffiths, Phillips. 1960. "How Can One Person Represent Another?" *Aristotelian Society* Supplement 34: 182–208.

Grimshaw, Jean. 1986. *Philosophy and Feminist Thinking*. Minneapolis: University of Minnesota Press.

Guinier, Lani. 1994. *The Tyranny of the Majority: Fundamental Fairness in Representative Democracy*. New York: Free Press.

Hafkin, Nancy, and Edna Bay, eds. 1976. *Women in Africa: Studies in Social and Economic Change*. Stanford, Calif.: Stanford University Press.

Haines, Herbert. 1984. "Black Radicalization and the Funding of Civil Rights: 1957-1970." *Social Problems* 32, no. 1: 31–43.

Hansen, Holger, and Michael Twaddle, eds. 1988. *Uganda Now: Between Decay and Development*. London: James Currey.

______. 1995. *From Chaos to Order: The Politics of Constitution-Making in Uganda*. Kampala: Fountain.

Hansen, T. Karen, ed. 1992. *African Encounters with Domesticity*. New Brunswick, N.J.: Rutgers University Press.

Harding, Sandra. 1991. *Whose Science? Whose Knowledge? Thinking From Women's Lives*. Ithaca, N.Y.: Cornell University Press.

Hare, Thomas. 1873. *The Election of Representatives, Parliamentary and Municipal*. 4th ed. London: Longmans.

Harris, Fredrick. 1994. "Something Within: Religion as a Mobilizer of African-American Political Activism." *The Journal of Politics* 56, no. 1: 42–68.

Harvey, William. 1966. *Law and Social Change in Ghana*. Princeton: Princeton University Press.

Henley, Nancy. 1977. *Body Politics: Power, Sex and Nonverbal Communication*. Englewood Cliffs, N.J.: Prentice-Hall.

Hermens, F. A. 1941. *Democracy or Anarchy.* Notre Dame, Ind.: University of Notre Dame Press.

Hess, Beth, and Myra Ferree, eds. 1987. *Analyzing Gender: A Handbook of Social Science.* Newbury Park, Calif.: Sage.

hooks, bell. 1984. *Feminist Theory: From Margin to Center.* Boston: South End.

______. 1994. *Outlaw Culture: Resisting Representations.* New York: Routledge.

Howard-Merriam, Kathleen. 1990. "Guaranteed Seats for Political Representation of Women: The Egyptian Example." *Women and Politics* 10, no. 1: 17–42.

Howard, Rhoda. 1985. "Women and the Crisis in Commonwealth Africa." *International Political Science Review* 6, no. 3: 287–296.

Hunt, Nancy. 1990. "Domesticity and Colonialism in Belgian Africa: Usumbura's Foyer Social, 1946–1960." *Signs: Journal of Women in Culture and Society* 15, no. 3: 447–474.

Huntington, Samuel. 1991. *The Third Wave: Democratization in the Late Twentieth Century.* Norman: University of Oklahoma Press.

Hyden, Goran. 1995. "Political Representation and the Future of Uganda." In Holger Hansen and Michael Twaddle, eds., *From Chaos to Order: The Politics of Constitution-Making in Uganda.* Kampala: Fountain.

Ibingira, G. S. K. 1973. *The Forging of an African Nation: The Political and Constitutional Evolution of Uganda from Colonial Rule to Independence, 1894–1962.* New York: Viking.

Imam, Ayesha. 1992. "Ideology, Women and Mass Media: A Case Study in Kano, Nigeria." In Ayesha Imam, Mounira Chelli, and Soha Abdel-Kadre, eds., *Women and the Mass Media in Africa.* Dakar: AAWORD.

Inter-Parliamentary Union. 1995. *Women in Parliaments, 1945–1995: A World Statistical Survey.* Reports and Documents Series, no. 23. Geneva: Inter-Parliamentary Union.

______. 1997. *Men and Women in Politics: Democracy Still in the Making.* Reports and Documents Series, no. 28. Geneva: Inter-Parliamentary Union.

ISIS-Wicce. 1993. "Uganda Does What It Can for Women." *ISIS Women's Health Journal* 4: 61–62.

Jacklin, Carol, and Laura Baker. 1993. "Early Gender Development." In Stuart Oskamp and Mark Costanzo, eds., *Gender Issues in contemporary Society.* Newbury Park, Calif.: Sage.

Jamal, V. 1978. "Taxation and Inequality in Uganda, 1900–1964." *Journal of Economic History* 38, no. 2: 418–438.

Jamison, Martin. 1992. *Idi Amin and Uganda: An Annotated Bibliography.* Westport, Conn.: Greenwood.

Jaros, Dean. 1973. *Socialization to Politics.* New York: Praeger.

Jennings, Kent. 1979. "Another Look at the Life Cycle and Political Participation." *American Journal of Political Science* 23, no. 4: 755–771.

Jjuuko, Frederick. 1993. "Matriarchy in Tribal Buganda, Uganda." *Journal of African Religion and Philosophy* 2, no. 2: 88–120.

Johnson, Marilyn, and Susan Carroll. 1978. *Profile of Women Holding Office II.* New Brunswick, N.J.: Center for the American Woman and Politics.

Johnston, Harry. 1902. *The Uganda Protectorate.* London: Hutchinson.

Johnson-Odim, Cheryl. 1991. "Common Themes, Different Contexts: Third World Women and Feminism." In Chandra Mohanty, Ann Russo, and Lourdes Torres, eds., *Third World Women and the Politics of Feminism*. Bloomington: Indiana University Press.

Joseph, Gloria, and Jill Lewis. 1981. *Common Differences: Conflicts in Black and White Feminist Perspectives*. New York: Anchor Books.

Kabaka of Buganda (Sir Mutesa II). 1967. *Desecration of My Kingdom*. London: Constable.

Kakwenzire, Joan. 1996. "Preconditions for Demarginalizing Women and Youth in Ugandan Politics." In J. Oloka-Onyango, K. Kibwana, and C. Peter, eds., *Law and the Struggle for Democracy in East Africa*. Nairobi: Claripress.

Kaleeba, Noerine. 1991. "Success Campaigns in Uganda." *Women's Global Network for Reproductive Rights* 34 (January): 50–51.

Kandiyoti, Deniz. 1988. "Bargaining with Patriarchy." *Gender and Society* 2, no. 3: 274–290.

Kanter, Rosabeth. 1977. *Men and Women of the Corporation*. New York: Basic Books.

Karugire, Samwiri. 1980. *A Political History of Uganda*. Nairobi: Heinemann.

______. 1988. *The Roots of Instability in Uganda*. Kampala: New Vision Printing and Publishing.

Kasfir, Nelson. 1995. "Ugandan Politics and the Constituent Assembly Elections of March 1994." In Holger Hansen and Michael Twaddle, eds., *From Chaos to Order: The Politics of Constitution-Making in Uganda*. Kampala: Fountain.

Kathlene, Lyn. 1989. "Uncovering the Political Impacts of Gender: An Exploratory Study." *Western Political Quarterly* 42, no. 2: 397–421.

______. 1990. "A New Approach to Understanding the Impact of Gender on the Legislative Process." In Joyce NcCarl Nielsen, ed., *Feminist Research Methods*. Boulder: Westview.

Keane, John. 1991. *The Media and Democracy*. Cambridge: Polity.

Kiguli, Susan, and Juliet Kiguli. 1997. "Representations of Women Leaders in the African Press: The Case of Uganda." Paper presented at the Faculty of Arts third annual conference, On Africa in World Affairs: Challenges to the Humanities, Makerere University, Uganda, March 6–8.

Kim, Chong, Joel Barkan, Ilter Turan, Malcom Jewell. 1984. *The Legislative Connection: The Politics of Representation in Kenya, Korea, and Turkey*. Durham, N.C.: Duke University Press.

Kirkpatrick, Jeanne. 1974. *Political Women*. New York: Basic Books.

Kisekka, Nakateregga. 1990. "AIDS in Uganda as a Gender Issue." *Women and Therapy* 10, no. 3: 35–53.

Kohn, Walter. 1980. *Women in National Legislatures: A Comparative Study of Six Countries*. New York: Praeger.

Krieger, Susan. 1985. "Beyond 'Subjectivity': The Use of the Self in Social Science." *Qualitative Sociology* 8, no. 4: 309–324.

______. 1991. *Social Sciences and the Self: Personal Essays on an Art Form*. New Brunswick, N.J.: Rutgers University Press.

Kwesiga, Joy. 1993. "Access of Women to Higher Education in Uganda: An Analysis of Inequalities, Barriers and Determinants." Ph.D. dissertation, University of London.

Kyomuhendo, G. 1992. "The Role of Women in Petty Commodity Production and Commerce: A Case Study of Rural Women in Uganda." Unpublished paper presented at a conference of the Center for Basic Research, Kampala.

Lapchick, Richard, and Stephanie Urdang. 1982. *Oppression and Resistance: The Struggle of Women in Southern Africa.* Westport, Conn.: Greenwood.

Laslett, Barbara, and Johanna Brenner. 1989. "Gender and Social Reproduction: Historical Perspectives." *Annual Review of Sociology* 15: 381–404.

Lebeuf, Annie. 1963. "The Role of Women in the Political Organization of African Societies." In Denise Paulme, ed., *Women of Tropical Africa.* Berkeley: University of California Press.

Lihamba, Amandina, and Penina Mlama. 1992. "Women in Communication: Popular Theatre as an Alternative Medium." In Ayesha Imam, Mounira Chelli, and Soha Abdel-Kadre, eds., *Women and the Mass Media in Africa.* Dakar: AAWORD.

Lind, Amy. 1992. "Power, Gender, and Development: Popular Women's Organizations and the Politics of need in Equador." In Arturo Escobar and Sonia Alvarez, eds., *The Making of Contemporary Social Movements in Latin America.* Boulder: Westview.

Lindeke, William, and Winnie Wanzala. 1994. "Regional Elections in Namibia: Deepening Democracy and Gender Inclusion." *Africa Today* 41, no. 3: 5–14.

Lofland, John, and Lyn Lofland. 1984. *Analyzing Social Settings.* 2d ed. Belmont, Calif.: Wordsworth.

Lopez, Eugenia. 1991. "Overcoming the Barriers: Women and Participation in Public Life." In Tina Wallace and Candida March, eds., *Changing Perceptions: Writings on Gender and Development.* Oxford: OXFAM.

Lorber, Judith. 1994. *Paradoxes of Gender.* New Haven: Yale University Press.

Lorde, Audre. 1984. *Sister Outsider: Essays and Speeches.* Trumansburg, N.Y.: Crossing.

Lugones, Maria. 1994. "Purity, Impurity, and Separation." *Signs: Journal of Women in Culture and Society* 19, no. 2: 458–479.

Maccoby, Eleanor, and Carol Jackin. 1975. *The Psychology of Sex Differences.* Stanford, Calif.: Stanford University Press.

MacKinnon, Catharine. 1979. *Sexual Harassment of Working Women.* New Haven: Yale University Press.

______. 1989. *Toward a Feminist Theory of the State.* Cambridge: Harvard University Press.

Mama, Amina. 1996. "Women's Studies and Studies of Women in Africa During the 1990s." CODESRIA Working Paper Series, no. 5. Dakar: CODESRIA.

Mamdani, Mahmood. 1976. *Politics and Class Formation in Uganda.* New York: Monthly Review Press.

______. 1986. "Contradictory Class Perspectives on the Question of Democracy in Africa." *OSSREA Journal* 2, no. 1: 45–64.

______. 1994. "Pluralism and the Right of Association." In Mahmood Mamdani and Joe Oloka-Onyango, eds., *Uganda: Studies in Living Conditions, Popular Movements and Constitutionalism.* Vienna: JEP.

Manning Lee, Marcia. 1976. "Why Few Women Hold Public Office: Democracy and Sexual Roles." *Political Science Quarterly* 91, no. 2: 297–314.

Martin, Patricia. 1990. "Rethinking Feminist Organizations." *Gender and Society* 4, no. 2: 182–206.

Massey, Marilyn. 1985. *The Feminist Soul: The Fate of an Ideal.* Boston: G. K. Hall.

Mba, Nina. 1982. *Nigerian Women Mobilized: Women's Political Activity in Southern Nigeria, 1900–1965.* Berkeley: Institute of International Studies, University of California, Berkeley.

Mbilinyi, Marjorie. 1993. "Struggles over Patriarchal Structural Adjustment in Tanzania." *Focus on Gender* 1, no. 3: 26–29.

McCaghy, M. D. 1985. *Sexual Harassment: A Guide to Resources.* Boston: G. K. Hall.

McClaurin-Allen, Irma. 1990. "Incongruities: Dissonance and Contradiction in the Life of a Black Middle-Class Woman." In Faye Ginsburg and Anna Tsing, eds., *Uncertain Terms: Negotiating Gender in American Culture.* Boston: Beacon.

McGlen, Nancy. 1980. "The Impact of Parenthood on Political Participation." *Western Political Quarterly* 33, no. 3: 297–313.

McRae, Susan. 1990. "Women at the Top: The Case of British National Politics." *Parliamentary Affairs* 43, no. 3: 341–347.

Means, Ingunn. 1972. "Women in Local Politics: The Norwegian Experience." *Canadian Journal of Political Science* 5, no. 3: 365–388.

Melady, Thomas, and Margaret Melady. 1977. *Idi Amin Dada: Hitler in Africa.* Kansas City: Sheed, Andrews, and McMeel.

Mezey, Susan. 1978. "Support for Women's Rights Policy: An Analysis of Local Politicians." *American Politics Quarterly* 6: 485–497.

Miers, David. 1989. "Legislation and the Legislative Process: A Case for Reform?" *Statute Law Review* 10: 26–36.

Michelman, Frank. 1986. "Traces of Self-Government." *Harvard Law Review* 100, no. 1: 4-77.

Mill, John Stuart. 1861. *Considerations on Representative Government.* London: Parker, Son & Bourn.

Mirabeau, Honoré Gabriel Riquetti. 1834. *Oeuvres De Mirabeau.* Paris: Lecointe et Pougin.

Mittelman, James. 1975. *Ideology and Politics in Uganda: From Obote to Amin.* Ithaca, N.Y.: Cornell University Press.

Mohanty, Chandra. 1991a. "Cartographies of Struggle: Third World Women and the Politics of Feminism." In Chandra Mohanty, Ann Russo, and Lourdes Torres, eds., *Third World Women and the Politics of Feminism.* Bloomington: Indiana University Press.

______. 1991b. "Under Western Eyes: Feminist Scholarship and Colonial Discourse." In Chandra Mohanty, Ann Russo, and Lourdes Torres, eds., *Third World Women and the Politics of Feminism.* Bloomington: Indiana University Press.

Mohanty, Chandra, Ann Russo, and Lourdes Torres, eds. 1991. *Third World Women and the Politics of Feminism.* Bloomington: Indiana University Press.

Molyneux, Maxine. 1985. "Mobilization Without Emancipation? Women's Interests, the State, and Revolution in Nicaragua." *Feminist Studies* 11, no. 2: 226–254.

Moraga, Cherrie, and Gloria Anzaldua, eds. 1981. *This Bridge Called My Back: Writings by Radical Women of Color.* Watertown, Mass.: Persephone.

Morris, Henry, and James Read. 1966. *Uganda: The Development of Its Laws and Constitution.* London: Stevens & Sons.

Mouffe, Chantal, ed. 1992. *Dimensions of Radical Democracy.* London: Verso.

Mudoola, Dan. 1988. "Political Transactions Since Idi Amin: A Study in Political Pathology." In Holger Hansen and Michael Twaddle, eds., *Uganda Now: Between Decay and Development.* London: James Currey.

Mueller, Carol. 1987. "Consensus Without Unity." *Journal of State Government* 60, no. 5: 230–234.

Mullen, Tom. 1988. "Affirmative Action." In Sheila McLean and Noreen Burrows, eds., *The Legal Relevance of Gender.* Atlantic Highlands, N.J.: Humanities Press International.

Murindwa, Rutanga. 1994. "People's Anti-colonial Struggles in Kigezi under the Nyabingi Movement, 1910–1930." In Mahmood Mamdani and J. Oloka-Onyango, eds., *Uganda: Studies in Living Conditions, Popular Movements and Constitutionalism.* Vienna: JEP.

Muscat, Richard, ed. 1984. *A Short History of the Democratic Party: 1954–1984.* Kampala: Foundation for African Development.

Museveni, K. Yoweri. 1997. *Sowing the Mustard Seed: The Struggle for Freedom and Democracy in Uganda.* London: Macmillan.

Musisi, Nakanyike. 1991. "Women, 'Elite Polygyny' and Buganda State Formation." *Signs: Journal of Women in Culture and Society* 16, no. 4: 757–786.

______. 1992. "Colonial and Missionary Education: Women and Domesticity in Uganda, 1900–1945." In Karen T. Hansen, ed., *African Encounters with Domesticity.* New Brunswick, N.J.: Rutgers University Press.

Mutibwa, Phares. 1992. *Uganda Since Independence: A Story of Unfulfilled Hopes.* London: Hurst.

Nabudere, Wadada. 1980. *Imperialism and Revolution in Uganda.* London: Onyx.

______. 1994. *The Impact of East-West Rapprochement on Africa.* Sapem Seminar Paper Series, no. 1. Harare: Southern African Political and Economic Monthly (SAPEM).

Nash, June, and Maria Fernandez-Kelly, eds. 1983. *Women, Men, and the International Division of Labor.* Albany: State University of New York Press.

National Assembly Official Reports: Uganda Parliamentary Debates. Entebbe: Uganda Government Printery.

NAWOU, National Association of Women's Organizations in Uganda. 1995. *Women's Landmarks in the Democratisation Process in Uganda.* Kampala: Friedrich Ebert Foundation.

Ngugi wa Thiong'o. 1986. *Decolonising the Mind: The Politics of Language in African Literature.* London: James Currey.

Nicholson, Beryl. 1993. "From Interest Group to (Almost) Equal Citizenship: Women's Representation in the Norwegian Parliament." *Parliamentary Affairs* 46, no. 2: 255–263.

Nicholson, Linda. 1986. *Gender and History: The Limits of Social Theory in the Age of the Family.* New York: Columbia University Press.

Norris, Pippa. 1985. "Women's Legislative Participation in Western Europe." *West European Politics* 8, no. 4: 90–101.

______. 1986. "Women in Congress: A Policy Difference?" *Politics* 6, no. 1: 34–40.

Norris, Pippa, ed. 1997. *Women, Media and Politics.* New York: Oxford University Press.

Norris, Pippa, and Joni Lovenduski. 1995. *Political Recruitment: Gender, Race, and Class in the British Parliament.* Cambridge: Cambridge University Press.

Nzomo, Maria. 1988. "Women, Democracy and Development in Africa." In Walter Oyugi et al., eds., *Democratic Theory and Practice in Africa.* Portsmouth, N.H.: Heinemann.

O'Barr, Jean. 1976. "Pare Women: A Case of Political Involvement." *Rural Africana* 29: 121–134.

Obbo, Christine. 1980. *African Women: Their Struggle for Economic Independence.* London: Zed.

______. 1986. "Stratification and the Lives of Women in Uganda." In Claire Robertson and Iris Berger, eds., *Women and Class in Africa.* New York: African Publishing.

Ogundipe-Leslie, Molara. 1994. *Re-creating Ourselves: African Women and Critical Transformations.* Trenton, N.J.: Africa World Press.

Ogunleye, Bisi. 1990. "Grassroots Development—A Nigerian Perspective." *Sage* 7: 43–45.

______. 1993. "Local Initiative: Key to Women's Voice in Global Decision Making for a Healthy Environment in Africa." *Women and Environments* 13, no. 3–4: 15–17.

Okeyo, Achola. 1980. "Daughters of the Lakes and Rivers: Colonization and the Land Rights of Luo Women." In Mona Etienne and Eleanor Leacock, eds., *Women and Colonization: Anthropological Perspectives.* New York: Praeger.

______. 1981. "Reflections on Development Myths." *Africa Report* (March-April): 7–10.

Okin, Susan. 1979. *Women in Western Political Theory.* Princeton: Princeton University Press.

Okoth, Godfrey. 1996. "The Historical Dimensions of Democracy in Uganda: A Review of the Problems and Prospects." In J. Oloka-Onyango, Kivutha Kibwana, and Chris Peter, eds., *Law and the Struggle for Democracy in East Africa.* Nairobi: Claripress.

Oloka-Onyango, J. 1991. "The National Resistance Movement, 'Grassroots Democracy,' and Dictatorship in Uganda." In Robin Cohen and Harry Goulbourne, eds., *Democracy and Socialism in Africa.* Boulder: Westview.

______. 1992. "The Legal Control of Tertiary Institutions in East Africa: The Case of Makerere University." *Africa Development* 17, no. 4: 47–66.

______. 1993. "Popular Justice, Resistance Committee Courts and the Judicial Process in Uganda, 1988–1992." *Beyond Law (Mas Alla Del Derecho)* 7:39–60.

______. 1994. "Judicial Power and Constitutionalism in Uganda." In Mahmood Mamdani and J. Oloka Onyango, eds., *Uganda: Studies in Living conditions, Popular Movements and Constitutionalism.* Vienna: JEP.

Oloka-Onyango, J., and Sylvia Tamale. 1995. "'The Personal Is Political,' or Why Women's Rights Are Indeed Human Rights: An African Perspective on International Feminism." *Human Rights Quarterly* 17, no. 4: 691–731.

Pateman, Carole. 1988. *The Sexual Contract.* Stanford, Calif.: Stanford University Press.

Paulus, Norma. 1987. "Women Find Political Power in Unity." *Journal of State Government* 60, no. 5: 227–229.

Patton, Michael. 1987. *How to Use Qualitative Methods in Evaluation.* Newbury Park, Calif.: Sage.

Perkins, Jerry, and Diane Fowlkes. 1980. "Opinion Representation Versus Social Representation: Or Why Women Can't Run as Women and Win." *American Political Science Review* 74, no. 1: 92–103.

Petchesky, Rosalind. 1979. "Dissolving the Hyphen: A Report on Marxist-Feminist Groups 1–5." In Zillah Eisenstein, ed., *Capitalist Patriarchy and the Case for Socialist-Feminism.* New York: Monthly Review Press, pp. 373–389.

Phillips, Anne. 1991. *Engendering Democracy.* University Park: Pennsylvania State University Press.

______. 1992. "Democracy and Difference: Some Problems for Feminist Theory." *The Political Quarterly* 63, no. 1: 79–90.

______. 1995. *The Politics of Presence.* Oxford: Clarendon.

Phillips, Melanie. 1980. *The Divided House: Women at Westminster.* London: Sidgwick & Jackson.

Pierce, Jennifer. 1995. *Gender Trials: Emotional Lives in Contemporary Law Firms.* Berkeley: University of California Press.

Pitkin, Hanna. 1967. *The Concept of Representation.* Berkeley: University of California Press.

Prabhavathi, V. 1991. *Perceptions, Motivations, and Performance of Women Legislators.* New Delhi: Classical Publishers.

Presley, Cora. 1988. "The Mau Mau Rebellion, Kikuyu Women, and Social Change." *Canadian Journal of African Studies* 22, no. 3: 503–527.

Pulme, Denise, ed. 1963. *Women of Tropical Africa.* Berkeley: University of California Press.

Randall, Vicky. 1987. *Women and Politics: An International Perspective.* 2d ed. London: Macmillan.

Ratan, Sudha. 1994. "Gender, Ethnicity, and Political Participation: A Case Study of Women in the Tamilnadu Legislative Assembly." *Journal of Third World Studies* 11, no. 1: 282–303.

Reagon, Bernice. 1983. "Coalition Politics: Turning the Century." In Barbara Smith, ed., *Home Girls: A Black Feminist Anthology.* New York: Kitchen Table Women of Color Press.

Reddy, Marlita, ed. 1996. *Statistical Abstract of the World.* 2d ed. Detroit, Mich.: Gale Research.

Reinharz, Shulamit. 1979. *On Becoming a Social Scientist: From Survey Research and Participant Observation to Experiential Analysis.* San Francisco: Jossey-Bass.

______. 1992. *Feminist Methods in Social Research.* New York: Oxford University Press.

Rich, Adrienne. 1976. *Of Woman Born: Motherhood as Experience and Institution.* New York: W. W. Norton.

Richards, Audrey. 1964. "Authority Patterns in Traditional Buganda and Traditional Values and Current Political Behavior." In Lloyd Fallers, ed., *The King's Men: Leadership and Status in Buganda on the Eve of Independence.* London: Oxford University Press.

Rinehart, Sue. 1992. *Gender Consciousness and Politics.* New York: Praeger.

Roberts, Helen, ed. 1981. *Doing Feminist Research.* London: Routledge.

Roberts, Pepe. 1984. "Feminism *in* Africa: Feminism *and* Africa." *Review of African Political Economy* 27–28: 175–184.

Robertson, Claire, and Iris Berger, eds. 1986. *Women and Class in Africa.* New York: Africana Publishing.

Robinson, Pearl. 1994. "Democratization: Understanding the Relationship Between Regime Change and the Culture of Politics." *African Studies Review* 37, no. 1: 39-67.

Roddan, G. M. 1958. "The Key Is Woman." *Corona* 57–59.

Rogers, Susan. 1980. "Anti-Colonial Protest in Africa: A Female Strategy Reconsidered." *Heresies* 3, no. 1: 22–25.

Rosaldo, Michelle. 1980. "The Use and Abuse of Anthropology: Reflections on Feminism and Cross-Cultural Understanding." *Signs: Journal of Women in Culture and Society* 5, no. 3: 389–417.

Roscoe, John. 1911. *The Baganda: An Account of Their Native Custom and Beliefs.* London: Macmillan.

______. 1924. *The Bagesu and Other Tribes of the Uganda Protectorate.* Cambridge: Cambridge University Press.

Rothchild, Donald, and Naomi Chazan, eds. 1988. *The Precarious Balance: State and Society in Africa.* Boulder: Westview.

Rubenstein, Michael. 1992. *Preventing and Remedying Sexual Harassment at Work: A Resource Manual.* 2d ed. London: Eclipse.

Ruddick, Sara. 1980. "Maternal Thinking." *Feminist Studies* 6, no. 2: 342–367.

Rule, Wilma. 1987. "Electoral Systems, Contextual Factors, and Women's Opportunity for Election to Parliament in Twenty-three Democracies." *Western Political Quarterly* 40, no. 3: 477–498.

Sadat, Jehan. 1987. *A Woman of Egypt.* New York: Simon & Schuster.

Saint-Germain, Michelle. 1989. "Does Their Difference Make a Difference? The Impact of Women on Public Policy in the Arizona Legislature." *Social Science Quarterly* 70, no. 4: 956–968.

______. 1993. "Paths to Power of Women Legislators in Costa Rica and Nicaragua." *Women's Studies International Forum* 16, no. 2: 119–138.

Salyaga, S. 1987. "RCs: A Path for Democracy?" *FORWARD* 9, no. 2: 2–29.

Sapiro, Virginia. 1981. "Research Frontier Essay: Where Are Interests Interesting? The Problem of Political Representation of Women." *American Political Science Review* 75, no. 3: 701–716.

______. 1983. *The Political Integration of Women: Roles, Socialization and Politics.* Urbana: University of Illinois Press.

Savane, Marie. 1982. "Another Development with Women." *Development Dialogue* 1, no. 2: 8–16.

Sawer, Marian. 1986. "From Motherhood to Sisterhood: Attitudes of Australian Women MPs to Their Roles." *Women's Studies International Forum* 9, no. 5–6: 531–541.

Sawer, Marian, and Marian Simms. 1984. *A Woman's Place: Women and Politics in Australia*. Sydney: Allen & Unwin.

Sawicki, Jane. 1991. *Disciplining Foucault: Feminism, Power, and the Body*. New York: Routledge.

Schmidt, Elizabeth. 1991. "Patriarchy, Capitalism, and the Colonial State in Zimbabwe." *Signs: Journal of Women in Culture and Society* 16, no. 4: 732–756.

Schiller, Laurence. 1990. "The Royal Women of Buganda." *The International Journal of African Historical Studies* 23, no. 3: 455–473.

Schreiber, Carol. 1979. *Men and Women in Transitional Occupations*. Cambridge: MIT Press.

Schreiner, Jenny. 1996. "Affirmative Action and Reconstruction: A Basis for Changing Race, Class and Gender Inequality." In Blade Nzimande and Mpumelelo Sikhosana, eds., *Affirmative Action and Transformation*. Durban: Indicator Press.

Scott, Catherine. 1995. *Gender and Development: Rethinking Modernization and Dependency Theory*. Boulder: Lynne Rienner.

Segers, Mary. 1983. "Justifying Affirmative Action." In James Foster and Mary Segers, eds., *Elusive Equality: Liberalism, Affirmative Action, and Social Change in America*. Port Washington, N.Y.: Associated Faculty Press.

Seidman, Gay. 1993. "'No Freedom Without the Women': Mobilization and Gender in South Africa, 1970–1992." *Signs: Journal of Women in Culture and Society* 18, no. 2: 291–320.

Seitz, Virginia. 1995. *Women, Development, and Communities for Empowerment in Appalachia*. New York: State University of New York Press.

Sender, Patricia, and Sheila Smith. 1990. *Poverty, Class, and Gender in Rural Africa: A Tanzanian Case Study*. London: Routledge.

Shapiro, Robert, and Herpreet Mahajan. 1986. "Gender Differences in Policy Preferences: A Summary of Trends from the 1960s to the 1980s." *Public Opinion Quarterly* 50, no. 1: 42–61.

Sibiya, Eunice. 1990. *Thoughts of An African Woman*. Braamfontein: Skotaville Publishers.

Sikhosana, Mpumelelo. 1996. "Affirmative Action: Possibilities and Limitations." In Blade Nzimande and Mpumelelo Sikhosana, eds., *Affirmative Action and Transformation*. Durban: Indicator Press.

Simon, Thomas. 1990. "Suspect Class Democracy: A Social Theory." *University of Miami Law Review* 45, no. 1: 107–158.

Sisulu, E., with A. Imam and M. Diouf. 1991. "Report on the Workshop on Gender Analysis and African Social Science held in Dakar, 16–21 September, 1991." *CODESRIA Bulletin* 4: 2–14.

Smith, Barbara. 1980. *Toward a Black Feminist Criticism*. Brooklyn, N.Y.: Out & Out Books.

Smith, Dorothy. 1974. "Women's Perspective as a Radical Critique of Sociology." *Sociological Inquiry* 44, no. 1: 7–13.

Smock, Audrey. 1977. "Ghana: From Autonomy to Subordination." In Janet Giele and Audrey Smock, eds., *Women: Roles and Status in Eight Countries.* New York: John Wiley.

Soh, Chung-Hee. 1993. *Women in Korean Politics.* 2d ed. Boulder: Westview.

Spelman, Elizabeth. 1988. *Inessential Woman: Problems of Exclusion in Feminist Thought.* Boston: Beacon.

Sreberny-Mohammadi, Annabelle, and Karen Ross. 1996. "Women MPs and the Media: Representing the Body Politic." *Parliamentary Affairs* 49, no. 1: 103–115.

Steady, Filomina. 1976. "Protestant Women's Associations in Freetown and Sierra Leone." In Nancy Hafkin and Edna Bay, eds., *Women in Africa: Studies in Social and Economic Change.* Stanford, Calif.: Stanford University Press.

Sudarkasa, Niara. 1986. "'The Status of Women' in Indigenous African Societies." *Feminist Studies* 12, no. 1: 92–99.

Stacey, Margaret, and Marion Price. 1981. *Women, Power and Politics.* London: Tavistock.

Stamp, Patricia. 1986. "Kikuyu Women's Self-Help Groups: Toward an Understanding of the Relation Between Sex-Gender System and Mode of Production in Africa." In Claire Robertson and Iris Berger, eds., *Women and Class in Africa.* New York: Africana Publishing.

Staudt, Kathleen. 1981. "Women's Politics in Africa." *Studies in Third World Societies* 16: 1–28.

———. 1989. "The State and Gender in Colonial Africa." In Sue Charlton, Jana Everett, and Kathleen Staudt, eds., *Women, the State and Development.* Albany: State University of New York Press.

Steady, Filomena. 1975. *Female Power in African Politics: The National Congress of Sierra Leone.* Los Angeles: California Institute of Technology, Munger Africana Library Notes.

Sterne, Simon. 1871. *On Representative Government and Personal Representation.* Philadelphia: J. B. Lippincott.

Sudarkasa, Niara. 1986. "'The Status of Women' in Indigenous African Societies." *Feminist Studies* 12, no. 1: 91–103.

Swabey, Marie. 1939. *Theory of the Democratic State.* Cambridge: Harvard University Press.

Tadria, Hilda. 1987. "Changes and Continuities in the Position of Women in Uganda." In P. D. Wiebe and C. P. Dodge, eds., *Beyond Crisis: Development Issues in Uganda.* Kampala: Makerere Institute of Social Research.

Tamale, Sylvia. 1992. "Rape Law and the Violation of Women in Uganda: A Critical Perspective." *Uganda Law Society Review* 1, no. 2: 195–211.

———. 1993. "Law Reform and Women's Rights in Uganda." *East African Journal of Peace and Human Rights* 1, no. 2: 164–194.

———. 1996a. "Democratization in Uganda: A Feminist Perspective." In J. Oloka-Onyango, Kivutha-Kibwana, and Chris M. Peter, eds., *Law and the Struggle for Democracy in East Africa.* Nairobi: Claripress.

———. 1996b. "The Outsider Looks In: Constructing Knowledge about American Collegiate Racism." *Qualitative Sociology* 19, no. 4: 471–495.

Tamale, Sylvia, and Joe Oloka-Onyango. 1997. "Bitches at the Academy: Gender and Academic Freedom at the African University." *Africa Development* 22, no. 1: 13–37.

Thernstrom, Abigail. 1987. *Whose Votes Count? Affirmative Action and Minority Voting Rights.* Cambridge: Harvard University Press.

Thomas, Linda. 1994. "African Indigenous Churches as a Source of Socio-Political Transformation in South Africa." *Africa Today* 41, no. 1: 39–56.

Thomas, Sue. 1990. "Voting Patterns in the California Assembly: The Role of Gender." *Women and Politics* 9, no. 4: 43–56.

________. 1991. "The Impact of Women on State Legislative Policies." *Journal of Politics* 53, no. 4: 958–976.

Thomas, Sue, and Susan Welch. 1991. "The Impact of Gender on Activities and Priorities of State Legislators." *Western Political Quarterly* 44, no. 2: 445–456.

Tosh, John. 1978. *Clan Leaders and Colonial Chiefs in Lango: The Political History of an East African Stateless Society, 1800–1939.* Oxford: Clarendon.

Toubia, Nahid. 1994. "Women's Reproductive and Sexual Rights." In Center for Women's Global Leadership, ed., *Gender Violence and Women's Human Rights in Africa.* New Brunswick, N.J.: Center for Women's Global Leadership.

Tripp, Aili. 1994. "Gender, Political Participation and the Transformation of Associational Life in Uganda and Tanzania." *Africa Studies Review* 37, no. 1: 107–131.

Tussman, Joseph. 1960. *Obligation and the Body Politic.* New York: Oxford University Press.

Ucko, Lenora. 1994. "Culture and Violence: The Interaction of Africa and America." *Sex Roles* 31, no. 3–4: 185–204.

UNESCO. 1993. *Statistical Year Book.* Paris: UNESCO.

Unger, R., and M. Crawford. 1992. *Women and Gender: A Feminist Psychology.* New York: McGraw-Hill.

UNICEF. 1994. *Equity and Vulnerability: A Situation Analysis of Women, Adolescents and Children in Uganda, 1994.* Kampala: UNICEF.

United Nations office at Vienna for Social Development and Humanitarian Affairs. 1992. *Women in Politics and Decision-Making in the Late Twentieth Century.* Dordrecht, Mass.: Martinus Nijhoff.

Urdang, Stephanie. 1989. *And Still They Dance: Women, War and the Struggle for Change in Mozambique.* London: Earthscan.

Uzoigwe, G. N., ed. 1982. *Uganda: The Dilemma of Nationhood.* New York: NOK.

Van Allen, Judith. 1976. "Aba Riot or Igbo Women's War? Ideology, Stratification, and the Invisibility of Women." In Nancy Hafkin and Edna Bay, eds., *Women in Africa: Studies in Social and Economic Change.* Stanford, Calif.: Stanford University Press.

Van de Walle, N. 1994. "Neopatrimonialism and Democracy in Africa with an Illustration from Cameroon." In Jennifer Widner, ed., *Economic Change and Political Liberalization in Sub-Saharan Africa.* Baltimore: Johns Hopkins University Press.

Vallance, Elizabeth. 1979. *Women in the House.* London: Athlone.

Walker, Cherryl. 1982. *Women and Resistance in South Africa.* London: Onyx.

Walker, Cherryl, ed. 1990. *Women and Gender in Southern Africa to 1945.* London: James Currey.

Wakoko, Florence, and Linda Lobao. 1996. "Reconceptualizing Gender and Reconstructing Social Life: Ugandan Women and the Path to National Development." *Africa Today* 43, no. 3: 307–322.

Waylen, Georgina. 1994. "Women and Democratization: Conceptualizing Gender Relations in Transition Politics." *World Politics* 46, no. 3: 327–354.

Weis, Lois. 1980. "Women and Education in Ghana: Some Problems of Assessing Change." *International Journal of Women's Studies* 3, no. 5: 431–453.

Weissberg, Robert. 1974. *Political Learning, Political Choice, and Democratic Citizenship.* Englewood Cliff, N.J.: Prentice-Hall.

Welch, Susan. 1977. "Women as Political Animals? A Test of Some Explanations for Male-Female Political Differences." *American Journal of Political Science* 21, no. 4: 711–730.

______. 1985. "Are Women More Liberal Than Men in the U.S. Congress?" *Legislative Studies Quarterly* 10, no. 1: 125–134.

West, Candace, and Don Zimmerman. 1987. "Doing Gender." *Gender and Society* 1, no. 2: 125–151.

Westcott, Marcia. 1990. "Feminist Criticism and the Social Sciences." In Joyce Nielsen, ed., *Feminist Research Methods: Exemplary Readings in the Social Sciences.* Boulder: Westview.

Whip, Rosemary. 1991. "Representing Women: Australian Female Parliamentarians on the Horns of a Dilemma." *Women and Politics* 11, no. 3: 1–2.

White, C. 1973. "The Role of Women as an Interest Group in the Ugandan Political System." M.A. thesis, Makerere University, Kampala, Uganda.

Williams, Christine. 1989. *Gender Differences at Work: Women and Men in Nontraditional Occupations.* Berkeley: University of California Press.

Wipper, Audrey. 1972. "African Women, Fashion, and Scapegoating." *Canadian Journal of African Studies* 6, no. 2: 329–349.

______. 1982. "Riot and Rebellion Among African Women: Three Examples of Women's Political Clout." In Jean O'Barr, ed., *Perspectives on Power: Women in Africa, Asia, and Latin America.* Durham, N.C.: Duke University Center for International Studies.

Wise, Sue, and Liz Stanley. 1987. *Georgi Porgie: Sexual Harassment in Everyday Life.* London: Pandora.

Wood, Julia. 1994. "Saying It Makes It So: The Discursive Construction of Sexual Harassment." In Shereen Bingham, ed., *Conceptualizing Sexual Harassment as Discursive Practice.* Westport, Conn.: Praeger.

Yoder, Janice. 1991. "Rethinking Tokenism: Looking Beyond Numbers." *Gender and Society* 5, no. 2: 178–192.

Young, M. Iris. 1990. *Justice and the Politics of Difference.* Princeton: Princeton University Press.

______. 1994. "Gender As Seriality: Thinking About Women as a Social Collective." *Signs: Journal of Women in Culture and Society* 19, no. 3: 713–738.

Zinanga, Evelyn. 1994. "Global Restructuring in Africa: The Impact on Women." *Kinesis* 11 (November): 17.

Index